Children
with Acquired
Aphasias

Second Edition

Children with Acquired Aphasias

Second Edition

Janet A Lees MPhil, MTh, MRCSLT

Honorary Research Fellow, Neurosciences Unit, Institute of Child Health,
University College, London.
Department of Human Communication Sciences, University of Sheffield.
Early Years Co-ordinator, Yorkshire, Humber and North-East, Scope.

Foreword by

Brian Neville FRCP

Professor of Paediatric Neurology, Institute of Child Health,
University College, London.
Honorary Consultant Paediatric Neurologist,
Great Ormond Street Hospital for Children NHS Trust, London.

W
WHURR PUBLISHERS
LONDON AND PHILADELPHIA

© 2005 Whurr Publishers Ltd
19b Compton Terrace, London N1 2UN, England and
325 Chestnut Street, Philadelphia PA 19106, USA.

British Library Cataloguing in Publication data

A catalogue record for this book is available from the
British Library.

ISBN 1 86156 490 2

Printed and bound in the UK by Athenaeum Press Limited,
Gateshead, Tyne & Wear.

Contents

Foreword   vii
    B.G.R. Neville
Preface   ix
Acknowledgements   xi
List of cases   xiii
Abbreviations   xv

Part One

Chapter 1   1

Introduction to the acquired aphasias of childhood

Chapter 2   20

Assessment of acquired speech and language problems in children

Chapter 3   33

Management of acquired speech and language problems in children

Part Two: Specific causes of ACA

Chapter 4   45

Paediatric stroke

Chapter 5   65

Head injury

Chapter 6   86

Cerebral neoplasm

Chapter 7   92

Cerebral infections

Chapter 8   100

Cerebral anoxia and prolonged coma

Chapter 9   105

Landau-Kleffner syndrome

Chapter 10   128

Other epileptic aphasias

Chapter 11   149

Other deteriorating conditions of childhood affecting speech
and language

Chapter 12   160

Conclusions

Appendix 1   168

Norms for the Graded Naming Test

Appendix 2   171

Story telling

References   173
Index   185

Foreword

Janet Lees is to be congratulated on producing a second edition of this book. Acquired aphasias in childhood remain relatively neglected by medical, therapy and educational services and a reminder of the extent of these problems is timely. Research and services related to childhood disability more generally remain under-resourced and this particularly applies to rehabilitation after acquired impairments.

Detailed case studies of the type presented in this book remain a valid contribution to science. Attempts at more fundamental studies tend to run into problems of classification and the problem of finding neurological and cognitive investigations that adequately describe the clinical phenomena or answer the critical question. Any general theory has to explain all phenotypes. An essential source of testable hypotheses in childhood aphasia is therefore well-documented clinical experience.

A developmental disability arising from damage to the central nervous system and defined by its phenotype contains the following elements:

1. It is occurring on a moving baseline of normal development upon which further development is to be expected.
2. The assessment tools need to be appropriate for the developmental age, and, in young children, this inevitably means that some functions will not be accessible.
3. Plasticity in the developing nervous system may allow the preservation of certain functions, particularly those related to language. From a theoretical standpoint, plasticity could involve relocation of function to the opposite hemisphere or elsewhere in the same hemisphere, or the accessing of a secondary, less efficient system.
4. Recovery from acute brain damage can be most dramatic. The mechanisms are poorly understood and can occur whether the person is 1 or 21 years old. This should not be confused with plasticity.

5. Critical periods for the development of a particular function may exist which may not be retrievable. Social communication is at relatively high risk in young children with, for example, early-onset epilepsy.
6. Adult models of acquired aphasia may be applicable to older children.
7. Any syndrome defined by the occurrence of acquired aphasia cannot, by definition, reflect the whole range of expression of the underlying pathologies.

These developmental dimensions both enliven and complicate the study of aphasia in the paediatric age group.

Modern imaging has advanced tremendously in the past decade and structural and functional magnetic resonance imaging are now being routinely used in children and adults. It is interesting how in adults the traditional speech and language areas of the brain have been largely confirmed. The application of these methodologies to children is at an earlier stage because of the level of co-operation required. Clinicians have to use the available assessment and descriptive tools but to be clear that the syndromes that we currently use may not be strictly biological but are a pragmatic solution to our incomplete understanding.

Research into the mechanisms of language function in the normal and pathological situations have many starting points. It could, for example, be examining the primacy of memory or the development of symbolic understanding or be looking at the primary drive to communicate. Research in this field may arise from the construction of theoretical models or be substrate-based.

It is into this largely uncharted area that Janet Lees has written this book. Such detailed clinical studies are a valuable starting point for clinical research. They also encourage therapists and doctors to develop their skills and widen their experience of these uncommon problems. This will, it is hoped, allow children who have acute language problems and their families to feel supported and understood, even if the professionals remain uncertain as to whether an intervention programme is effective.

Janet Lees' approach is essentially one of flexible problem-solving. If the child's condition does not conform to a classical syndrome the closest condition(s) are used to assess possible management and outcome. Assessments are to be used to attempt to understand the child's strengths and weaknesses using either available tests or modified or invented ones if necessary. There is no such thing as a routine assessment. Management has to be flexible and inventive, looking for tactics to help the child to communicate.

I commend this book as an important and very practical contribution to the subject.

B. G. R. Neville

Preface

The first edition of this book was published over ten years ago. It had its beginnings in my interest in acquired childhood aphasia as a student at the School for the Study of Disorders of Human Communication in London, now more than 20 years ago.

At that time clinical work with children who had acquired aphasias was not common.

There was something of a mystery surrounding this group of conditions. Papers written in the 1940s were the first published studies with this clinical group yet there seemed to have been little progress up to the late 1970s. I was resolved to learn more and was fortunate to have the opportunity to discuss the whole matter with one of the leading aphasiologists of the day, H. Hecaen, whose 1976 paper on ACA was about the most widely available at the time. Others have commented on the willingness of Professor Hecaen to discuss anything with even the newest student and in my faltering French I was no exception.

By 1984 I had seen just four children with ACA when I began working at Guy's Hospital, where I met Brian Neville. From then on I had the opportunity to study so much ACA that a longitudinal study became a real possibility. I began this at the end of 1984, when Professor Bob Fawcus offered me a place to study for a postgraduate degree at the new Department of Clinical Communication Studies at the City University, London. That longitudinal study was supervised by Dr Dorothy Bishop, then at Manchester University, now at Oxford, who has researched widely in paediatric language disorder, both developmental and acquired.

Throughout the 1980s there were many exciting and challenging developments. One of the best aspects for me must be the many friends and colleagues I made in this time. Because of the small numbers of children seen at any one centre the study of ACA gradually developed into a network, mainly across Europe. This afforded many opportunities to meet with colleagues in the Netherlands, Belgium, Switzerland, Ireland and Portugal particularly.

By the time I finished my MPhil in the late 1980s I was at Mansfield College, Oxford, preparing for the ordained ministry in the United Reformed

Church. This by no means signalled the end of my work with ACA. The first edition of this book came out just as I finished that course. When I returned from South Africa, about a year later, I once again began working with Brian Neville. The team that came together in the mid-1990s at the Institute of Child Health provided new opportunities for clinical and research work with children who had epilepsy and their families. The focus of our attention was the complex Landau-Kleffner syndrome.

It was particularly important to be involved in the early years of the family support group, Friends of Landau-Kleffner Syndrome (FOLKS) that now has a national profile. Towards the end of the 1990s I was glad to be asked to take a supervisory role in a study carried out in Kenya by Julie Carter, considering the speech and language abilities of children who survived severe malaria. Her help in the preparation of this second edition has been invaluable.

In the introduction to my MPhil thesis I said that I had learnt much from the children I had worked with and that 'not all of that was about acquired childhood aphasia'. Human development is a fascinating area of study that benefits from the interaction of many disciplines. The speech and language therapist works best as a member of a team. Speech and language therapy is itself a discipline that combines a number of ways of thinking and working integrating medical, educational, psychological, linguistic and sociological models. It is the integration of these perspectives into an holistic child-centred model which is fundamental to speech and language therapy as outlined both in *Children with Language Disorders* (Lees and Urwin, 1991 and 1997), in which some of my earlier work on ACA is discussed alongside work on developmental language problems, and this present book.

As a speech and language therapist who is also a theologian I must also say that the study of ACA is a pilgrimage in faith; mostly exciting and fun, sometimes sad, difficult and also frustrating. It is still ongoing. It did not end when I finished my thesis, or when I was ordained, and I therefore doubt it will end with the second edition of this book. In science we test hypotheses and I continue to be stimulated by the questions asked of me by students, parents and others. In Christian theology we use a method of action/reflection that calls us to critically examine our experiences and from that reflection, take the next step in faith. I employ both of these methods as a speech and language therapist. This book is a reflection on over 20 years of study of ACA, of discussions and developments in the light of research by myself and with others. To remain true to my model the next step has to be taken in faith; the faith that the revelation continues and that ultimately we shall know and be known. As Sydney Carter, who died in the spring of 2004, has it in his hymn: 'One more step along the world I go ... and it's from the old I travel to the new'. And so I do.

Janet A. Lees
Sheffield, UK
Pentecost 2004

Acknowledgements

The clinical work that first informed this book was undertaken at the Newcomen Centre, Guy's Hospital in the 1980s. I have many memories of the colleagues and friends of those days.

In over 20 years of clinical work in speech and language therapy I have been particularly grateful for the company and support of speech and language therapists throughout the country.

The first edition of this book, based on the work of my MPhil at City University, London, was written during my ordination training at Mansfield College, Oxford. Many members of the United Reformed Church in local churches, regionally and nationally, have also supported this work since then.

New colleagues and friends are continually being added to the number of people who have influenced my thinking, particularly at the Institute of Child Health and Department of Human Communication Science, both at University College, London, and most recently at the Department of Human Communication Sciences, University of Sheffield.

Brian Neville and Julie Carter, of the Institute of Child Health, have been very supportive colleagues, and their help in the preparation of this volume is gratefully acknowledged. Any errors or omissions that remain are my responsibility.

Family members have also played an important part, in support and encouragement. My father, Doug Lees, did the two illustrations in Figures 1.1 and 10.1. My husband, Bob Warwicker, made the computer work. My mum was there. The first edition was published the month our daughter Hannah was born in 1993. Now eleven years old, this second edition is dedicated to her.

List of cases

Case 1: Developmental language disorder after a neonatal unilateral lesion of Broca's area [*]

Case 2: Aphasia after unilateral cerebrovascular lesion at age 4;5 years

Case 3: Aphasia after unilateral cerebrovascular lesion at age 13;5 years [+]

Case 4: Aphasia after unilateral cerebrovascular lesion at age 8;2 years

Case 5: Aphasia after unilateral cerebrovascular lesion at age 8;3 years [+]

Case 6: Aphasia after head injury at age 5;3 years

Case 7: Aphasia after head injury at age 12 years [*]

Case 8: Aphasia after head injury at age 11;6 years [*]

Case 9: Loss of language after removal of dysembryoplastic neuroepithelial tumour (DNET) and response to pharmacological treatment

Case 10: Aphasia after cerebral abscess at age 15 years [+]

Case 11: Aphasia after meningitis at age 15;7 years

Case 12: Aphasia after viral encephalopathy at age 6 years

Case 13: Landau-Kleffner syndrome (acute onset) at age 12;7 years [+]

Case 14: Landau-Kleffner syndrome (fluctuating onset) from age 9 years

Case 15: Landau-Kleffner syndrome (progressive deterioration) from age 5 years

Case 16: Landau-Kleffner syndrome (progressive deterioration) from age 6;9 years [*]

Case 17: Aphasia after convulsive status at age 8;3 years

Case 18: Aphasia as a post-ictal phenomenon from 5;6 years

Case 19: Epileptic aphasia after neurosurgery at age 10;10 years

Case 20: Aphasia with minor epileptic status and congenital hemiplegia [*]

Case 21: Aphasia with minor epileptic status

Case 22: Unexplained language regression at 14 months of age

Case 23: Late onset autism at age 3;4 years

Case 24: Rett's syndrome

Case 25: Sturge-Weber syndrome [+]

Note: The cases marked [+] were first described by Lees and Neville (1990) and those marked [*] by Lees and Urwin (1991).

Abbreviations

AAC	alternative and augmentative communication
ACA	acquired childhood aphasia
AEDs	antiepileptic drugs
Aud Assoc	auditory association subtest
AVM	arteriovenous malformation
BRE	Benign Rolandic Epilepsy
CAST	Children's Aphasia Screening Test
CNS	central nervous system
CSF	cerebrospinal fluid
CSWSS	continuous spike and wave in slow sleep
CT	computed tomography
dB	decibel
DNET	dysembryoplastic neuroepithelial tumour
EEG	electroencephalogram
ESES	electrical status epilepticus in sleep
fMRI	functional Magnetic Resonance Imaging
GCE	General Certificate of Education
GCS	Glasgow Coma Score
GCSE	General Certificate of Secondary Education
GNT	Graded Naming Test
HI	head injury
Hz	hertz
IQ	intelligence quotient
kg	kilogram
LKS	Landau-Kleffner syndrome
MRI	magnetic resonance imaging
NMR	nuclear magnetic resonance
PET	positron emission tomography
PICAC	Porch Index of Communicative Ability in Children
POSP	Paediatric Oral Skills Package

RDLS	Reynell Developmental Language Scales
sd	standard deviation
Sent Rep	sentence repetition subtest
SLT	speech and language therapist
TROG	Test for Reception of Grammar
UK	United Kingdom
WFVT	Word Finding Vocabulary Test
WISC(R)	Wechsler Intelligence Scale for Children (revised)
wte	whole time equivalent

Part 1

Chapter 1
Introduction to the acquired aphasias of childhood

The acquired aphasias of childhood are those language disorders that appear after a period of normal language development and are secondary to cerebral dysfunction. There have been no large-scale studies of epidemiology of acquired childhood aphasias (ACA). A small-scale study (Robinson, 1991) suggested that they are considerably more rare than developmental language impairments, accounting for less than 10 per cent of children presenting with language impairment in childhood. There is also a 'grey area' somewhere between developmental and acquired problems. Clinically it can be a struggle to answer the question 'When is a problem acquired?' Robinson (1991) pointed to a group of about 7 per cent of his sample for whom the origin of their language problem was uncertain. These included children who had an incident within the first year or two of life which was later thought to have contributed to their communication problem, and children who clearly did have delayed development but also lost more skills later in childhood, whether gradually or suddenly. Van Hout (1997) states that a disruption to language development caused by a brain lesion acquired before the age of two years should not be referred to as ACA. Rather it should be described as a 'disruption of language milestones' or a 'developmental language breakdown'. She selects the age of two years as being 'the mean age of acquisition of first sentences' and further stipulates that ACA implies that there are 'disruptions in the symbolic aspects of oral communication' (Van Hout, 1997), not just speech abnormalities. Examples where a child may or may not have what could be termed an acquired aphasia continue to arise, amongst those with epilepsy, cerebral infections and other subgroups.

Although few speech and language therapists (SLTs) may presently have much experience with this population, there is an increasing likelihood that they will find children with acquired aphasias under their care. Improvements in paediatric intensive care facilities mean that more children will survive serious brain injury, one of the potential causes of ACA. Additionally, in the long term, the statutory provision of assessment of special educational needs under the 1981 (and subsequent) Education Act means that those surviving will need to be provided with appropriate assessment and management services. The full integration of children with impairments in mainstream education in the United Kingdom has gradually become recognized as the preferred educational option for the majority, but it requires significant resources if it is to be successful. Once again SLTs will have a larger role to play in identifying these requirements.

There are a number of different ways of understanding the strengths and needs of children with acquired aphasias. Previous research over the last 60 years has tended to follow a medical model, organizing acquired childhood aphasias according to their medical cause. A more limited amount of research has, in the last 20 years, investigated the types of language impairments seen in ACA. During this time the rise of the social model of disability and its aim of inclusion for people with disabilities has also affected the way in which children with ACA are treated in our society. The clinical and research work of this book has tried to integrate these models, although it is primarily organized according to the various causes of ACA. Because the book is for SLTs there is information about the types of language impairment, their assessment and management in each section. Examples of the language impairments of children with ACA are given. Further, each child with ACA has the right to full inclusion in education and social life and where possible these issues are also addressed.

The causes of loss or deterioration of language in childhood

Most clinicians will probably think of the results of severe brain injury, particularly after closed head injury, as a typical case of ACA. However, there are many causes of loss or deterioration of language in childhood as can be seen in Table 1.1, earlier versions of which have appeared in Lees and Urwin (1991 and 1997) and Lees (2001). Some of these causes have attracted greater research interest to date than others. Previous research is summarized in the subsequent chapters concerned with specific subtypes.

Whilst children have probably been suffering from ACA in its many forms for centuries it has only recently (since about 1978) become the subject of significant research and clinical interest. Traditionally researchers have divided these language problems into two broad groups: those aphasias of traumatic origin and those where the origin is thought to be connected to epileptic activity. This division was also followed in the first edition of this book, which had separate parts for 'traumatic' and 'convulsive' aphasias. Due to changes in terminology and further developments in our understanding of brain injury this division has attracted less interest recently.

Table 1.1 Causes of acquired speech and language problems in childhood

Damage	Impairments	Prognosis
Head injury open or closed		
Diffuse and often bilateral, but may be combined with additional focal damage.	May include motor, cognitive and sensory deficits. Epilepsy may be a sequela.	Poor when initial aphasia is very severe and persists for more than 6 months. In young children, later acquisition of written language may be impaired.
Unilateral cerebrovascular lesions		
Usually focal.	Visual field defects and hemiplegia may also occur. Epilepsy may be a sequela.	Good, even when initial aphasia is severe, if there is a return to within 2 s d for verbal comprehension score within 6 months of onset.
Cerebral infections: meningitis, encephalitis, cerebral malaria and cerebral abscess		
Ranges from diffuse to focal depending on aetiology, and response to treatment of the infection.	Additional motor, cognitive and sensory deficits are common in severe cases.	Where the damage is purely cortical the aphasia is usually only moderate to mild.
Cerebral tumour		
Usually focal, but disruption of wider cerebral function may be seen if the tumour extends or after the effects of radiotherapy or chemotherapy.	An initial delayed period of mutism is common after surgery for some posterior fossa tumours. Epilepsy may be a sequela.	Any additional treatments for the more malignant tumours (radiotherapy and chemotherapy) can also affect prognosis for subsequent speech and language abilities.
Epileptic aphasia		
Aphasia may occur as a consequence of convulsive status, as a post-ictal phenomenon, or as a feature of minor epileptic status.	Other learning problems may also occur in association, particularly after long and repeated convulsive status.	Language disturbance may be fleeting, short term (less than 24 hours), more long term or fluctuating.

(contd)

Table 1.1 (contd)

Damage	Impairments	Prognosis
Landau-Kleffner syndrome		
May be preceded or followed by epilepsy but one-third of cases never have epilepsy. CSWSS is implicated as an underlying mechanism.	Severe receptive aphasia; other language processing problems including word-finding and expressive language problems.	Poor when language comprehension deteriorates over a long period and where this shows little recovery over first 6 months. Good when loss of language comprehension is acute, sometimes in association with another illness, and where recovery is good in first 6 months (to within -2 sd). Variable when language comprehension continues to fluctuate in association with temporal lobe EEG abnormalities. Moderate to good when these fluctuations can be controlled by antiepileptic drugs.
Other syndromes and conditions		
Parasites; tapeworm Focal damage due to tapeworm parasite in the left temporal lobe has been reported.	Receptive aphasia and epilepsy.	Only one reported case.
Late onset autism Of uncertain origin, but probably related to epileptic aphasias and LKS. A pervasive developmental disorder of the autistic type that is preceded by a period of normal development.	Loss of social and communication skills, with severe receptive language disorder. There may be an accompanying deterioration in other cognitive skills.	A few of these children have been shown to regain some social and cognitive skills with the use of antiepileptic drugs.
Rett's syndrome Developmental disorder in which motor and cognitive skills are lost between 6 and 12 months of age. All known cases are girls.	Inappropriate social interaction, slowing of head growth, severe communication difficulties, abnormal oral movements.	Very poor. No known recovery.

(contd)

Table 1.1 (contd)

Damage	Impairments	Prognosis
Other syndromes and conditions (contd)		
Other disorders of developmental regression in childhood		
The term 'developmental regression disorders' includes acquired, late-onset or otherwise deteriorating conditions of unknown aetiology.	These are as yet poorly identified but include cognitive, social and language skills.	In general, those in which the greatest range of skills is lost, in which severe epilepsy occurs and in which little progress is made in the first 6 months after onset are associated with a poor prognosis.

The traumatic group was always problematic as it included various types of direct cerebral damage or invasion of cerebral tissue including ischaemia and invasion by viral and bacterial agents. On the fringes of the traumatic group there was cerebral anoxia. The term 'convulsive aphasia' has largely been replaced by 'epileptic aphasia'. The relationship between the various epilepsy syndromes of childhood in which speech and language deficits are reported, such as Benign Rolandic Epilepsy (BRE) and Landau-Kleffner syndrome (LKS), is still under discussion. There was always a group of conditions in which the aetiology remained unknown, as the loss of language in childhood is just one symptom of a range of regressive conditions. Furthermore, it was thought that this division between traumatic and convulsive aphasias over-emphasized the medical aspects of ACA and that a consideration of the presenting features of the language disorders would be more useful to the clinician.

The range and types of language disorders encountered in ACA will not be overlooked, but there is at present no universally agreed system of classification of language disorders in childhood that is in general use. A number of different models of the classification of language disorders and their application to ACA will be discussed. It is to be hoped that further research into the language disorder subtypes presenting in ACA and the language processing skills of these children will allow for the development of a more appropriate linguistic classification in the future.

Throughout this book the aim is to provide information and a framework for assessment and management that can be related directly to clinical practice. Thus a wide range of cases will be discussed and details of assessment procedures, short- and long-term recovery and management strategies will be given. Whilst not claiming to represent the whole possible range of ACA, it is hoped that this will establish a basis from which the clinician can work with such children. The way in which the cases are presented here has formed the basis of recent clinical research into ACA (Lees, 1989; Lees and Neville, 1990; Lees, 1993, 1997 and 2001). It has been used to present cases of children with language disorders, both developmental and acquired, by Lees and Urwin (1997) and can also be seen in use with other client groups in Brindley et al. (1993).

A history of the study of ACA

Before the 1940s

The modern study of aphasia can be traced back to the work of Broca (1824–80) and Wernicke (1848–1905). Both neurologists, they were responsible for the beginnings of a clinically scientific method of describing language loss, at least in adults, due to cerebral disease. It was on the basis of observations of this kind that the lesion-based maps of the cerebral cortex were developed which attributed certain aspects of language function to specific locations within the cerebral hemispheres, a simplified version of which is shown in Figure 1.1.

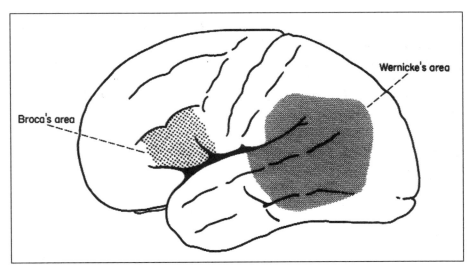

Figure 1.1 Diagrammatic representation of the left cerebral cortex showing Broca's and Wernicke's areas.

This school of thought continues to have a significant influence on our understanding of language breakdown in adults, although it has been recognized to have more limited application to the study of childhood language disorders, both developmental and acquired. It is clear that whilst we are a long way from understanding the way in which the brain responds to injury in childhood, research in brain structure and function, often from clinical examples, continues to inform our understanding. Variables such as age at injury, the nature, location and extent of brain injury and the path of recovery have all been considered in ACA research. Bishop (1988) said 'anyone attempting to assimilate the literature on acquired aphasia in children soon becomes frustrated at the paucity of the data and the lack of detail given in many of the published cases'. An outline of some of the major past studies demonstrates some of these problems.

1940–1970s

It was not until 1942 that large numbers of children presenting with ACA began to be reported in the literature in any systematic way. Guttman (1942) reported a series of 16 children with ACA from a range of aetiologies. His report seemed to suggest that aphasia after right hemisphere lesions was more common in children than in adults. This was later restated by Hecaen (1976). It was not until 1982 that Carter, Hohenegger and Satz tackled this controversy. They concluded that when early studies, in which the incidence of ACA was conflictingly reported, were excluded and the evidence from later studies was amalgamated then the data were consistent with the electrophysiological, neuro-anatomical and behavioural data in support of the developmental invariance position (i.e., that in most human beings the left cerebral hemisphere is organized as dominant for language function before birth).

Similarly studies of traumatic ACA between 1942 and 1976 emphasized the rapid and complete recovery of the speech and language skills of such children. It could be said that this view led to the neglect of the study of ACA by aphasiologists as the dominant view was that aphasia in a child was seldom of long-term significance (Lesser, 1978). It was also accepted that ACA was characterized by a nonfluent language disorder. Guttman (1942) set the trend when he reported that ACA was a 'motor aphasia' and he noted the absence of 'sensory aphasia' even when temporal lobe lesions were reported. This view went more or less unchallenged until 1978 when Woods and Teuber (1978) reported a series that included a five-year-old boy with jargon aphasia. Since then a number of cases, including some small groups, with fluent aphasias have been reported. Satz (1991) reviewed the relative incidence of fluent versus nonfluent aphasias in children, noting that they are predominantly single case reports. He concluded that fluent aphasias were significantly less common than nonfluent aphasias, when compared to adult studies. He stated that 'it seems reasonable to conclude that the symptom picture in childhood aphasia is predominantly nonfluent' and using the previous three largest series estimated that it was probably in excess of 85 per cent in children. Examples of children with both fluent and nonfluent aphasias will be included in later chapters of this book.

In 1957, a type of ACA that did not appear to be related to trauma was first described. This puzzling syndrome has many names, most commonly 'acquired receptive aphasia with convulsive disorder' or the Landau-Kleffner syndrome (Landau and Kleffner, 1957). Researchers have now spent nearly 50 years trying to decide whether it is one syndrome and what part epilepsy plays in the aetiology, amongst other questions.

For all aetiological groups the main problems of the pre-1978 period were the small numbers of cases being reported and the rather ad hoc methodology employed in the studies. Thus it was very difficult to make meaningful comparisons between studies on the basis of either neurology or the language problems observed. With the small numbers of children being reported it was difficult to draw comprehensive conclusions from any individual study. Whilst most studies of traumatic aphasias concluded that the prognosis for recovery in this group was good as compared to the reverse in studies of convulsive, or epileptic, aphasias it was difficult to see that these claims could be substantiated when few studies used appropriate forms of longitudinal assessment of language impairments and little actual language data was reported.

This led to the development of the view that there were two distinct clinical pictures of acquired aphasias in childhood. The traumatic aphasias were characteristically short-term problems and complete recovery was the rule. The language impairments were usually nonfluent aphasias in which there was an initial period of post-traumatic mutism. There were usually some comprehension problems, but the most persistent symptoms were word-finding problems. There was a noted absence of paraphasias or jargon but sometimes dyslexia and dysgraphia were observed.

By contrast the convulsive aphasias were reported as long-term problems in which complete recovery was rare. The language impairment was usually a severe receptive aphasia that was often described as a verbal auditory agnosia. Different patterns of onset were noted including a gradual deterioration in language skills or an acute aphasia with or without epilepsy.

1980s onwards

However, in 1978, the series reported by Woods and Teuber not only included one child with the unusual pattern of a fluent 'jargon' aphasia and severe comprehension problems but their paper was to prove to be a new starting point in the study of ACA. They tried to document the long-term recovery of the group using more suitable assessment techniques. This has been a continuing trend and has led to reports of an increasing range of aphasic symptoms in ACA, including a wide range of paraphasias (Van Hout et al., 1985) and several other reports of fluent aphasias including Van Dongen et al. (1985) and Van Dongen and Pacquier (1991).

Van Hout (1997) reports the use of more appropriate language assessment techniques as being one of the recent contributions to progress in studying ACA. However, she favours the view that the subtypes of ACA should be described in comparison to the aphasic syndromes of adults, and reviews these. This view has been contested by Lees (1993), and that discussion is pursued in detail later in this chapter. Van Hout (1997) advocates a language assessment procedure that includes:

- fluency of language production, including mean length of utterance;
- naming, usually to visual confrontation with an object or picture;
- auditory comprehension;
- sentence repetition;
- articulation.

Neurosurgery is sometimes necessary in children who have severe cerebral disease. There have been a number of significant reports in this period concerning the effects on language in children who have undergone some of the more common neurosurgical procedures: hemispherectomy, resection and multiple subpial transaction (MST).

There are two types of hemispherectomy: anatomical hemispherectomy, in which the whole of one cerebral hemisphere is removed, has largely been replaced by functional hemispherectomy. The latter is a combined process of central resection and disconnection of the commissures that join the affected hemisphere to the normal one (Lees and Neville, 1996). Vargha-Khadem et al. (1991) reported a series of six cases who had undergone hemispherectomy. These were made up of three pairs, each pair including one with a right and one with a left hemispherectomy. The three pairs were those who had sustained damage in a) early childhood; b) middle childhood; and c) late childhood.

A number of measures including language were carried out to determine the effects on outcome of the side of hemispherectomy and age at initial damage. They stated that 'the degree of selective language impairment after left hemispherectomy remained roughly constant, irrespective of age at injury for some measure, but not all'. Overall they concluded that the earlier the left hemisphere injury the less severe the residual language deficit. For children who had undergone right hemispherectomy, language functions were most affected when injury was early, with those who had acquired damage from middle childhood onwards having the least impaired language.

Neville et al. (1997) reported two cases of children who had a history of autistic regression, who had then undergone neurosurgical resection of dysembryoplastic neuroepithelial tumours (DNET). They suggested that early surgery was important if developmental potential is to be preserved as much as possible.

Multiple subpial transaction (MST) was described by Morrell et al. (1995) as a treatment for LKS. Theirs was the first series to report outcomes on a number of children who had undergone this process. A more recent UK series of children who had MST was reported by Irwin et al. (2001). Not all children who have had MST have made a favourable recovery and the variables that affect outcome are still under discussion. The working hypothesis for the mechanisms causing language regression and recovery in the brain in the context of focal epilepsy is, according to Lees and Neville (1996), that 'sub-clinical seizure activity may be more important than overt seizures in the developing brain'. Discharges, often at a high rate in sleep, may prevent language areas on the opposite (normal) side of the brain, or even those close to the origin of the epilepsy on the same side, from functioning. By removing the epileptogenic zone, or disconnecting it from the normal language areas, some amount of recovery of these functions may be possible.

Problems in the study of ACA

Although this is a brief overview, it shows some of the problems in the study of ACA. A more detailed review of previous studies will be given in each chapter as they relate to the specific aetiological groups. Here we will discuss some of the problems in the study of ACA in general, together with some potential solutions.

Rarity of the problem

It has already been pointed out that ACA is a rare cause of language disturbance in childhood when compared with problems of developmental origin. However, most clinicians are familiar with children with a history of a short arrest or possible deterioration in early language development, which is sometimes associated with an illness or even a psychological event. There is a grey area between clear-cut cases of ACA that are preceded by a recognizable period of normal language development and those children who never develop language normally, in which it is difficult to rule out some interference in language development. However, it is often difficult to establish specific evidence for this. We will return to consider this group in Chapter 11.

For the most part we will concern ourselves with clear-cut cases of ACA, in which it has been possible to establish, even if usually by informal reports only, that the child had a period of normal, or near normal, language development before the onset of the aphasia. The cases reported were all seen by the author and represent part of a larger group of more than 150 cases seen over 20 years. Such a group is by no means representative of an ordinary clinical caseload for the average speech and language therapist but rather is the result of a research interest in this area. Bishop (1988) stated that 'Given the rarity of acquired aphasia in children, it is unlikely that progress will be made unless researchers start to co-operate in multi-centre studies', a view which has been well recognized by those working in this field in Europe. Whilst cooperative studies are still relatively new this philosophy has led to the growth of a European study group and even joint work as reported by Martins et al. (1991).

Inadequacy of language tests used

Bishop (1988) stated that 'In this field small numbers of subjects are inevitable, but poor measurement of language function is not', yet time and time again studies have failed to report language function and aphasic symptoms in sufficient detail. Most early studies, like Collignon et al. (1968), relied on subjective reports of informal assessments and bedside observations of the aphasia. Where concern was expressed about long-term recovery of children with ACA, as in Alajouanine and Lhermitte (1965), reference to peer group norms was not given. It was therefore impossible to determine what a good or poor recovery might actually have been. Van Hout (1997) noted that the Token Test, which has often been cited in ACA studies, although supposed to measure syntactic comprehension, has a high load in respect of memory and attention. She also stated that 'recovered aphasic children may still earn abnormal scores [on the Token Test] in the long term'. However, like too many writers, she did not define 'recovery'.

Bishop (1988) hoped that 'future studies will increasingly supplement clinical observation with objective and standardised measures'. The cases reported in this book have been selected with this aim in view. However, the selection of appropriate assessment procedures can still be a problem for the inexperienced clinician seeing a child in a local clinic. Such problems also exist when trying to select assessments for children whose first language is not English or who are bilingual and require assessment in more than one language. The assessment needs of children in non-Western cultures who may have ACA, for example those surviving cerebral malaria in Kenya, have also been the subject of a few recent studies (Carter, 2002).

The comprehensive assessment of the child's language to produce a detailed language profile is one of the first stages of management by an SLT. Lees and Urwin (1991 and 1997) suggested there were five major purposes for the comprehensive assessment of a child's language problem:

- the establishment of a baseline of that child's language impairment;
- from there to contribute to the setting up of an appropriate management plan;

- to help the child, family and others come to terms with the history and implications of the condition;
- to help in the recognition of the condition if it reoccurs, either in the same family or in others;
- to allow longitudinal monitoring of the child's condition as well as cross-child comparison in clinically based research.

However, it is not altogether obvious what assessment material would be most suitable for these tasks in children with ACA. Previous studies have often used unsuitable materials, including tests that were designed for developmental problems (Huskisson, 1973), like the Reynell Developmental Language Scales (RDLS) (Reynell, 1985), or tests designed for adults with aphasia. In many ways it is difficult to get away from some of these problems. There are very few tests that were designed primarily for children with ACA. The issues related to the assessment of children with ACA by an SLT are discussed in Chapter 2.

Lesion-based studies

The use of the lesion-based model, from its basis in the work of Broca and Wernicke to its development by Goodglass and Kaplan (1972) has already been mentioned. Most of the early studies were based on this model, even when lesions could not be anatomically confirmed. With the development of neuro-radiological techniques such as computed tomography scanning and magnetic resonance imaging, which have improved the identification of lesions, most studies have retained the use of this model. This is despite that fact that it is difficult to apply to understanding the pathology of those children who do not present with identifiable lesions. This includes the majority of children with the Landau-Kleffner syndrome and other epileptic aphasias. It is also of limited application to children with closed head injury. Those with severe head injuries are likely to have bilateral lesions and those with more minor injuries may have areas of contusion and oedema that are a different type of cerebral injury, although they often lead to significant deficits.

A predominantly lesion-based perspective on ACA may also overlook the underlying ongoing development of the child. With a model based in adult studies it is all too easy to forget that that child, and the child's brain, are still developing and maturing. This can lead to the child's needs and rights being overlooked, particularly in educational terms. It is important to work within a child-centred model.

A further criticism of the Goodglass and Kaplan (1972) model is that it is of limited application even in adults (Marshall, 1986). Although we clearly do need a model from which to develop and test our hypotheses, that model should not be so rigid as to rule out significant numbers of the children seen. If this is so then the model has clearly ceased to be applicable and must be discarded in favour of another that will help to generate new hypotheses. The Goodglass and Kaplan model cannot be used alone as the major model for the study of aphasia, for it fails to explain significant numbers of aphasias in childhood. The development of a more appropriate model is an urgent need. It is to be hoped that such a model may be developed from the clinical study of ACA.

The treatment effect and concept of recovery

Most early studies emphasized the good prognosis for recovery from ACA of traumatic origin, despite being unable to measure the severity of the aphasia or provide peer group norms. In some studies this claim is clearly false. Alajouanine and Lhermitte (1965) reported that two-thirds of their 32 children had regained 'normal or nearly normal' language one year after onset, yet went on to report severe residual motor problems, EEG abnormalities and problems at school with the majority of these. Such claims can only lead to clinicians wondering what 'recovery' might be. Too many recent reports, for example Martins and Ferro (1991), concentrate on a return to a 'normal' score on one or more standardized language tests as the measure of recovery. However, too often it is the lack of objective measures that has hindered our understanding. Surely complete recovery can only be claimed when a child is able to resume all activities appropriate to the peer group, both educational and social. The woman from Mozambique who told me that she knew her daughter had recovered from her illness because 'she could now carry a full container of water on her head without spilling any' was using a functional assessment relevant to her culture. The concept of recovery requires analysis of more than test scores alone, but also a closer look at the child's learning abilities and quality of life. One of the problems of such a definition is that it seems likely that from this wider perspective few children can really be said to recover completely from ACA. The extent and severity of residual problems must be reported carefully and taken seriously if appropriate plans are to be made for the children's needs.

Few studies have investigated any treatment effect in ACA. There are many reasons for this, some of which include those outlined here, but others relate to the whole range of problems in setting up treatment studies in children. It is only when a clear picture of the residual deficits of a child is produced that clear aims and objectives of long- and short-term management can be produced. If treatment studies are to be set up then a clearer understanding of recovery is required.

However, when considering the long-term recovery of a child, we cannot abstain from short-term intervention, even in the acute period. It is therefore important that we document as fully as possible the progress of children with ACA at all stages of recovery. It is hoped that the cases presented here will demonstrate one way of doing that.

Management within a multidisciplinary team

Because ACA usually arises from complex neurological conditions most children will see a range of professionals during their recovery. In the acute stages this may include those who will have a smaller part to play in long-term rehabilitation and vice versa. The child and family will be called upon to relate to many different individuals, each with a part to play in the child's management. For both the long-term wellbeing of the child and family, for ease of management and for the development of a better understanding of ACA, a multidisciplinary team approach is to be recommended.

It is often difficult for different professionals to see each other's point of view because their view is largely obscured by what they see as the pressing needs of the child in respect of their own service. Thus acute medicine may fail to communicate to therapy and both may fail to communicate with educational services. Such a state of affairs cannot be tolerated if the wellbeing of the child is really of prime concern, and all clinical guidelines should be multidisciplinary. The aim must be to operate as a multi-disciplinary team in which views are exchanged and an holistic picture of the child's needs developed and acted upon. Such a team may well need a leader and to meet regularly if it is to work efficiently. Families often prefer a 'keyworker' to relate to, although the person taking this role may differ between settings. Thus a pattern and a style of management need to be agreed and set up for each child, although of course the way in which this works may well differ significantly across aetiologies and during recovery. The needs of the head-injured child in intensive care are obviously quite different from those of a child with Landau-Kleffner syndrome in residential education. Specific differences will be referred to in the relevant chapters that follow. For now it is enough to emphasize that whilst the team may have many different members according to the situation, the child and immediate family are always the central members of it. Other issues about the management of ACA by an SLT are discussed in Chapter 3.

Classifying language disorders in childhood

A wide range of presenting language problems has been reported in ACA across aetiologies by various authors (Deonna et al., 1977; Van Hout et al., 1985). Severe receptive aphasia, the major feature of the Landau-Kleffner syndrome, can also be a feature of the acute phase of traumatic aphasia. Similarly word-finding problems and paraphasias can occur in both the traumatic and epileptic groups. The most commonly encountered language, speech and social communication problems are listed in Table 1.2.

A number of methods have been used to classify language deficits amongst groups of language-impaired individuals. It would seem sensible to

---

Table 1.2 Most commonly encountered acquired speech and language problems in childhood

---

Language problems or aphasias
- both nonfluent and fluent aphasias do occur, but the former is more common;
- paraphasias, lexical organization and naming problems can be persistent;
- comprehension and auditory processing problems occur in the majority;
- written language problems are a more likely consequence of cerebral damage before age five years.

Speech problems or dysarthrias
- dysarthrias arise in some conditions more often than in others (for example when injury or dysfunction of the cerebellum is indicated, after surgery to remove tumours in the fourth ventricle or head injury at the base of the back of the skull);
- can co-occur with aphasias or other cognitive deficits;
- can co-occur with swallowing problems (dysphagia).

Social communication disorders or autism
- the causes and effects of autism in childhood are complex;
- acquired autistic symptoms have been reported after a range of neurological diseases after 3 years of age (3 years of age is the upper age limit for one definition of infantile autism) including a 14-year-old girl who had Herpes Simplex encephalitis (Gillberg and Coleman, 1992).

---

review the reasons for adopting a system that would allow for the classification of types of aphasia. The purpose of defining language disorder syndromes is: to outline natural history and substantiate prognosis, allocate appropriate treatment and/or management, enable appropriate comparisons between children and to facilitate research.

The main classification system in common use for the assessment of adult aphasia was described by Goodglass and Kaplan in 1972. Some authors have used this classification for children with acquired aphasias (Van Dongen et al., 1985; Martins and Ferro, 1987; Paquier et al., 1989). It is interesting to note here that studies of the use of this classification system in adult aphasia have found that between 30 and 50 per cent of cases cannot be classified into one of these traditional syndromes (Marshall, 1986).

Reference to the Goodglass and Kaplan categories will demonstrate that although they define aphasic symptoms according to a limited number of parameters, the overall descriptions are rather general and few specific indications of severity or level are given. The parameters used include a measure of verbal comprehension, naming (including vocabulary and the presence of paraphasias), sentence repetition and the fluency of expressive language. However, terms such as 'severe' are not defined objectively, i.e. in terms of a particular level or test score. Neither is any information given

Table 1.3 The main aphasic syndromes as described by Goodglass and Kaplan (1972)

Syndrome	Comment
Broca's aphasia	A non-fluent aphasia with awkward articulation, restricted vocabulary and grammar, and well-preserved auditory comprehension
Wernicke's aphasia	A fluent aphasia with impaired auditory comprehension, paraphasic speech and word-finding difficulty
Anomia	Severe word-finding problems; speech is fluent with few paraphasias
Global aphasia	Severe deficit in verbal comprehension, vocabulary and grammar with speech restricted to stereotyped utterances
Conduction aphasia	A fluent aphasia in which sentence repetition appears selectively impaired in relation to auditory comprehension
Transcortical sensory aphasia	A rare aphasia with severe deficit in verbal comprehension, normal or near normal sentence repetition, and severely impaired naming with paraphasias and perseverations and little extended expressive language
Pure word deafness or verbal auditory agnosia	No verbal comprehension
Mixed non-fluent aphasia	A tendency to non-fluent speech, moderate verbal comprehension problems but some expressive language

about how the pattern of language deficit in these aphasic syndromes might change during recovery.

The problem of appropriate terminology for language disorders in childhood was addressed by Bishop and Rosenbloom (1987). They demonstrated that no consistent approach has yet been adopted. In developmental language disorder, six language disorder subtypes were proposed by Rapin and Allen (1987). Some of these language disorder subtypes have been compared to types of aphasic language disturbance seen in adults. They have been used to confirm that the communication disorders of children with developmental language disorders and autistic spectrum disorders are the same, but that the prevalence of the syndromes differs in the two groups.

Clearly, Rapin and Allen's categories also present some problems. Two of the categories are named with neurological aspects in mind: dyspraxia and agnosia. The other categories contain strictly linguistic terms. As with Goodglass and Kaplan there is no attempt to give objective definitions of 'severe' or other similar terms. However, they have attempted to describe the probable prognosis of each subtype with a brief description of the clinical picture that may be seen in an older child, although this is also in

Table 1.4 Six language disorder subtypes as described by Rapin and Allen (1987)

Disorder subtype	Comment
Verbal auditory agnosia	Also called word deafness. There is no auditory–verbal comprehension. The problem is thought to have a poor prognosis and children need to be taught to understand language through the visual channel
Semantic-pragmatic deficit	Fluent and well-formed speech which initially is echolalic and delayed echolalia, progressing onto well learnt monologues. Auditory-verbal comprehension is literal and the child often responds to key words in the sentence. Other features of expressive language include verbal stereotypes, perseveration and circumlocution; said to have features of transcortical sensory aphasia
Lexical-syntactic deficit	A severe word retrieval difficulty alongside a difficulty forming connected utterances and understanding complex grammar. The child may produce paraphasias; said to share features with both anomia and conduction aphasia
Phonological-syntactic deficit	Speech is dysfluent in short utterances, usually with morphological errors. Comprehension may be impaired but less so than expression and phonological contrasts are reduced; said to be reminiscent of Broca's aphasia
Phonological programming deficit	Utterances are longer but there is a moderate-to-severe problem of speech intelligibility. Speech–sound contrasts are severely reduced
Verbal dyspraxia	Speech is very dysfluent and severely unintelligible. There is usually evidence of a motor planning deficit and possibly other more general motor deficits

very general terms. Whilst they admitted that the boundaries between the syndromes may be blurred Rapin and Allen (1987) stated that this 'does not suggest to us that they are invalid or but variants of a single disorder with unequal severity, any more than the fuzzy edges of the acquired aphasias negate their validity'. I would suggest that the validity or otherwise of such syndromes is borne out by the extent to which they can usefully classify language impairments and the contribution they make to our understanding of these.

Whilst there has been an increase in the number of studies containing detailed clinical reports of the language profiles of children with acquired aphasia, there has been no consistent use of a classification system for these disorders. The most commonly used system remains that developed by Goodglass and Kaplan (1972). Only recently (Lees, 1993b) has there been any discussion of how unsatisfactory this or any other classification system is for the subtypes of language disorder seen in acquired childhood aphasia. In that study the language profiles of 34 children with ACA from a range of aetiologies were compared with the categories of aphasia described by Goodglass and Kaplan (1972) and the language disorder subtypes of Rapin and Allen (1987) to see how many children had language deficits which could be classified according to these two systems.

Analysis of the profiles showed that 53 per cent of the children could not be allocated to one of the Goodglass and Kaplan categories. Of those who could not be classified:

- four children presented with fluctuating aphasias which included periods of word deafness, anomia and Wernicke's type aphasia;
- eight had closed head injuries and, as a result, a slowing in speed of auditory verbal processing and lexical recall;
- five had short periods of paraphasias followed by mild word-finding problems.

Similarly 59 per cent of the children could not be allocated to one of the Rapin and Allen subtypes. Of the 20 who could not be classified the same four with fluctuating aphasias had periods of verbal auditory agnosia and semantic–pragmatic deficit as well as severe word-finding problems. Of the remainder:

- 13 were head-injured and showed a range of problems with the speed and volume of auditory verbal processing, auditory verbal comprehension problems, word-finding difficulties including some paraphasias but no expressive phonological problems;
- two had aphasic periods of short duration in which verbal comprehension problems and paraphasias were the most common features;
- one had the Landau-Kleffner syndrome and passed through periods of verbal auditory agnosia, semantic–pragmatic deficit and lexical syntactic deficit.

The study suggested that the classification of language deficits in acquired childhood aphasia cannot be adequately undertaken using either the Goodglass and Kaplan or the Rapin and Allen categories.

Marshall (1986), in his criticism of the use of the traditional classification of aphasic syndromes in adults, noted that 'all clinical definitions are replete with such words as "some", "typically", "often" and so forth' and further stated that perhaps we should accept that 'the classical taxonomy only accepts a minority of patients within its confines'. This may be so and no doubt it will continue to be of interest to describe children with acquired aphasias whose symptoms concur with those syndromes seen in aphasic adults. However, the whole process by which we describe language disorder in children requires further consideration. Rapin and Allen (1987) reported that their six language disorder subtypes accounted for types of language deficits seen in two groups of children, with developmental language disorder and autism. The data presented by Lees (1993b) suggested that the same subtypes were not so useful in classifying the language deficits of acquired childhood aphasia. One factor which Rapin and Allen did not consider was the way in which the language disorder changed during the natural history, something which is perhaps more obvious in recovery from ACA. Neither do they accept the possible overlap between syndromes, where children seem to present with features of more than one subtype. Bishop and Rosenbloom (1987) concluded that 'we need more information about the time course, patterns of evolution and the natural and modified histories of children with language disorders' as they recognized that our present classificatory systems have largely been based on short-term observations and cross-sectional rather than longitudinal data.

Data from a longitudinal study of children with acquired aphasia (Lees and Neville, 1990) suggested that the language deficit presented differently during the course of recovery. Even children with traumatic aphasia had an initial short period of word deafness and those with fluctuating aphasias had repeated short periods like this. Recovery could include a period in which literal comprehension prevails and in which jargon is produced. There was a gradual recovery of flexibility of auditory–verbal comprehension and a variable period in which paraphasias were produced. The final stage was often a high-level problem with speed and volume of auditory verbal processing and lexical recall. This description of the natural history makes it clear that these stages might reasonably require selective treatment or management. They described the use of a consistent assessment battery to allow for comparison of language recovery profiles across children. From a series of such profiles it might be possible to hypothesize a classificatory system that better identifies the nature and course of the heterogeneous language deficits that we call acquired childhood aphasia. The language profiles of all the cases in this book will be presented in this way. It is hoped that this will allow careful consideration of this method. Whilst ACA is related to aphasic syndromes in adults as well as developmental language disorder our understanding of acquired childhood aphasia would proceed better if we respected the need to describe it carefully rather than resort to means previously designed to describe other phenomena. This point will be addressed again in the conclusion.

Chapter 2
Assessment of acquired speech and language problems in children

When an SLT receives a referral for a child with ACA the next step will be determined by a number of factors including:

- how familiar the clinician is with children who have these disorders
- the setting in which the clinician works
- the settings in which the child could be seen
- the resources immediately available.

The SLT needs to consider where to start.

Knowing what to do

According to Coombes (1987), there are four questions each SLT thinks about at the beginning of a consultation:

1) knowing what to do
2) who to do it with and where
3) when to do it
4) when to stop.

Assessment helps us to establish 'what to do'. It continues throughout clinical involvement with the child because it also includes an evaluation of:

- the child's progress with treatment
- whether the child's problems have resolved
- whether new problems can be identified.

Assessment can be complicated when the child has an acquired communication problem because most SLTs see few or no children with these disorders, and the SLT may not be familiar with what assessments to use or how to interpret the results.

This may mean referral to another more experienced SLT. Further, the complex inter-relationship between speech and language problems and other impairments (sensory, cognitive, motor) will require the input of a multidisciplinary team for further advice. Comprehensive assessment is fundamental because treatment needs to be based on clear evidence and the development of a hypothesis to have any significant impact on the child's communication difficulties. As stated by Howard et al. (1996), clinicians 'are being pulled in opposing directions by the conflicting demands of political agendas which cut and constrain the time and resources, and theoretical developments which advocate broader ranging, more detailed, and more time consuming assessments'. It is hoped that the information in this chapter will help the clinician with the demands of this task.

Assessment approaches are generally twofold: formal or informal. In respect of children with acquired aphasias it is generally true that:

- informal methods may be more useful than formal in the very early stages of recovery;
- a full assessment of strengths and weaknesses will probably require both formal and informal assessment methods;
- there are few formal assessments designed for use with children with ACA;
- both psychometric and functional assessments have their place in exploring fully a child's strengths and needs, particularly when considering educational placement;
- an assessment with a multidimensional scoring system is probably more useful in the long-term management of a child than one with only a plus/minus scoring system.

Scoring systems

An assessment, like the Reynell Developmental Language Scales III (Edwards et al., 1997), or any of its predecessors (Reynell 1977, 1985), involves only one level of scoring. The items a child gets correct are calculated versus the number the child gets wrong. The number correct forms the raw score and, in a formal standardized procedure, this is related to normal data collected from the general population in order to show how the child compares with that population. The majority of standardized speech and language assessments for children use such a plus/minus scoring system (Lees, 1999). Whilst it may be possible to determine from the pattern of errors which sections of the test cause the child most difficulty, and thereby what aspects of speech and language are most affected, such a system does little to help the assessor understand what other problems may be contributing to low scores (poor attention, motor problems, slow response time, etc.). The main advocate for multidimensional scoring for children and adults was Porch who, in the 1970s, developed his Porch Index of Communicative Ability in Children (Porch, 1972; an adult version is also available). In his 16-point multidimensional scoring system Porch provided a systematic way of analysing the child response style that gives further insight into why the child gets an item wrong; clearly an important issue when trying to develop a management/treatment hypothesis. However, Porch's 16-point system never became hugely popular and few therapists use the whole scale.

Some other formal assessments recognize the importance of understanding what makes children fail the test. Bishop (1983) provided a vocabulary checklist in the first version of her Test for Reception of Grammar (TROG) to ensure that children are not diagnosed with grammatical problems when it is the vocabulary content of the sentences that have led to the error. In the manual Bishop also identified two other types of response for which it is important not to penalize children: the slow response and the child's need for an item to be repeated. Neither of these two response styles should be counted as errors in a test for grammar. Only errors of grammar are true errors on such a test. Unfortunately TROG does not include data on the number of slow responses or repeated instructions which a child might be expected to include while doing the test. However, clinical experience working with children with ACA suggests that it is helpful to look for patterns of speed of response and attention problems when scoring tests like TROG.

For therapists who are convinced by this argument and have not developed their own qualitative scoring system Lees and Urwin (1997) described a simple one which can be used alongside a test like TROG: a five-point code which notes when responses are delayed but accurate, or accurate after requested repetition, or self-corrected (see Table 2.1).

Table 2.1 A five-point qualitative scoring code (Lees and Urwin, 1997)

1. All accurate and complete responses not requiring a repetition or cue will not receive any additional annotation (in other words, just score correct responses according to the usual method on any specific test).
2. All complete and accurate responses carried out after a delay of up to 10 seconds (this is an accurate but delayed response).
3. All complete and accurate responses carried out after the tester repeats the instructions.
4. All complete and accurate responses carried out after the child requests a repetition.
5. All complete and accurate responses after the child initially chooses another response and then changes her or his mind (a self-corrected response).

Obviously this is not the only way of ordering such observations and clinicians are encouraged to develop a system that works for them, so that more data on the quality of children's responses during assessment, and also treatment, might be made available.

Some standardized tests do include information about response style, when it is a recognized part of the presenting difficulty. For example, German (1986) included information about patterns of response in her original version of the Test of Word Finding, as she recognized that patterns of cueing and delay are important in understanding children's lexical recall problems and developing a treatment hypothesis. Again, a correct or incorrect response will only provide so much information about a child's naming problems. Naming difficulties may include different kinds of paraphasia (naming errors) such as those related semantically or phonemically to the target item as well as unrelated strings of phonemes (neologisms). Naming may be helped with gestural self-cueing or when phonemic cues are provided, for example. This can help to generate treatment hypotheses based on suggestions about how the child's lexicon is organized and accessed. Knowing how a response relates to the target response is therefore as important as knowing if the response is correct or not.

Types of assessments

Cross and Ozanne (1990) outlined one possible model for the assessment of children with ACA. Their proposed assessment included standardized tests, informal or non-standardized tests and observations as well as samples of spontaneous language and play. Within the area of language assessment they use the form/content/use division of language (Bloom and Lahey, 1978) to look at syntactic, semantic and pragmatic abilities, and additionally reading, writing and speech production. They gave a comprehensive overview of a number of tests that could be used with this population. Another summary of test procedure used with ACA can be found in Lees and Urwin (1997), who also reviewed a wide range of speech and language test material across the age range.

The actual tests a clinician may choose will depend on many things, but most often the availability of different test procedures and her/his familiarity with these. A survey carried out in 1986 asked SLTs seeing children with ACA in the UK about the assessment procedures they used. Collated results from 27 replies gave quite a long list of tests (see Table 2.2).

It is interesting that this list contains material designed for use with both children and adults and that few of the tests were designed for this specific population. Of those listed only two: the Test for Reception of Grammar (TROG) (Bishop, 1983) and the Children's Aphasia Screening Test (CAST) (Whurr and Evans, 1986) could be said to fulfil this criteria. Bishop (1982) reported that her trial version of the TROG was used with a group of children with the Landau-Kleffner syndrome while Whurr and Evans essentially adapted the adult version of Whurr's Aphasia Screening Test (1974) for use with children. They aimed to provide a simple yet sensitive

Table 1.2 Assessments used by speech and language therapists seeing children with ACA in the UK*

Title	*Author(s)*
Test for Reception of Grammar (TROG)	Bishop (1983)
Frenchay Dysarthria Test	Enderby (1983)
Reynell Developmental Language Scales (RDLS) (revised)	Reynell (1985)
Children's Aphasia Screening Test	Whurr and Evans (1986)
English Picture Vocabulary Test	Brimer and Dunn (1973)
Symbolic Play Test	Lowe and Costello (1976)
Graded Naming Test	McKenna and Warrington (1983)
Porch Index of Communicative Ability in Children	Porch (1972)
Illinois Test of Psycholinguistic Abilities	Kirk, McCarthy and Kirk (1968)
Derbyshire Language Scheme	Knowles and Masidlover (1982)
Boston Aphasia Test	Goodglass and Kaplan (1972)
The Token Test for Children	Di Simone (1978)
Action Picture Test	Renfrew (1988)
Word Finding Vocabulary Test (WFVT)	Renfrew (1977a)
Receptive and Expressive Emergent Language Scale	Bzoch and League (1970)
Language Assessment, Remediation and Screening Procedure	Crystal, Fletcher and Garman (1989)

* Replies from 27 clinicians are given in order of preference, from a survey carried out by the author in 1986.

test to identify language disorder in brain-injured children. In the clinical situation it is more sensitive to younger children's needs in the acute stages than for longer term follow-up or use with older children as in both of the latter situations the test ceiling is often reached. The Reynell Developmental Language Scales (III) (Edwards et al., 1997), continues to be widely used by SLTs. It continues to be of limited value for children with ACA, and more difficult than earlier versions to use with children who have severe motor impairments (Lees, 1999).

Of the adult tests used the Frenchay Dysarthria Test (Enderby, 1983) was the most popular. This probably indicated the paucity of formal assessment techniques to investigate oral dysfunction in children. More newly developed procedures like the Paediatric Oral Skills Package (Brindley et al., 1993) have helped to remedy this problem. This detailed observation schedule aims to look at all areas of oral function in children aged 0–16 years and can be used alongside other techniques like radiographic investigations to help create a detailed profile of a child's oral skills.

The assessment procedure used with the cases outlined in this book was developed in a clinical situation. Its aims were to provide as comprehensive an assessment of speech and language as possible within 30–45 minutes (considered to be the average time available for initial assessments), using tests as far as possible suitable for the age group under examinatic familiar to most speech and language therapists (or at least not requi lengthy time to learn the test procedure), having peer group norms where possible, which could be repeated at regular intervals during the recovery process without compromising the validity of the tests.

This does not cover all possibilities. New tests are continually becoming available and old ones are updated. Some younger children or those with severe involvement of motor or perceptual skills may need to use adapted tests or even computerized assessment procedures. Similarly where specific deficits are revealed a more detailed procedure, perhaps specific to that child, may need to be developed to look at particular impairments. For a general review of speech and language tests available the reader is referred to summaries published elsewhere (Bishop and Mogford, 1988; Cross and Ozanne, 1990; Lees and Urwin, 1997).

The assessment of speech and language reported here formed the basis of the study of 34 children with ACA which was reported by Lees (1989). Longitudinal data from a study of five children with ACA using this test battery was reported by Lees and Neville (1990). A follow-up study of 24 children using the same battery was published by Lees (1997). The tests used are listed in Table 2.3.

Table 2.3 Speech and language tests used by Lees 1997

1. For auditory–verbal comprehension: The Test for Reception of Grammar (Bishop, 1983, 2003).

2. For confrontational naming: The Word Finding Vocabulary Test (Renfrew 1977a) for children up to 10 years, and The Graded Naming Test (McKenna and Warrington, 1983) for children over 11 years, using norms by Lees (1989).

3. For naming by association: The Auditory Association subtest of the Illinois Test of Psycholinguistic Abilities (ITPA) (Kirk et al., 1968).

4. For short term auditory-verbal memory and repetition: The Sentence Repetition subtest (Spreen and Benton, 1969) using the norms of Gaddes and Crockett (1975).

5. A sample of expressive language was elicited using a story telling technique (after Mandler and Johnson, 1977), the texts of which are in Appendix 1 (see also Lees and Neville, 1990; Lees and Urwin, 1997).

The results from these tests were evaluated both quantitatively and qualitatively. Tests scores were converted to z-scores and displayed graphically over time to show the child's progress during recovery. These test results are also used to determine the extent of the child's recovery. The z-scores on both the TROG and a naming test are used for outcome in comprehension and expressive language respectively according to the classification shown in Table 2.4.

Table 2.4 Severity groups according to z-scores

Severity group	Z-score
Normal to above average	Any score over 0 to +1
Normal to mild deficit	0 to −1
Moderate deficit	−1 to −2
Severe deficit	Any score below −2

This classification of severity was used to determine outcome in the longitudinal study, (Lees, 1989) and has more recently been used in a study of outcome in children with developmental disorders by Haynes (1992).

Two tests that can include a qualitative analysis of errors are the Test of Word Finding (German 1986, 2000) and the Test for Reception of Grammar (Bishop 1983, 2003). Errors such as delay in response time, number of self-corrected errors, number of repetitions a child requires, types and number of paraphasic errors, syntactic errors, perseverations, can all be coded and compared both during the child's progress or between children. However, as yet no normalized data is available in respect of qualitative errors for children with ACA. The need for clinicians to develop ways of recording qualitative assessment data in all types of childhood language disorder cannot be over-emphasized. When moving from assessment to planning treatment it is often the quality of the child's responses and the types of cues a child uses that will be most helpful in promoting functional communication.

Informal language assessments

Initial assessment in the acute stage needs to establish which skills have been affected and how. The Children's Aphasia Screening Test (Whurr and Evans, 1995) can form the basis of such a 'bedside' assessment of communication skills in the early stages of recovery, as can the Derbyshire Language Scheme (Knowles and Masidlover, 1982). As with any child it is important to establish how other skills are affected including play and nonverbal communication (see Lees and Urwin, 1997).

Formal language assessments

During the stages of recovery, depending on the age of the child, the clinician will need to establish a profile of language skills. A formal assessment battery may be used for this (see Table 2.2). Some clinicians prefer one test battery that covers many component skills, like the CELF third UK edition (Semel et al., 2000) or preschool UK version (Wiig et al., 2000). Others will choose different individual tests that tap particular skills

as described by Lees (1993a, 1993c), some of these like the T[
Reception of Grammar (Bishop 1983, 2003) and the Test of Word F[
(German 1986, 2000) have already been mentioned.

A revised version of the TROG is now available (Bishop, 2003). The format remains essentially the same but the range of difficulty of grammatical structures tested has been increased. The age range of the standardization sample has also been extended to 4–16 years and further includes 70 adults. The data from the 2001 national census was used to stratify the sample for age, gender, geographical distribution and socio-economic status. German's Test of Word Finding has also been revised (2nd edition, German 2000). This test has an age range from 4 to 12 years 11 months, eliminating the need to have more than one test to cover the age range.

Bishop (2003b) has also published a story-telling test similar to the story recall activities used in studies by Lees (Lees, 1989; Lees and Neville, 1990; Lees and Urwin,1997). Called the Expression, Reception and Recall of Narrative Instrument (ERRNI), it provides an assessment of the child's ability to relate, comprehend and remember a story, with and without visual clues. The age range of the test, using two stories called the beach story and the fish story, is from 6 years to adults with norms available from 4 years. It is quick to administer, taking around 10 minutes for each child, and can provide information about fluency, syntactic structures and the cohesion of narrative.

More recently, work has begun on using the psycholinguistic profiling techniques of Stackhouse and Wells (1997) to develop a hypothesis-led treatment programme. Assessments that are compatible with a psycho-linguistic framework include Gathercole and Baddeley's (1996) Children's Test of Nonword Repetition. For an age range 4 to 8 years this test takes 15 minutes to administer to each child. The 40 nonwords are presented on a prerecorded audio-cassette to standardize presentation. It is said to provide an excellent predictor of later achievement in reading and writing. Two assessments that go beyond nonword repetition to sample a wider range of phonological abilities are Dodd et al. (2000) Preschool and Primary Inventory of Phonological Awareness and Mutter et al. (1997) Phonological Abilities Test. Both have UK norms and cover basically the same age range (4 to 7 years) sampling a number of phonological abilities including awareness, detection and production of rhyme, letter and phoneme knowledge. Like Gathercole and Baddeley (1996) these authors are interested to make the link between early phonological skills and later reading and writing abilities. This is of interest to clinicians working with ACA, given the number of reports that include reference to ongoing literacy problems in this group (Chadwick et al., 1981; Aram et al., 1989).

Informal speech assessments

Most approaches to motor speech problems in children are informal and depend on local circumstances. If such an approach is used it needs to be as comprehensive as possible. A structured approach as outlined by the Paediatric Oral Skills Package (POSP) (Brindley et al., 1996) has the advantage of being repeatable and communicable to other professionals. It includes a multidimensional scoring system. Other systems, like the Nuffield Centre Dyspraxia Programme (2004), now revised in accordance with a psycholinguistic model, can also be helpful with a rare subset of children for whom an acquired motor programming deficit is the problem.

Formal speech assessments

Objective assessment can be difficult with children who have acquired motor speech problems, and has rarely been used to date. Murdoch (1998) included a number of physiological approaches to the measurement of motor speech difficulties both developmental and acquired.

Videofluoroscopy has become invaluable to the management of dysphagia and if necessary a child should be referred to a centre where this is available.

Psycholinguistic assessment

A number of psycholinguistic models of different complexity have begun to be used increasingly to understand and remediate speech and language problems in childhood. Chiat et al. (1997) described some of the basic stages of processing on the input and output sides of the model (see Table 2.5)

Table 2.5 Stages of input and output processing (Chiat et al., 1997)	
Input	*Output*
Auditory input	Semantics
Phonology	Phonology
Semantics	Motor output

There are a number of reasons why a child may have input problems including:

- hearing impairment;
- difficulty identifying speech from non speech sounds;
- difficulty segmenting speech into word units;
- difficulty storing sound patterns of words;
- difficulty linking sound patterns to word meanings.

Similarly a range of output problems could be identified:

- selecting a sound pattern for the correct word meaning;
- storing a motor plan for the sound pattern;
- planning the motor pattern for the sound pattern;
- executing motor pattern.

Using a model of this kind as the basis for speech and language assessment enables closer identification of the place where the language processing breaks down for the child with language impairment. For children with acquired disorders this may make an important contribution to the management of the difficulties, if we are able to locate stages in language processing that are directly affected by, for example, ongoing epileptic activity. Few reported examples have so far used this approach. An interesting exception is Vance (1997).

Informal assessments of social communication

A scale was devised by the Epilepsy Research Team at Great Ormond Street Hospital to compare developmental level with the extent of interference by social communication deficit in the treatment of children with epileptic aphasias including early onset LKS. The scale has already been used to demonstrate improvement in 52 per cent of a group of 20 such children treated with antiepileptic drugs including steroids in a recent study (Lees et al., 1998).

Formal assessments of social communication

A number of more formalized scales can be used to assess social communication including the Checklist of Everyday Communication Skills by Dewart and Summers (1995). A study of a small group of children with epileptic aphasias by Hand (1996) used this assessment effectively in an ABA design. Bishop's (2003c) Children's Communication Checklist is the second edition of this 70-item questionnaire which, like Dewart and Summers, is for parents/caregivers. Whilst primarily for the identification of pragmatic impairments in children it claims to be useful in identifying children who may have autistic spectrum disorders. It can be used with children aged 4–16 years.

Some tests are more suitable for use with ACA than others. The Test for Reception of Grammar (Bishop 1983, 2003) was designed to assess children with language disorders including some with the Landau-Kleffner syndrome (Bishop, 1982) and is widely used with this group. Some adult aphasia tests have been adapted for use with children by the addition of normal data for at least part of the age group. Gaddes and Crockett (1975) have produced norms for 6–13-year-olds on the Spreen-Benton Aphasia Tests (Spreen and Benton, 1969) and Lees (1989) includes some norms for teenagers on the

Graded Naming Test (McKenna and Warrington, 1983). Other problems related to assessment will be discussed further as they relate to each subtype in subsequent chapters.

Cultural issues in speech and language assessment

Culture is defined as the set of values, beliefs, perceptions, institutions, technologies, survival systems and codes of conduct held by members of a particular group of people (Payne and Taylor, 2002). Super and Harkness (1986) described a framework that they call the 'developmental niche' within which the link between culture and child development can be discussed. This framework suggests components of the child's environment that are shaped by features of the wider sociocultural setting. Three principal groups of factors are described, which operate together as a system. These are described in Table 2.6.

Table 2.6 The 'developmental niche' framework according to Super and Harkness (1986)

1. Physical and social settings of everyday life: where, with whom and in what activities children spend their time.
2. Culturally regulated customs of childcare: the caretakers' repertoire of normative approaches to child rearing, such as length of breastfeeding and traditional methods of discipline.
3. Psychology of the caretakers: parental theories and beliefs about children's behaviour and development, for example the locus of authority and the economic value of children.

A culturally valid assessment is one in which the procedure only discriminates between the normal and impaired behaviour under observation, in this case acquired communication problems, and does not work against the child for other cultural reasons. Some relevant cultural issues include the child's:

- familiarity with testing situations;
- experience of formal education;
- preferred language.

Isaac (2002) lists some activities that can be used for a culturally appropriate informal assessment of a child's communication skills. These include:

- culturally relevant books, songs, rhymes and stories;
- photographs of family and community events;
- toys and objects that reflect the child's culture;

- dolls that reflect the child's culture and ethnicity;
- games and activities from the child's experience (e.g., making cha[   ] using a wok or chopsticks).

She also discusses the procedures to consider when using interpreters in the assessment process. These include:

- pre-session briefing between assessor and interpretor;
- collaborative models of partnership between assessor, interpretor, the child and family.

Low performance on formal tests has, in some studies, been shown to be due to lack of experience and familiarity with the formal testing situation, particularly the way in which the child is expected to interact with the tester. For example, in Carter's (2003b) study of children surviving severe malaria in rural Kenya, one-to-one interaction with an unknown adult was not a situation that children would commonly encounter. They would more normally relate to each other in age groups. In Kenyan culture social rules mean that children would keep their gaze averted and voice low to an unknown adult. In addition, a proportion of children will not have attended school, and thus would not be familiar with the educational style of assessment used by SLTs in which a child is required to exhibit their best behaviour or performance to an unfamiliar adult in a structured and unfamiliar environment. There is evidence to suggest that schooling itself has an influence on the development of cognitive processes and on the language children use. There are also expectations about concentration and attention for children who go to school.

Language use is social and embedded in culture. Thus translation from one language to another often presents problems. What is one word in one language may not be so translated in another. What is a common vocabulary item in one language will not be so well known, if at all, in another. Although this might be said to be obvious, translation effects have been found in a number of studies of the use of formal speech and language assessment material across cultures. For example Pahl and Kara (1992), who translated the WFVT for a South African context, found that children considered to have normal language abilities by their teachers consistently underperformed by comparison to the age levels of the British norms. They had difficulty with specific test items like 'spire/steeple'. When planning to test vocabulary in this type of exercise it is important to establish that the intended test items are culturally appropriate and test this out in advance if necessary.

Multidisciplinary assessment

The child with ACA will be seen by a number of professionals and each will assess the situation from their perspective. Thus the speech and language data will be a part of the overall profile which may include information about neurological status, including investigations like CT or MRI scan and perhaps angiography or EEG, an assessment of mobility, hearing, neuro-psychology, etc., depending on the situation. It is the role of the speech and language therapist to carry out a comprehensive assessment of the child's speech and language skills and to evaluate these in order to draw up a profile of the child's strengths and weaknesses on which future management may be based. There will be situations in which the SLT's assessment will be used for a purpose other than planning speech and language therapy. A neurosurgeon may base surgical intervention in part on evidence from a speech and language therapist or a paediatric neurologist may base antiepileptic drug treatment on such information. The choice of the speech and language assessment procedures will be determined by a number of factors: the child's age and level of ability, the presence of co-existing disabilities like motor or perceptual problems, the assessment procedures available and the experience of the clinician as well as the need for repetition of the assessment at any stage during recovery.

Summary

The speech and language assessment of children with acquired communication disorders should:

- include all areas of communicative function;
- identify strengths as well as weaknesses;
- include all stages of speech and language processing;
- allow assessment in depth and over time;
- be carried out in step with other treatment programmes;
- include skills that may be particularly at risk depending on the natural history of a syndrome;
- be culturally appropriate.

Chapter 3
Management of acquired speech and language problems in children

There are no set SLT remedies for children with acquired speech and language disorders. A few techniques have been reported in a few children (single case studies like Vance 1991, 1997; Swinburn 1999). We might assume that the more like the child described our child is, the more likely the same approach is to work. But speech therapy is as much an art as a science and must always be adapted to the individual child's needs. Some of the methods described for these children include:

- augmentative communication: sign and symbol languages, pictures, objects and communication aids which may develop into a total communication approach (i.e., all modes of communication in a 24-hour programme) (Vance, 1991);
- a psycholinguistic framework for speech, reading and spelling difficulties (Stackhouse and Wells, 1997; Vance, 1997);
- structured grammatical training: John Lea Colour Scheme and Language Through Reading (Lea, 1970; Vance, 1991);
- sentence processing therapy in nonfluent aphasia (Swinburn, 1999).

Models of speech and language therapy

Different SLTs will base their therapy on different models. SLT is a discipline that integrates a number of ways of thinking and working. However, this eclectic working is not an excuse for being muddle-headed. If clients or their carers challenge our approach we should always be ready to enter an informed discussion. There is no need to be unnecessarily defensive. The ideal situation is a dialogue, with parents/carers and professionals working in partnership. The more SLTs involve and encourage parents, the more likely they are to express their views, and SLTs must be prepared to listen, explain and modify their approach when necessary. The three issues amongst those most commonly raised during the rehabilitation of a child with ACA are:

33

- the use of nonverbal communication which may or may not lead on to more formalized alternative/augmentative communication therapy;
- the use of individual versus group therapy;
- the differences in models and methods adopted by different SLTs.

Decisions about the allocation of therapy should be based on the comprehensive assessment of the child and on a child-centred model of management. SLTs should feel empowered by the assessment process and speak up for the child's best interests in respect of therapy. The SLT should work in partnership with the parents to implement the best therapy plan possible.

Augmentative or total communication

Some families see nonverbal communication as 'the thin end of the wedge'; a sign that verbal language will not be regained or is not seriously being pursued as an option. Nonverbal communication is regarded as 'dumbing down' to a lower level of ability and may even be considered a social stigma. There is a need for SLTs to clearly advocate the totality of communicative methods and the role nonverbal communication plays for us all, as well as a need to challenge the verbal bias of our society. We all use and benefit from nonverbal communication all of the time.

Where augmentative and alternative communication (AAC) is required either short- or long-term, the SLT might need to act as an advocate, informing any of those concerned about these methods. It is important that it is 'no longer considered the "last chance" for children with chronic speech impairments' (Clarke et al., 2001). The types of AAC to consider are (Bochner and Jones, 2003):

- gestures
- signs
- objects
- photographs
- symbols
- electronic devices.

Clarke et al. (2001) provide a comprehensive summary of the decision making process when assessing children to use AAC. These include assessment of sensory impairments (vision and hearing), mobility, posture and hand control as well as symbolic understanding.

Morris (2002) says 'Never believe it if someone says to you "he can't communicate".' It may take time to tune into the way an individual expresses him or her self. Further, a young person's communication needs will change over time, especially over major life transitions and should therefore be assessed regularly. Neither is it just a question of providing a method or device and leaving families to 'get on with it'. If AAC is to keep pace with the child's needs, new vocabulary and syntax will be required. The user will want to expand the range of communicative intentions that can be accessed if communicative experiences are to continue to be novel and creative and not always passive and predictable.

Group versus individual therapy

Equally the different benefits to be gained from group or individual therapy need to be clearly explained. Communication is a social activity. It is not therefore necessarily more beneficial to spend 40 minutes a week in a very small room engaging in some unnatural oral behaviour with another person than it is to spend time in groups of different sizes doing what comes naturally in terms of communication. When children acquire language normally they do so within a range of human interactions (Bochner and Jones, 2003). Whilst theirs is a developmental approach, it is important not to forget the vital role interaction plays in language learning when planning intervention to re-acquire lost communication skills.

Riley (2001) has clearly summarized the advantages and disadvantages of individual versus group therapy with children. Where an individual's needs might be best targeted in an individual therapy session clearly this can also create an artificial environment. However, when learning new skills a safe situation can be a positive advantage. There is more time to give explanations or demonstrations of techniques to parents, to monitor change and keep notes and so adjust therapy in changing circumstances. However, the process is time-consuming, often inhibits generalization and parents have little contact with others in the same situation.

If group therapy can provide a social environment for learning communication skills it may not suit every child. Some will not do well in a group for personal reasons; not everyone will be able to learn from other group members or thrive in a competitive atmosphere. A more economical use of time both in clinical and classroom settings, the initial setting up of a group requires time for planning, organization and identifying resources. SLTs planning to use group therapy may also have the opportunity to work together in a supportive atmosphere, or with other staff for skills sharing.

Setting up a group requires a clear sense of function and purpose. The entry to the group should be clearly defined and the group composition and balance considered. The group needs clear aims and a structure for each session. The SLT should refrain from taking children into the group against these multiple considerations. The group leader/s need to develop the skills necessary to ensure the success of the group, to enable the group dynamics and deal with disruptive or non-participating members. Group therapy for children with ACA is unlikely to involve a whole group of children with such problems unless it is in a specialist facility. However, a child with ACA could be a member of a more diverse group providing s/he fitted the membership criteria.

However, the choice of individual therapy also requires just as many considerations in terms of planning, aims and resources. It is little help to set up an individual therapy contract and then discover that it cannot be implemented due to resource restrictions. This does not mean that such restrictions should limit the therapist's choice of management options. If the child requires individual therapy, then say so.

For several decades the 'expert model' has dominated the way SLTs work with clients (Bray, 2001). Fitting as it does with the medical model of 'diagnosis-treatment-cure' it has, however, begun to give way to other models. Bray (2001) suggests that 'people do not take advice easily' and clearly adherence is an important issue. However, models that encourage parental participation may also have their disadvantages. 'It is difficult to be both parents and "teacher" to a child', Bray (2001) says. This may lead to parents becoming over-demanding or over-critical of their children. A balance where parents and professionals work together in the decision making process recognizes the skill and expertise that parents have as parents. However, this process can be time-consuming and parents must be willing and able to take part in it for it to succeed.

Bilingual or multilingual client groups

Thankfully more attention is now being paid to the needs of the bilingual or multilingual child with a communication difficulty and their family. Some cultural issues were discussed in Chapter 2. Any child may present with ACA, and thus children from dual language backgrounds may just as commonly be seen in the developed urban contexts of western Europe as in the developing contexts of Africa and Asia. An SLT should refer to a specialist colleague if not themselves experienced in working with this client group. There have been reports of adults with aphasia in whom selective impairment of one or more languages occurs. Reports of ACA are as yet too few to confirm this but it cannot be ruled out. Furthermore, it is not just a question of providing assessment and therapy in the dominant language of the culture (usually English in the UK). Social, educational and interpersonal communication should be facilitated in the language of choice for the child and the family. Where a preschool child is cared for by family members who do not use the culturally dominant language, or a young person from a refugee or asylum-seeking family is admitted with ACA, or a family expresses a wish for the child to take part in faith-based cultural activities that use 'mother-tongue', then the SLT should listen and try to facilitate by liaising with relevant community workers.

Where it is necessary to work with interpreters then Isaac (2002) is a good source of advice about these issues. She discusses the linguistic differences that arise in the interpreting process when:

- there is a lack of common language between the child and the SLT;
- there are differences in word meaning between the languages they use;
- there are differences in explaining culture-specific behaviours or technical information;
- miscommunication results from literal translation of a message.

Isaacs highlights the need for SLTs to be aware of the professional jargon they use and the sentence lengths they employ when working with interpreters. It takes time to build up a partnership between an SLT and an interpreter, and Isaacs lists a number of questions that need considering when doing this, as well as future considerations for the profession in respect of working in situations of cultural and linguistic diversity.

When to do it

Lees and Urwin (1997) say about SLT for children with speech and language disorders (including children with acquired disorders):

- it should begin early;
- it should be intensive;
- it should be specific to the child's needs;
- it should be structured rather than just involving general language stimulation principles;
- it should be consistent;
- it should be built on the child's success.

SLTs and parents do ask if therapy should begin in the earliest days of recovery from an acute neurological incident. Some professionals appear to advocate that the child does not need structured intervention until the period of fastest recovery is over and the situation has stabilized, so that residual deficits are more apparent. To the child, and also the family, loss of communication skills can be every bit as catastrophic as for an adult. Reactions to this loss can vary but those observed do include selective mutism. Early intervention by an SLT is about supporting both child and family in a situation of communication loss. The exploration of modes and methods of communication that are functional for child and family are important in this phase, even if these methods are only used for a few days or weeks. The SLT has a role in building up awareness of communication skills and strategies for everyone involved in working with the child.

Where dysphagia is part of the initial presentation, then a specialist paediatric dysphagia therapist needs to be involved in establishing the extent and severity of the problem and advising about management, for example type of feeding and type of food. Most specialist dysphagia therapists work as part of a dysphagia team that will include other specialists such as the dietician, psychologist, physiotherapist and radiologist, for example. Anderson (2001) states that:

> Non-oral feeding is often the management of choice for children with neurological impairments who have poor nutrition due to persistently inadequate oral intake or where aspiration presents a serious health risk.

The two options are gastrostomy or feeding by nasogastric tube but any decision should be taken by a specialist team that includes the parents. For children with acquired problems some will have long-term impairments that necessitate such actions, but even in the short to medium term they can significantly improve the quality of life and aid further recovery.

Although there are few studies about efficacy of SLT in acquired aphasia, what has been shown about SLT in other client groups suggests that therapy that is not specific or intensive is rarely, if ever, useful. Equally a deficit-based approach, although common, is hardly motivating.

Swinburn (1999) described a successful course of therapy for a boy who had sustained a cerebral haemorrhage when aged 15 years. This therapy began 19 months post-onset of his aphasia by which time it was said that he 'communicated relatively well despite his impairments'. The therapy was based on language assessment at the single word and sentence levels, including TROG (Bishop, 1983). On this test he was said to have difficulty beyond two-item commands and comprehending reversible sentences. The therapy was carried out over eight weeks and consisted of one hour twice a week. A system of colour coding was used where each phrase type was always the same colour (e.g., red was used for verb) which is similar to the John Lea colour scheme (Lea, 1970). A story-telling test was also used to measure progress in spontaneous verbal output. Post-therapy outcomes included the observation that the boy was using more language and therefore took longer to complete the language sample, with an increase in the length and complexity of the phrases he used. Swinburn (1999) stated that 'this improvement had a direct and positive effect on his ability to convey information verbally'. She stated that given that the therapy had been carried out 19 months post-onset it was unlikely to be attributable to spontaneous recovery.

Therapy in the teenage years is important when we remember that language development is ongoing in the second decade of life. Nippold (1988) has assembled a wealth of evidence concerning the growth in syntactic, semantic and pragmatic language skills both in verbal and written language during this age period. A child who has ACA and who demonstrates good initial progress such that s/he is once again able to communicate verbally, and may even pass some language assessments at or near age level, can nonetheless go on to experience significant language difficulties when they are unable to learn these more advanced language skills. Rather we see the gap between the aphasic teenager and their peers opening up as the language skills of the former can remain more or less static by comparison.

When to stop

A child's need for SLT will change and develop on account of:

* the course of recovery;
* changes due to drug treatment or surgery;
* changes due to developmental progress;
* changes due to social situation.

There are three phases in recovery from an acquired aphasia in childhood. The length of each phase will vary depending on the child, the cause of the aphasia and its severity, so it is not possible to say that phase one will last three days and phase two six weeks, for example. The main variable in each phase is the speed of change in the child's communication skills; how quickly goals are reached. The three stages: acute, steady progress and plateau, are described in more detail by Lees (1993a). The main decision making issues in each stage need to be based on comprehensive observation and discussion with parents/carers and child. Any techniques used should be based on sound hypotheses and aim towards success for the child.

Children can go on receiving SLT in the transition to adulthood if they need it (there is no age limit), but provision for those whose communication problems began in childhood (whether developmental or acquired) needs to be understood by those who provide services to adult clients.

Managing challenging behaviour

There is evidence that children with ACA are at increased risk of behavioural difficulties (Neville et al., 2000; O'Brien and Cheeseburgh, 2000; Yeates, 2000). This can be difficult to manage and lead to exclusion from education and community services, which could include SLT. Managing behaviour is a serious issue that requires time, a consistent approach and teamwork if it is to be really effective. Remember that the attitudes of others may affect the behaviour of a child with disabilities. Where a child presents with mild impairments that are not readily apparent, scapegoating and bullying may result. Other children and adults may judge the impaired child as behaving inappropriately, for example being attention seeking, when they are actually behaving in a way that is life-preserving and self-affirming. Promoting good behaviour is not necessarily straightforward although the maxim 'Do more of what works and less of what does not' is worth remembering.

The most ineffective way of managing problem behaviour is the 'shout-threat-punish' strategy. This method is more likely to result in an escalation of inappropriate behaviours. Rather, it is better to try to address the child's unmet need that has led to the behaviour. It is important to be assertive with the child rather than aggressive. An assertive approach means being firm, clear and consistent about your expectations. If you expect the child to listen quietly then say: 'I expect you to sit quietly'. If the child does not, then repeat your expectation as a reminder, adding an alternative outcome if the requirement is not met: 'I expect you to sit quietly, or else you will leave the room'. If the expectation is not met then the alternative should be carried out.

For children with difficult behaviour there may be many underlying factors including low self-esteem and low self-confidence. Everyone needs to feel valued and it is important that children with ACA can use strategies to build up their vocabulary about feelings of esteem and confidence. Where communication problems persist an approach that emphasizes the essentials of 'living in community, relating to each other; building friendships, enjoying emotional and psychological well-being and adaptive coping skills' is advocated by Nash et al. (2002). They define a persistent communication difficulty as one:

- that has continued past the age of school entry;
- where progress has plateaued;
- where the child has become demotivated and is at risk for psychosocial difficulties.

For children with ACA the problem may not begin until after school age, but even so the other aspects of this definition are useful. Whilst much of the work of Nash et al. (2002) was with children who were living with the long-term effects of cleft palate the intervention programme, with its psychosocial, cognitive and emotional dimensions, is also useful for ACA where these factors can also be a feature of long-term recovery. The programme was developed for residential groups but can be adapted. The resource sheets are available in a photocopiable format.

Many schools now have anti-bullying policies that include strategies like:

- circle time: a whole-class format for peaceful problem solving;
- circle of friends: a peer group strategy for supporting and including potentially isolated children;

- peer mediation: a whole-school strategy by which trained peers deal with general bullying and conflict issues.

Basic to most of these approaches is a thinking and learning strategy that empowers children through active listening to help and support each other. The education inclusion coordinator or educational psychologist should be a source of information about such strategies.

Summary

By now it will be clear that:

- acquired speech and language problems pose particular difficulties to the child, the family and those professionals involved in their rehabilitation;
- some progress has been made in managing this client group but it is a rapidly changing field in which the practitioner needs to keep abreast of current research;
- the relatively uncommon nature of these problems for most SLTs makes them quite a challenge and means teamwork is particularly important.

Whilst a small number of case studies have been able to demonstrate responses to specific SLT techniques, it is hoped that many other largely unanswered questions about treatment and rehabilitation will be the focus of renewed clinical and research interest in the coming decade.

Part 2
Specific Causes of ACA

Chapter 4
Paediatric stroke

Pathology

Although in clinical and research terms it could be argued that stroke in childhood is a neglected area, it actually affects around 1,000 children a year in the UK (Paediatric Stroke Working Group, 2004). Children with certain types of medical conditions, such as cardiac disorders and sickle cell disease, may be particularly vulnerable to stroke. Two kinds of pathology commonly occur in stroke: haemorrhage and infarction. Cerebral haemorrhage occurs when a cerebral blood vessel ruptures and blood escapes into the brain. This may be into the subarachnoid space, the substance of the brain or into the ventricles, called a subarachnoid, an intracerebral or an intraventricular haemorrhage respectively. Wherever the blood collects, a blood clot, or haematoma, may form. Obviously head trauma is a potential cause of bleeding within the brain. This will be considered in Chapter 5. In this chapter the focus is on types of cerebrovascular disease, particularly those that lead to focal unilateral brain lesions including what is commonly referred to as stroke.

Most speech and language therapists will be more familiar with the management of adult stroke survivors, which is more often subsequent to infarction. This occurs when a cerebral vessel becomes blocked by a blood clot or thrombus, reducing or interrupting the supply of blood, and therefore oxygen in the blood, to the surrounding cerebral tissue. Aphasia resulting from unilateral lesions of vascular origin is more common in adults than in children. However, the latter group should not be ignored. For more than a century children with acute hemiplegia have been reported in the literature. Whilst this is a recognized sign of cerebral dysfunction, there has been much historical speculation about its causes in childhood. The advent of non-invasive vascular imaging rapidly clarified this subject. The presence of congenital hemiplegia, and occasionally other deficits, further serves to complicate the issue. When an infant presents with a mild hemiplegia,

45

attributing this to pre-natal or post-natal causes may take considerable investigation, although the majority appear to be caused by intrauterine ischaemia or early embryological defects.

Cerebral palsy is a term often used to refer to a wide range of motor disorders of varying severity in childhood. This was defined by Bax (1964) as a disorder of movement and posture due to a defect or lesion of the immature brain. Both the lesion and the disorder are non-progressive and may arise in the pre-natal period, at the time of birth, or in the neonatal period. The subsequent discussion here is not concerned with the motor and/or cognitive impairments of cerebral palsy.

Early cerebral lesions

There has been considerable research into the long-term effects on speech and language development of early cerebral lesions, defined as those acquired before one year of age. Bishop (1988) reviewed much of this material because of her interest in language development 'in exceptional circumstances'. She noted that 'we might expect to find that left-hemisphere damage early in life would preclude language development, but this is not so'. As early as 1897, Freud remarked on the rarity of persistent language disturbances in children with congenital right hemiplegia. More recent research has often used an experimental design which has compared groups of children with early (acquired before one year of age) focal lesions of either the left or right hemispheres with groups of children with late (acquired after one year of age) focal lesions of either hemisphere. The children are then asked to carry out different types of tasks, either linguistic, visuo-spatial or other cognitive tasks. The results are used to conclude that either there are, or are not, specific effects of early and late brain lesions but also that there is, or is not, evidence to support the hypothesis that the left cerebral hemisphere is predisposed to be dominant for language development from before birth. Similar studies have been carried out by other authors including Vargha-Khadem et al. (1985), Aram et al. (1987), Aram and Ekelman (1988a, 1988b), Aram (1991b) and Riva et al. (1991). Most have supported the hypothesis that the left hemisphere is predisposed before birth to a dominant role in the development of language.

However, the debate is by no means concluded. More recent studies that include the use of functional MRI (fMRI) are still providing new insights. Hertz-Pannier et al. (2002) used pre- and post-operative fMRI tasks with a child who underwent hemispherectomy at age 9 years. This child had had a period of normal language acquisition before developing intractable epilepsy related to Rasmussen's encephalitis at age 5;06 years. Pre-operative fMRI confirmed left hemisphere lateralization for word fluency. Post-operative fMRI at age 10;06 showed activation in the right hemisphere during expressive and receptive language tasks. Although these regions had not shown as active pre-operatively they did mirror those areas active in the left hemisphere before hemispherectomy. They concluded that the brain is capable of developmental reorganization for language at a later age than had previously been thought.

Some studies have looked at quite specific aspects of functioning. Eisele (1991) carried out a detailed study of language comprehension. She had two groups of children with unilateral lesions to right and left hemispheres respectively and two control groups individually matched with the experimental groups for age, sex and race. The onset of the cerebral lesions ranged from the peri-natal period to 9 years of age, but none were clinically aphasic at the time of the study. The children were asked to make 'truth-value judgements' on ten complex sentence types which were chosen to 'involve the integration of syntax as well as semantic and pragmatic language knowledge', with the aim of demonstrating whether or not subtle aspects of language function might be impaired by early right hemisphere injury as well as the more usually reported effects on language of early left hemisphere injury. Eisele claimed that her results did uphold this hypothesis and went on to conclude, perhaps not too surprisingly, that 'a complete acquisition of language depends on the normal functioning of both hemispheres throughout the course of development'.

Aphasia after stroke in childhood

It is those children who present with acute aphasia in childhood, with or without hemiplegia, as a result of cerebrovascular disease, who we shall discuss here in more detail, both vascular malformations and cerebrovascular occlusion disorders. The various subtypes of these conditions were well documented by Isler (1971), who presented a wide range of cases and considered both the neurological management of each and their prognosis.

Few other studies have considered this aetiological group exclusively, and none specifically from the point of view of presenting speech and language disorder, except for a single case by Dennis (1980). In most studies of ACA children with unilateral cerebrovascular disease are mixed together with other traumatic aetiologies so that the underlying neuropathological mechanisms and their different effects are glossed over. It is acknowledged that these disorders are a rare cause of morbidity and mortality in the first two decades of life (Kelly et al., 1978). Isler (1971) and Kelly et al. (1978) both agree that the sex ratio of incidence indicates that boys are almost twice as likely to present with arteriovenous malformations than girls. By contrast, in Moyamoya syndrome, a disorder associated with multiple intra-cranial arterial occlusions that can be caused by a range of pathologies, Isler's review of the literature demonstrated that it was more common in girls.

Natural history

The effect of an acquired vascular lesion on a child's language appears to vary considerably from child to child. Factors such as site of the lesion, age at which the lesion is acquired and the initial severity of the disorder have been suggested as the major variables related to prognosis. The way in which these variables interact is not understood but, as with developmental language disorder, it is obviously far from simple. In defining ACA it is usual to include only those children whose cerebral lesions were obviously acquired after spoken language had become established. As already stated, children with congenital lesions may be included in the group described as cerebral palsied but they may also occasionally be included with children with developmental language disorders. Recent research has considered the long-term effects of early unilateral cerebral lesions but few cases of severe language disorder in childhood have been reported. Case 1 is an example of a boy with a unilateral cerebral lesion arising in the neonatal period who presented with a developmental language disorder. The definition of ACA does of course leave a grey area, roughly between six and 20 months of age, when it is problematic to decide whether a child should be considered to have an acquired problem or not. A case of aphasia in which an unexplained period of regression and deterioration of communication skills in early childhood has been reported will be considered in Chapter 11.

Few studies have specifically documented the natural history of aphasia subsequent to unilateral cerebral lesions, except for a few individual case studies. Because these are highly variable, only preliminary conclusions can be drawn. Firstly, acute expressive aphasia appears to be rare in childhood. In the majority of reported cases, where the results of formal language tests are included, the presence of comprehension disorders as well as expressive language difficulties has been clearly demonstrated. Secondly, a general picture of an initial period of quite fast recovery that gradually tails off has also been shown (Lees and Neville, 1990), to the extent of this period being a major determiner of final outcome. Lees (1989) suggested that where children reached the level of >2 standard deviations from the mean in verbal comprehension up to six months post-onset then prognosis is usually good. Those who failed to reach this level were more likely to have significant long-term language deficits.

Paraphasias

Paraphasic naming errors have been reported in children with unilateral cerebral lesions. Three types of paraphasia are usually recognized: semantic paraphasias where the error is semantically related to the target item (a 'table' is named as a 'chair'), phonemic paraphasias where the error is phonemically related to the target item (a 'thimble' is called a 'thrimble') and neologisms where so many phonemic errors occur that it is impossible to see any relationship between the named item and the target item.

Van Hout et al. (1985) reported a series of cases, not all of whom had the same aetiology, with a wide range of paraphasias, both as temporary initial features of the aphasia and as more persistent long-term problems. In the 11 children aged from four to ten years, semantic or phonemic paraphasias always occurred. The tendency to perseverate these naming errors was also reported as quite a frequent occurrence. They postulated that the lack of previous reports of paraphasia in cases of ACA of this kind (essentially the view before 1978) may have been due to the fact that language investigations were not always carried out as soon as reasonably possible. Where the paraphasic period was short (perhaps only a few days) they would therefore have been missed. Clinical experience of seeing children from acute onset to long-term follow-up supports the view that detailed assessment at all stages of recovery is important for a full understanding of ACA. Lees (1989) reported that the majority of the children in that study who were in this aetiological group produced paraphasic errors at some time during the recovery period. This data further supports Van Hout et al. (1985), that a paraphasic period longer than six months was a poor prognostic sign.

Pitchford et al. (1997) reported the case of a of a girl who at the age of 6;07 years suffered a left hemisphere stroke that initially left her mute. They used a cognitive neuropsychological approach to monitor the recovery of her language processing over two years. The features of the recovery of her language were:

- an initial period of mutism;
- rapid reappearance of spoken language, the vocabulary suggesting a recovery of previous language rather than relearning;
- a nonfluent aphasia, characterized by word-finding difficulties and semantic and phonemic paraphasias, with distorted intonation;
- poor confrontation naming, but the use of phonemic cues helped lexical access;
- comprehension of single words only, and problems with sentence comprehension.

Within two years this girl's language had recovered to normal levels for naming and above normal levels for verbal comprehension. However, her written language skills remained severely affected.

The role of the speech and language therapist

A comprehensive assessment procedure will be required to determine the child's strengths and needs. Various tests and informal measures have been advocated. Dennis (1980) used the Neurosensory Centre Comprehensive

Examination for Aphasia (Spreen and Benton, 1969) with the norms for children prepared by Gaddes and Crockett (1975). It may be useful to select some of these subtests to investigate specific functions like naming, repetition, fluency or reading. The specific situation will determine whether or not the whole test battery is used. Dennis (1980) also advocated the use of the story-telling techniques proposed by Mandler and Johnson (1977) for the analysis of expressive language. This can be useful where children are reticent, especially after a period of mutism as may be observed after stroke, and has been used in other studies (Lees and Neville, 1990). Unfortunately peer group norms are not available.

A review of studies of children presenting with traumatic aphasias reveals the use of a wide range of assessment material. Aram (1991a) reviewed this subject and suggested a number of different tests, but the list had a predictably North American bias. Quite a number of studies have used tests originally designed for the assessment of adult aphasia. For some of these, peer group norms for children are available, as with the Spreen-Benton test, or there is a child's version, as with the Token Test (Di Simoni, 1978). However, many use the Boston Diagnostic Aphasia Examination (Goodglass and Kaplan, 1972) and also use their diagnostic categories. A discussion of the limitations of these is provided in the introduction to this volume.

There are three levels at which the language of aphasic children could be evaluated: clinical rating, psychometric assessment and linguistic study. Each level will require a different amount of time to complete and provide different types and amounts of data. Equally each level may require a different amount of training to carry out. However, as Aram (1991a) concluded, 'whatever level of description used or specific tests selected or developed, the overwhelming conclusion that emerges ... is that as an area of study, we have only begun to describe and understand factors related to the language of brain-lesioned children'. Until we begin to report the language of aphasic children in greater detail in relation to different aetiological groups we will not be able to say which tests suit which subgroups within this population better than others, if indeed that is shown to be the case.

When determining the need for therapy directed at the child's naming difficulties an analysis of the types of cues the child uses, whether self-generated or supplied by others, is an important consideration. Children and adults without language problems use self-generated and environmental cues to aid naming when necessary. It is possible to help the aphasic child regain an understanding of cueing that in turn may improve naming. Some details of the cues used to aid naming by normal teenagers doing the Graded Naming Test (McKenna and Warrington, 1983) are provided in Appendix 1. By observing which cues the child finds most helpful, the therapist can prepare a programme to reinforce these in a range of individual and group tasks for confrontational and association naming, as well as in spontaneous language. Initially tasks will involve naming in a structured but non-pressurized situation. Gradually the structure can be altered to include recall of names in other situations, ranging from more informal tasks to formal timed tasks. If feasible, the child should be encouraged to keep a notebook to record situations in which naming has proved difficult for later discussion with the therapist. These can then be re-enacted in a role-play and the child can work through the range of strategies that would help naming if a similar situation were to recur.

Multidisciplinary management

For those children admitted with acute aphasia after a stroke, a range of investigations may be used to determine the aetiology. The investigations used by the acute medical team will depend on the local situation. They include CT or MRI scanning and angiography. Magnetic resonance imaging is being used increasingly, as it gives better definition of the brain in children, as is non-invasive vessel imaging including Doppler ultrasound. Occasionally a stroke-like syndrome can be caused by some investigations of cerebral vascular disorders. Angiography may not therefore be indicated in all cases. When it is carried out the angiogram can provide a radiological picture of the arrangement of the cerebral vessels and show up any malformations that may be present. Figure 4.1 is an example of an angiogram of a child with a large congenital arteriovenous malformation on the surface of the left cerebral hemisphere (see case 25 for further details). CT scans of the brain provide a different type of radiograph that gives information about the density of the cerebral matter. Thus they are able to demonstrate haemorrhage, infarction, haematoma or neoplasm. They will also show if there is general atrophy of the cerebral hemispheres or a shift in the position of the lateral ventricles, for example. Figure 4.2 shows a CT scan of a child with a large haematoma in the posterior part of the left temporal lobe from a haemorrhage of a congenital AVM (see case 3 for further details).

Two other imaging techniques that have become more available for the investigation of children with cerebral dysfunction are magnetic resonance imaging (MRI) and positron emission tomography (PET). Like CT scanning, MRI is a non-invasive investigative technique. However, MRI scanning is said to have several advantages over CT scanning for investigations in children. These include a greater sensitivity to blood flow, oedema, haemorrhage and the extent of myelination (Gooding et al., 1984). By contrast with both CT and MRI scanning PET allows for the study of brain physiology and chemistry. Cerebral blood flow and oxygen or glucose metabolism can be examined. Metter (1987) reported the use of PET to investigate cerebral physiology in 70 adult aphasic patients and identified five abnormal patterns of activity. He claimed that the results showed that not only cortical but also subcortical connections were vital for competent language function. This

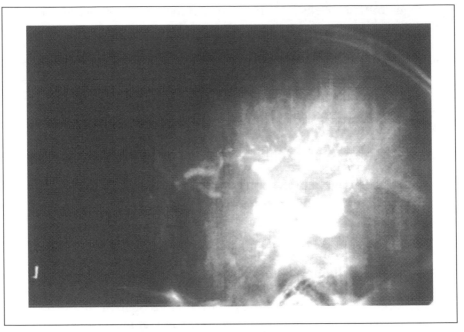

Figure 4.1 Angiogram of Case 25.

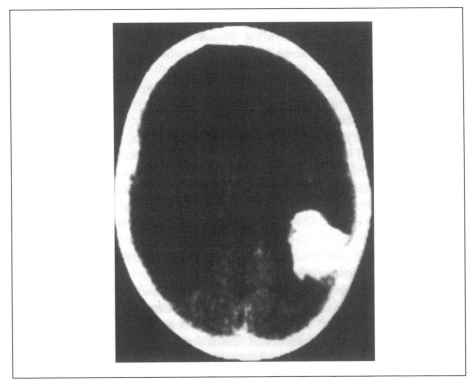

Figure 4.2 CT scan of Case 3.

technique has not been used extensively in ACA and therefore no comparable study yet exists. However, Robinson (1992) reviewed studies of using PET scanning in aphasia and concluded that it is 'for very good reason why everyone is rethinking the neurophysiology of language, not in terms of the strict one-to-one site-to-function relationship' of the lesion-based model but 'in terms of functionally overlapping networks'.

Rehabilitation

A recent review undertaken to produce clinical guidelines for the management of paediatric stroke states that 'There is little evidence of the effectiveness of rehabilitation interventions specifically for children affected by stroke' (Paediatric Stroke Working Group, 2004). It is advised that the management of problems that occur after stroke should aim to achieve relevant skills in all domains of activity and care appropriate to a child's home, school and community context.

A number of other deficits can occur after stroke, particularly motor or sensory deficits. However, there is mounting evidence to suggest that aspects of development such as mood, behaviour and memory can also be affected. Where the lesion is in the posterior part of the temporal lobe then visual field defects may occur, whereas a more anterior lesion encroaching on the motor cortex can lead to hemiplegia. The severity of the latter can vary to include the face, arm and/or leg. Equally variable recovery is reported. The three girls reported later in this chapter (cases 3, 4 and 5) provide good examples of the variability of the presenting deficits and their duration. Thorough assessment by a number of different professionals will be required to establish the extent of any coexisting problems. This will include audiological and opthalmological investigations as well as assessment by a physiotherapist and occupational therapist.

In the long term the child is likely to need assessment for educational placement. Such assessment 'should aim to document a particular aspect of function, impairment and/or disability as objectively as possible' (Paediatric Stroke Working Group, 2004). It is not enough to presume that any child who can walk can return to her/his previous school without any further discussion. Even if the child makes a good recovery (i.e., scores return to within 2 standard deviations within six months of onset) it is advisable to make an annual follow-up for at least two years post-onset to rule out any specific educational needs. We know very little about the long-term learning capacities of children who sustain unilateral cerebrovascular lesions, and certainly not enough to presume that any fast initial recovery curve will indicate a return to previous learning abilities. Therefore some level of surveillance until school leaving age is both a sensible precaution and would begin to provide some of the information lacking about these children.

Clinical experience with children placed in a wide range of educational situations has led to a view that where a child does have special educational needs and these are identified, the advantages of close cooperation between the education and health services and also with the family are of greatest benefit. Some education authorities will make creative attempts to meet these children's needs to good effect (for example case 3). In other situations special educational needs will not be properly identified and the child will have an ongoing experience of failure and frustration (for example case 5). There can be no general rules about specific educational provision for these children. Rather, comprehensive assessment of each individual is required so that each one has a profile of strengths and needs which can be translated into aims, goals and strategies. This has to be the right of every child.

Examples of children with unilateral cerebral lesions

Case 1: A boy with a developmental language disorder from neonatal stroke

This boy (first described by Lees and Urwin, 1991) was born at 34 weeks gestation. He was the second child of two healthy unrelated parents. At 29 weeks of pregnancy there was a history of a small amount of bleeding, but this did not give cause for further concern. His birth weight was 2.3 kg and he was considered rather small for dates. His parents began to be concerned when his motor development appeared rather different from his older, healthy and normally developing brother. At the age of six months a right hemiplegia was confirmed. He also had eczema but was otherwise well. A CT scan showed atrophy of the left cerebral hemisphere. There was an area of low density in the posterior part of the left frontal lobe in the region of Broca's area, and other smaller patches in the left temporal and parietal lobes that suggested an old left middle cerebral artery infarct. With physiotherapy his motor skills improved. He walked independently at 26 months.

Parental concern increased when it was noted that the boy was not speaking at that age, although his comprehension appeared good. Formal testing, using the Reynell Developmental Language Scales (revised) (Reynell, 1985) confirmed that comprehension was within normal limits at age 2;6 years and remained so throughout the period he received speech therapy. He was using a few vowel sounds to communicate as well as pointing and pulling. A programme of therapy that included introducing the Makaton Vocabulary (Walker, 1980), a gestural system, was commenced and he soon learnt a useful number of signs. Despite his hemiplegia, he managed signing quite well and within two months was making up his own signs and linking signs accompanied by vowel sounds. He was over three years old before he developed a small vocabulary of single words. These were simple combinations of long vowels and glottal stops that had to be clarified by signing. Over the next year he received speech therapy twice weekly on an individual basis and once weekly in a small group. He made good progress with communication and became more verbal as he mastered first velar and then bilabial, nasal and plosive sounds. Signing remained vital for intelligibility.

The boy was admitted to a preschool language unit at age 4 years. By this stage his verbal language consisted of a wide vocabulary of open syllables in which the consonant-vowel combinations were predominantly plosives or nasals with long vowels and some glides. These were joined in short sequences of three of four words often with glottal stops between each one. He continued to rely on signing for communication.

For this child, it is clear that the normal sequence of speech sound acquisition was disrupted, resulting in a severe difficulty in communication through verbal language. Whilst it is not possible to say that all of his impairments were related to the early cerebral injury, it is difficult to suggest that it played no part in the aetiology of the problem. The case confirms that early lesions of the left cerebral hemisphere, and Broca's area, can interfere with language acquisition to the extent of affecting a child's educational needs. Careful study of children presenting with early unilateral cerebral lesions involving areas thought to be primary for language processing is to be recommended.

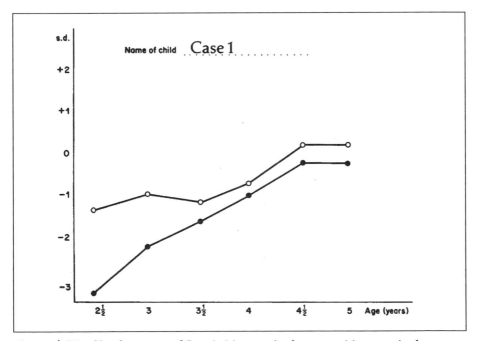

Figure 4.3 Profile of recovery of Case 1: (o) receptive language; (•) expressive language.

It has generally been considered that children with unilateral cerebral lesions with onset before the age of five years recover quickly and well where they are no other complications. It is probably more helpful to say that each child requires consistent long-term follow-up to determine the rate and extent of recovery well into school age, as the following example demonstrates.

Case 2

This boy presented with an acute aphasia at the age of 4;5 years. He had a history of normal development, although his parents had recently become concerned about the persistence of a developmental dysfluency and had seen a speech therapist about this. Before his admission, his parents had noticed a slight asymmetry of his face, with his mouth turned down on the right side, for the preceding two days. His behaviour was also described as 'odd'; he would walk around aimlessly, appeared quiet and uninterested in play. On admission he was found to have a moderate right hemiplegia and an acute aphasia, such that his speech was slurred and expressive language was reduced to jargon. CT scan confirmed a small lesion in the territory of the left middle cerebral artery in the anterior part of the left temporal lobe.

The boy's right hemiplegia gradually resolved over four days. There was no evidence of visual field defect and hearing was normal. During the first week the jargon persisted and he communicated by pointing, pulling and other gestures. He was producing neologisms and parpahasias as well as perseverated errors. Formal testing using the Test for Reception of Grammar (Bishop, 1983) confirmed a severe comprehension deficit.

However, by the second week his language showed a marked improvement and he was no longer jargoning. Comprehension was still impaired, as was naming. There was evidence of sentence formulation problems in expressive language. By six months post-onset scores for both verbal comprehension and naming had regained the normal range. However, there was still some evidence of grammatical problems in expressive language and some naming difficulties. Examples of his expressive language, taken from responses to the Renfrew Action Picture Test (Renfrew 1988 and 1997, in Table 4.1) show how this improved over the two years of follow-up. Initially there was evidence of unintelligible jargon and incomplete sentences that developed into a more nonfluent pattern. This later resolved into short sentences with some minor grammatical errors. He began his education in a mainstream nursery class without additional support at the expected time. Only long-term follow-up will confirm whether this period of language disturbance will have a significant effect on his communication and more especially on his ability to acquire written language skills.

Table 4.1 Examples of responses for Case 2 on the Action Picture Test*

Onset (age 4;5 years)
1. That's her ... doing ... cuddling teddy
2. Putting her /dɒz/ on
3. He got stuck /tʌt/
4. The man ... doing a lot of jumps
5. Did the ... er ... cat did
6. Her ... [unintelligible]
7. I don't know
8. The man ... doing lots of jobs
9. Happen to his shoe
10. They ... [unintelligible]

Three months post-onset (4;9 years)
1. There's a girl and a panda bear
2. There's a girl ... she's putting his sandals on ... it's snowy time
3. It goes next to there ... he pushed him
4. Jumping the horse ... he's a policeman
5. He feed the cats ... he feed the mouse
6. He got broken glasses ... he fellen down the stairs
7. Putting the letter ... post ... it's a boy
8. Laddering the cats
9. He got his slippers off
10. He got fall the apples ... the girl fall the apple ... that's the road

Six months post-onset (4;11 years)
1. Girl got her teddy bear
2. Putting his boots on 'cos it's snowing
3. Going to get that wall off him ... someone take him
4. Man going to jump the horse and the gate
5. Cat going to get mice
6. He fell over and broke his glasses
7. Going to lift him up 'cos he's going to put post up
8. The man is going ... climb up ladder ... and get the cat
9. Boy's crying ... lost his slipper ... the dog take it
10. Apples ... the boy put apples ... the lady carry the bag ... she dropping apples ... the boy doing picking apples

One year post-onset (5;8 years)
1. Cuddling ... she put her hands round her and cuddle the baby
2. Putting her boots in ... she's pulling her chair and she's rocking it backwards and she's fell off the chair
3. He get ... he some ... naughty boys tie him round 'cos he don't want to bite every children
4. He's jumping over the fence
5. He's chasing the mouse over the track
6. Fallen down step and broken his glasses
7. She's put the post in

(contd)

Table 4.1 (contd)

8. The man's doing ... he's got a ladder and he's fixing the roof and trying to get the cat away from it
9. He's taking his slipper and he's crying
10. She's dropped some apples and he pick the apples up

Two years post-onset (6;7 years)
1. She's cuddling a teddy 'cos she likes it
2. She's putting her boots on 'cos she's going outside ... or to the farm
3. He's tied round 'cos the man doesn't want the dog to go away. He's car parked there while he gets some dog food
4. He's having a race jumping over the gate
5. He's chasing the mouse 'cos he wants to eat them with his claws
6. She fell over by accident ... She's broken 'cos she fell over ... 'cos she broke her glasses
7. Putting the letter ... posting 'cos he can't reach it ... 'cos it's high for him that's why she lift him up
8. He's climbing up so he can get the cat down from his roof
9. He's crying 'cos that dog got his slipper
10. The lady brought a apple and it's dropping out of her ... and that boy picked it up and he told the lady there's a hole in ... and he picked them up to give them to the lady who dropped them

*Renfrew (1988, 1997).

These expressive language samples show the gradual expansion of the boy's telegrammatic utterances over two years as well as a resolution of unintelligibility. Residual features of nonfluency at two years post-onset were predominantly excessive pausing and repetition of phrase structure. The graph of his overall language recovery is shown in Figure 4.4.

In order to demonstrate the variability of children presenting with ACA after stroke, three girls who had lesions of the left hemisphere at different ages, all of which resulted in a severe acute aphasia, are presented next. They all recovered differently and further confirm the way in which the complex interaction of variables like age at onset, lesion size and site, occurs in children with ACA. The first, and the eldest, did very well to recover from a complete aphasia at age 13 years. At age 17 she had a mild high-level language problem in speed and volume of processing and recall and a risk of epilepsy. The second girl recovered well in terms of language skills but had a residual right hemiplegia. However, the later stages of assessment showed that she was unable to learn at the same rate as her peers and so she did not return to mainstream school. The third girl, although similar in age to the second, showed the least recovery of language and also had a severe right

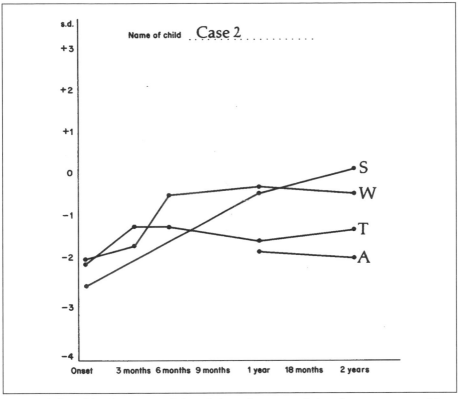

Figure 4.4 Profile of recovery of Case 2: A, auditory association; S, sentence repetition; T, TROG; W, Word Finding Vocabulary Test.

hemiplegia. Their recovery profiles (Figures 4.5, 4.6 and 4.7) are placed side by side so the patterns can be compared more easily. They are not intended to represent all the possible outcomes for this group, but rather to highlight the inadequacy of considering any one variable, in this case age, for the determining of eventual outcome.

Case 3

This girl (first described by Lees and Neville, 1990) had a normal developmental history when she presented with an acute aphasia at 13 years of age. CT scan and angiography revealed a large posterior temporoparietal haemorrhage from an AVM (this CT scan is Figure 4.2). Right-sided deficits included right hemianopia and very mild hand incoordination.

Initially she had a severe deficit in both receptive and expressive language; comprehending only single nouns and producing both semantic and phonemic paraphasias. Pure tone audiometry confirmed normal hearing. On discharge from hospital she continued to receive speech therapy from her local service once weekly for at least a year. Eleven months post-onset she was readmitted with a small episode of language disturbance following a severe and prolonged headache, and some right-sided signs. There was some deterioration in her auditory-verbal processing and an increase in paraphasias. This appeared to resolve within one week. Two years after the initial event another short episode of the same kind occurred. She was treated with carbamazepine and had stereotactic radiotherapy to a residual piece of the original AVM deep in the left temporal lobe. Her full-scale WISC IQ one month after the first episode was 76, and one year later it had improved to 96.

This girl was one of the children followed up by Lees (1997). She had a statement of educational needs that made provision for a personal tutor and integration to mainstream comprehensive school. By age 17 years she had passed three GCSE examinations and was studying for three more. She continued to experience high-level difficulties in the verbal comprehension of complex instructions in a noisy environment and had occasional word-finding problems. She was successfully weaned off her antiepileptic drugs by age 18 years.

During the course of her aphasia this girl did produce a range of paraphasias. These were predominantly phonemic and an increase in these always accompanied subsequent episodes. Some examples of these phonemic paraphasias include: (two months post-onset) 'scarecrow' was called 'scarescrow', 'handcuffs' were 'handcrups', 'sporran' was called 'skoran'. Similar errors occurred over the next two years but there were never more than this in one session.

Expressive language in a story-telling task was always nonfluent in the early recovery period, as this example of the Dog Story at three months post-onset shows:

> There was a dog and he wented down to the canal and he walked a p...(6 attempts at this) plank. And he went down... he and with his piece of ... meat and he looked into the ... canal and he saw his new...he saw his own reflection. He thought it was another dog and he ... did sort of throw... he dived in dived in and he never s... and he never saw his meat again.

Case 4

This girl, with a normal developmental history, presented at age 8;2 years with an acute aphasia. She had had a flu-like illness and headache for three days. Examination revealed a dense right hemiplegia and complete aphasia. This was diagnosed as a left middle cerebral artery infarct after a ruptured angioma of the left internal carotid artery and confirmed with CT scan and angiography. She was aphasic for one month during which time she was unable to comprehend anything more than single words. She then had a six-month period of producing paraphasic errors during which time the hemiplegia persisted. She also dribbled out of the right corner of her mouth. Up to one year after the event she continued to have word-finding and spelling difficulties. Pure tone audiometry confirmed normal hearing. Her IQ on the WISC was 83 (performance 94 and verbal 74). Eighteen months post-onset her aphasia appeared to have resolved to a high-level word-finding deficit, with comprehension essentially normal. The right hemiplegia persisted. She was placed in a school for children with physical difficulties.

The girl's response to a story-telling task confirms that expressive language regained a good level of fluency and accuracy within six months of onset with this example of the Dog Story:

> There was a dog and he had a piece of meat and he was going home. As he was going home he had to cross a bridge. When he looked down he could see his own reflection but he didn't know it was his reflection. So he opened his mouth to snap at the other piece of meat. His piece of meat was gone.

Although conversation was a little more stilted it was not grossly impaired, as this short one about her holiday recorded six months post-onset shows:

> There are small countries. There are some countries that are smaller...hotter than England; Jamaica, Barbados, St Kitts. Do you know any more ? [*hesitation*] America is hotter but it's too hot to stay outside and sunbathe. And I've been to Disney World.

Case 5

This girl (first described by Lees and Neville, 1990) had a normal developmental history when she presented with an acute aphasia and a right hemiplegia at age 8;3 years. CT scan and angiography revealed severe arterial disease involving the left terminal internal carotid, left proximal middle cerebral artery and distal middle cerebral artery, with a large infarct. Pure tone audiometry confirmed a mild conductive hearing loss of less than 30dB that was of long standing. She had a severe receptive and expressive aphasia such that she did not even respond to single words and she was essentially anomic. There was some improvement in all areas but three years post-onset she remained severely language disabled. She continued to receive speech and language therapy on a weekly basis from her local service for two years post-onset. The right hemiplegia persisted. Six months post-onset her WISC IQ was recorded as performance 86 and verbal 52. The local authority made no alternative or additional provision for her educational needs, and she continued in a mainstream comprehensive school where she made very poor progress. Her right hemiplegia persisted unchanged.

This girl produced very little language, and was particularly reluctant to name items to confrontation. Therefore few naming errors were recorded and those few given here suggest a general naming impairment: (at three months post-onset) 'basket' was called 'purse' as was 'case'; 'saw' was called 'knife'.

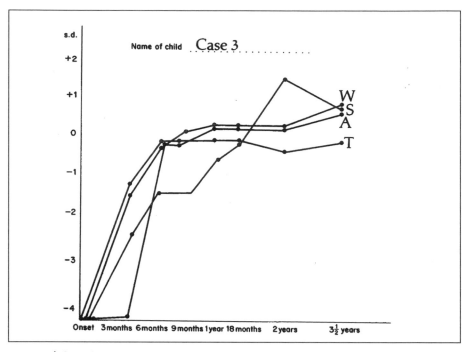

Figure 4.5 Profile of recovery of Case 3: A, auditory association; S, sentence repetition; T, TROG; W, Word Finding Vocabulary Test.

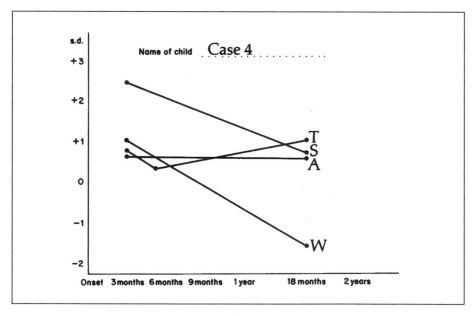

Figure 4.6 Profile of recovery of Case 4: A, auditory association; S, sentence repetition; T, TROG; W, Word Finding Vocabulary Test.

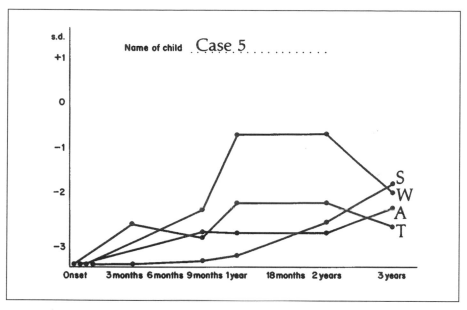

Figure 4.7 Profile of recovery of Case 5: A, auditory association; S, sentence repetition; T, TROG; W, Word Finding Vocabulary Test.

Very little spontaneous expressive language ever occurred but some short phrases were produced in a story-telling situation. This example of the Farmer Story was recorded nine months post-onset:

The farmer and the donkey go in barn. He pushed him... He pulled him... no go. Tell the cat scratch dog. Cat scratch him. Dog bark. He went in barn.

Conclusions

Clearly we cannot draw simple conclusions about age of onset and duration or severity of aphasia. The traditional view that unilateral cerebrovascular lesions in childhood rarely have significant long-term effects is not upheld by recent studies. However, the range and extent of recovery seen is highly variable and the way in which the numerous variables interact to influence this is not understood. Whilst there are a few studies which suggest the interaction of the variables of age, extent and nature of lesion, type and severity of initial aphasia, in determining prognosis in this group (Loonen and Van Dongen, 1990; Van Hout, 1991; Martins and Ferro, 1991), in many respects, it would be helpful to pool data across a number of centres to improve our understanding. Few centres have enough children to provide useful studies of this group otherwise. This would mean agreeing on a collaborative protocol. Recent work on national clinical guidelines for the client group indicates that this issue is still outstanding.

Unlike the adult group, there have been very few studies of treatment in children. Lees (1989) noted that the children in that study received varying amounts of speech and language therapy and it was therefore not possible to draw any conclusions about this. Children who survive stroke and their families are often faced with uncertainty about educational placement and rehabilitation. With the uncommon nature of this disorder support is not necessarily easy to access. A group called Different Strokes[1] seeks to support young survivors, mainly young adults, through a telephone helpline staffed by stroke survivors. They also offer counselling and information on benefits, further and higher education, special training and work opportunities.

---

[1] Different Strokes, 9 Cannon Harnett Court, Wolverton Mill, Milton Keynes MK12 5NF. Tel: 08451 307172. Fax: 01908 313501.

Chapter 5
Head injury

Pathology

The largest group of children with acquired language problems are those who suffer head injuries of varying severity. In the UK the number of children with head injuries has been rising annually since the 1980s (Middleton, 1989). Whilst severe injuries are known to potentially produce profound long-term effects the view that mild injuries, which do in fact predominate, do not produce significant cognitive or psychological sequelae, has been challenged. As Middleton (1989) said 'children, once seen as having an advantage over adults with regard to recovery, may in fact be more vulnerable and have a poorer prognosis'. Despite this, adequate rehabilitation facilities are still not available in the United Kingdom for children who survive head injuries.

Most of the early mixed series of ACA (1942 to 1978) included a substantial number of head-injured children. In most of these series there was little attempt to differentiate the possible underlying neuropathology and its implication for prognosis. More recent studies have recognized some of these implications and have given more details of the aetiological subgroups in mixed studies (Loonen and Van Dongen, 1990).

According to Ewing-Cobbs et al. (1985), head injury (HI) is the commonest cause of death in children. Middleton (1989) reported that four children in every 10,000 die from HI in the UK. Ewing-Cobbs et al. (1985) discussed the mechanisms of trauma and the response of the injured brain. Although diffuse cerebral injury at impact is the major initial effect, other forces of acceleration, shearing and stretching occur subsequently, resulting in widespread injury to the cerebral tissues. This damage is sometimes shown up by advanced radiographic techniques like magnetic resonance imaging. Chapman et al. (1995) also point out that focal lesions can occur, particularly in the frontotemporal cortex. These include contusions and haematomas and commonly result from 'transient in-bending of the skull or from penetration of a bone fragment subsequent to depressed skull fracture'.

Chapman et al. (1995) also review the use of the Glasgow Coma Scale to describe the severity of HI. They state that:

- severe HI is a score of 8 or less for a period of 6 or more hours in the acute phase (although recently the 6-hour requirement has been withdrawn);
- moderate HI is a score of between 9 and 12, which indicates that consciousness is impaired but without coma;
- mild HI is a score from 13–15 where the child is confused and disorientated.

Few studies have documented the recovery of cognitive and language skills in HI children. The series of 100 children under 19 years of age with severe head injuries was reported by Ward and Alberico (1987), and is an example of such studies. Severe head injury was defined by a Glasgow Coma Scale score of less than 7 on admission. Ninety-four per cent of the children had intracranial pressure monitoring and 24 per cent of them died from their injuries, while 68 per cent were said to have had a good or moderately impaired outcome. However the parameters of this were not defined further. The resolution of acute neurology is only a small measure of recovery in children who have sustained complex brain injury. Long-term neuro-psychological deficits are more likely to affect the quality of life, return to former community and progress within school; therefore these must be more carefully defined.

Since the early 1980s the number of children referred with acquired language problems after head injury has increased. This seems to be due to two factors: firstly better intensive care facilities, including the use of intracranial pressure monitoring, leading to more child survivors of severe HI, and secondly the introduction of the 1981 Education Act, which makes provision for the assessment of children with special educational needs. As we shall see, the residual language problems after HI in childhood can cover a wide range and require comprehensive assessment if they are to be suitably managed. As Ylvisaker (1985) stated, in a discussion of the neuro-psychological sequelae of head injury in children, 'the traditional view that children are relatively impervious to the effects of acquired brain injury has obviously been overstated' as more and more evidence of the long-term effects of childhood head injury become available.

Natural history

There are three stages to the recovery of a head injured child. The length of the stages is variable and probably depends on the severity of the injury.

1. The acute period lasts from emergency admission to the re-establishment of the stable conscious state. The trauma team will be at its most active during this period. Neurosurgery, various investigations and intensive care monitoring may all be a necessary part of the management. A small number of children may return to a situation of having wake/sleep cycles but unfortunately make no further progress. This is described as a 'persistent vegetative state'.

2. From the re-establishment of the stable conscious state a period of consistent recovery usually begins. This period may be very short in the mildly or moderately injured child or may last for several months in a more severely injured child. It is a time for therapy and educational input to maximize recovery. Thorough and ongoing assessment needs to be carried out and a goal-oriented treatment programme used which aims toward functional rehabilitation. Where progress through this period is fast, the child may appear to quickly regain the normal range on a number of skills. This does not mean that more long-term difficulties may not develop later, particularly when the child returns to school where learning may not be sustained.

3. Towards the end of this period a slowing down of progress such that recovery appears to plateau will be observed. At this stage long-term residual deficits will become apparent. The time it takes for the child to reach this stage will again depend on the severity of the injury. Only consistent and comprehensive assessment will reveal if progress is tailing off. Where there is a return to more or less normal previous levels, at least in some skills, long-term residual problems in others may be overlooked. Where there are multiple persisting deficits a consistent, specific and intensive approach to treatment is probably necessary.

Chapman et al. (1995) define two stages of recovery: early, which is equal to the first six months, and long-term, which is anything after that. In order to establish the short-term needs of these children, Ewing-Cobbs et al. (1985) looked at the language function of a group of children five months after closed HI. They found aphasic language problems in less than 10 per cent of the sample and concluded that language difficulties after paediatric HI were 'non-specific in nature, and did not vary consistently with the type of cerebral involvement'. The need for long-term follow-up was also emphasized, particularly as it had been suggested that problems in the later acquisition of language skills such as reading may be delayed following HI, particularly in younger children (Chadwick et al., 1981). Their study of the intellectual performance, scholastic achievement and reading skills of 97 children at least two years after HI lead them to conclude that 'brain injury is more likely to impair the acquisition of new skills than to cause the loss of well-established old skills'. They particularly noticed that this was true for children less than five years of age at the time of injury in respect of their later acquisition of written language skills. This was an important finding in helping to dispel the old myth that brain injury in young children had few serious long-term consequences.

There is little consensus about the length of follow-up time that constitutes a long-term study. This is of particular relevance to children in the third stage of recovery. Jordan et al. (1988) examined a group of 20 children aged 8 to 16 years who had sustained CHI at least 12 months previously. They found language test scores of the HI group to be significantly lower than their control group. The performance of both groups on the Frenchay Dysarthria Test (Enderby, 1983) was well within the normal range, so they do not appear to have had motor speech problems, which can complicate the clinical presentation after HI in childhood. They concluded that it was important to include both long- and short-term monitoring of language in this group.

The role of the speech and language therapist

Assessment

Speech and language therapy intervention needs to begin with appropriate assessment and diagnosis. However, for the HI child with ACA there are several factors that can complicate this clinical task:

- traumatic brain injury, both localized and diffuse, is likely to give rise to a complex association of motor, cognitive, perceptual, emotional and communication problems;
- there is little formal assessment material available which is specifically designed to meet the needs of these children;
- the previous outline of the stages of recovery indicate that the deficits are likely to change from day to day, week to week or month to month, depending on the stage the child has reached;
- traumatic brain injury is still uncommon enough to mean that the majority of staff are relatively inexperienced in this area and that few specialists are available.

Reassessment is clearly important for measuring recovery. As each individual child's response to brain injury will vary, the only way to know what stage the child is at and how to establish the next goal for intervention is to use an appropriate protocol. This is particularly necessary in the following circumstances:

- during the second stage of recovery where the child's situation is changing rapidly and/or often so that intervention keeps up with these changes;
- during the third stage of recovery where the situation is rather static in order to draw up a comprehensive profile of the child's specific deficits;
- at any stage where therapy is being given, to evaluate its effect and redirect goals as necessary;
- at any time when the child is said to have 'recovered' but is still experiencing difficulty at school, to see if any residual problems have been overlooked.

Informal assessment and screening procedures like the Children's Aphasia Screening Test (Whurr and Evans, 1986) may be useful in the initial stages, particularly in young children. However, the mildly or moderately aphasic child soon reaches the ceiling on such tests and they rarely provide a detailed enough profile for long-term use with the severely aphasic child. The choice of formal assessment will depend on the stage of recovery the child is at and the level of cooperation. It should be emphasized that developmental assessments like the Reynell Development Language Scales (Reynell, 1985) are rarely able to describe the specific difficulties of this group. A discussion of the tests used in both clinical situations and research studies is outlined in Chapter 2, although it does not claim to include all the tests which could be used with this group.

Speech problems

It is important to remember that language problems after HI in childhood are likely to occur alongside speech production problems such as dysarthria and dyspraxia. More fundamental oral dysfunction problems are likely to dominate rehabilitation in the early stages. Where there is any doubt about the competence of the swallowing mechanism, an examination using videofluoroscopic radiology should always be carried out. The differential diagnosis of dysphasia and dysarthria, while theoretically straightforward, may be less so in practice. Although the primary concern here is language, some of the difficulties in managing motor speech problems need to be briefly outlined. The problems are similar to those encountered when assessing the children's language. With very little specific assessment material available the use of two types of assessments predominate:

1. The use of adult material. In this respect the Frenchay Dysarthria Test (Enderby, 1983) is most commonly used by speech and language therapists. However, it is difficult to use this test successfully with children under 8 years of age and almost impossible where they have difficulties with attention and compliance.

2. The use of informal material. Most therapists use their own informal assessments. These should include assessment of head position and general posture (in conjunction with a physiotherapist), the presence or absence of oral reflexes, the control of respiration and phonation, observation and movement of the facial musculature, dentition, swallowing and the control of saliva. The major problem in the use of informal assessments is in developing a scoring or recording scheme which allows the therapist to document the presenting situation and which allows for reliable reassessment measures.

The Paediatric Oral Skills Package (Brindley et al., 1996) has set out to do this. It aims to provide a profile of a child's oral skills and can be used with those aged between 0 and 16 years. There are three scales: observation, examination (for eating and drinking) and performance. Any combination of these can be chosen depending on the child's needs, age, and ability to cooperate. The profile that is produced is then used as the basis upon which the clinician can formulate a hypothesis about the improvement of oral function for the individual child.

The problem of treatment is complicated by the fact that most HI children do not present with one 'pure' type of dysarthria. Usually the motor pattern is mixed and may include both upper and lower motor neurone signs. Most therapists initially become familiar with the assessment and treatment of oral motor problems in children through working with those with cerebral palsy. Although such experience is useful, the motor problems of HI children are different. This is not only because of the mixed neurology arising from the diffuse cerebral damage but also because of the acquired nature of the problem. The HI child, depending on the degree of recovery, has had a wealth of pre-traumatic experience. The way in which the child remembers this will vary, but must be a consideration when planning treatment. It is certainly different from the child with the congenital motor disorder who has no previous experience of unimpaired function. The presence of other problems, particularly in language and cognition, but also possibly sensorimotor, may make it difficult for the HI child to understand what is required during treatment. Models need to be clearly presented within a structured framework. Frequent repetition of the desired target is also required in order to accommodate these difficulties and the variable attention span, which may also be a feature.

AAC

In the very earliest stages of recovery the HI child may have no communication at all, or only be able to communicate nonverbally. It is not appropriate to leave a child with severe communication difficulties, and the family, without speech and language therapy support in the initial period of rapid recovery, even if you think the child will improve. Informed and sensitive help will be required by both the child and the family if they are to cope with communication difficulties that are likely to arise. Alternative or augmentative communication may be appropriate in the immediate post-trauma period to ease communication problems. However, it is not a straightforward matter of supplying a communication aid and leaving the child, family and other staff to get on with it. The following considerations are important:

1. The child's reaction to sudden loss of communication and other skills: this has not been studied extensively but it is recognized that brain injury is a catastrophic insult that is likely to leave the child confused and fearful. After HI in children a condition of post-traumatic mutism has been commonly encountered. Levin et al. (1983) stated that mutism is more common after HI in children than in adults. They gave an account of the recovery of a 12-year-old girl who was mute for three weeks post trauma. It is not clear whether mutism is primarily related to the overall effect of the cerebral damage or if it is a psychological reaction to loss of function. There have been varied reports concerning the length of the period of mutism. Hecaen (1976) reported a range up to 21 days. It may affect all communication modalities or be specifically related to the use of verbal language. The child may or may not be interested in using an alternative communication device during this time.

2. The family may insist on 'normality' of approach: this is especially true where they equate alternative communication with the acceptance of handicap. The traumatic effect of the head injury is not only in relation to the injury to the child's brain. The family too is 'injured' and will need to work through reactions of grief and loss. 'Coming to terms' with the effect of the injury has been described by families as mourning for the child they have lost and getting to know the head-injured child as a new member of the family. This reaction probably relates to the considerable physical, cognitive and personality changes that can be the sequelae of severe HI.

3. The associated motor, visual and perceptual problems may limit the choice of system or device: whilst these problems are not insurmountable in the long term, assessment for such devices is probably best carried out at a specialist centre. The provision of computer hardware, software and switches, is a complex area requiring the combined approached of an experienced multidisciplinary team. A number of national centres exist to advise about the provision of communication aids. However, in the short term, a less 'hi-tech' approach and the use of common sense may be the best answer.

4. The underlying language and cognitive problems: the presence of such impairments may mean that, where complex instructions are required, the child cannot understand how to use the device. Nonverbal demonstration is probably the best answer to this problem. Time spent just playing alongside the child and being with the family, seeing what fits their communication needs, is also essential.

5. The speed at which the situation changes: this may mean the device is only appropriate for a short time and needs frequent changing or adjustment. It is important that the changing situation is reviewed regularly.

With regard to these points, the following methods are recommended, particularly in the early stages of recovery:

1. Gestural communication: this may be introduced informally and later developed into a more formal system if necessary. The framework of the Makaton vocabulary (Walker, 1980) is recommended as it is adaptable, fairly simple, already known in many places and training courses are readily available. Where basic gestures/signs have been introduced, they should be used consistently by all those working with the child: nurses, therapists, medical staff, teachers, etc. It is usually helpful to ask the family to suggest the things they want to communicate to/with the child. Where possible the child's own suggestions should also be included. Some children will readily make up their own signs or use mime to communicate.

2. Communication boards: these should be tailored to the child's needs as much as possible. Personal photographs are often a good idea to stimulate interest, add a real element of communicative intent and aid recall. They may also help the family to become involved in the project. Although some ready-made boards are available, a multipurpose perspex board, in which the pictures or symbols can be changed regularly, is often more flexible in keeping up with the child's changing needs. Avoid static pictures of uninteresting objects. Rather, choose life-like objects and actions within a contextual setting.

In the later stages of recovery, before any effective therapy programme can be implemented, the severity of the specific deficits should be carefully investigated. A goal-orientated approach that is regularly reviewed is recommended for the following reasons:

1. It can be graded in a step-like manner and should be based on the child's strengths and needs. Thus, when working through the range of auditory processing difficulties, for example, it is important to begin therapy in a distraction-free environment as far as auditory interference is concerned, where the child can function well. Then work up through various situations that the child may encounter with less ease, including those

found at home and school, both formal and informal. Where possible try to use both individual and group situations.

2. When teaching syntax a structured approach is preferred. Both the Colour Pattern Scheme (Lea, 1970) and the Derbyshire Language Scheme (Knowles and Masidlover, 1982) are useful. For review of ways to use the Derbyshire Language Scheme, for both assessment and management of various age groups, see Lees and Urwin (1997).

3. A consistent approach to the use of cueing to aid confrontational naming and word finding allows the child to generalize these skills more readily. Experience suggests the child may pass through different stages at which different types of cues aid recall. Work in adult aphasia (Howard et al., 1985) has suggested that different types of cues may be effective over different time periods. Clinical experience suggests that children may use different cues even within the normal population. Commonly the cues used early in recovery are gestural, with verbal description and phonemic cues developing as later strategies.

4. The child should be encouraged to develop a capacity for the self-monitoring of errors. For the long-term benefit of the brain-injured child, relearning a self-monitoring strategy is of greatest importance, both for social independence and educational placement. The use of video in small group sessions may be a helpful technique, particularly with teenagers in the later stages of recovery.

5. Long stretches of individual therapy in traditional treatment centres may not always be the most appropriate management for children and teenagers with long-term problems. The therapist needs to be as flexible as possible when considering the place, timing and style of therapy offered and its effect on motivation.

Pragmatics

Pragmatic language impairments have been reported after HI in childhood (Yeates, 2000). These include difficulties such as making inferences and interpreting ambiguous sentences. Studies show that the quality and organization of discourse is often poor, normally measured using story recall, which is significant even after verbal memory and word knowledge are controlled. This indicates that it is a problem with the use of language and not due to injury-related deficits in word knowledge memory. Research also shows that discourse skills are often affected in children after HI despite their apparently adequate performance on standardized language tests, and present as long-term sequelae. A lack of age appropriate pragmatic development for children after HI, especially for children younger at the time of the HI may continue for more than three years post injury. Yeates (2000) suggests this discourse deficit may account for some of the academic difficulties that children with closed head injuries often experience.

Rigaudeau-McKenna (1998) reported a study of the metalinguistic awareness of a 15-year-old boy, 20 months after HI. She defined metalinguistic knowledge as 'the explicit knowledge of the structure and functions of language' that is self-reflective in nature. Her case study investigated how aphasia 'affects the adolescent's conception of language' by assessing his ability to reflect on syntactic forms of sentences and judge both their grammatical accuracy and correcting syntactic errors. Her detailed study illuminates the strengths and weakness of this boy's language processing skills and shows how they would affect his educational and social functioning.

Written language problems

Problems with written language can occur after HI in children. Age at injury does appear to be one of the prognostic factors. Ewing-Cobbs et al. (1985) reported that head-injured children demonstrated greater difficulty with written language tests than head-injured adolescents, regardless of the severity of the injury. The few studies with this population have failed to establish the specific ways in which the processing of written language breaks down. Neither have they outlined the strategies used by HI children to overcome reading and spelling problems. These are two important considerations when therapists and teachers seek to plan remedial programmes. When seeing a HI child with reading and spelling problems it is therefore important that comprehensive language assessment should be carried out to confirm that other difficulties really do not exist.

Children referred with persisting spelling problems frequently also have high-level auditory comprehension problems, auditory discrimination problems and other difficulties with the discrimination and manipulation of phonemes, as well as word-finding problems, both general and specific. These high-level language problems may have been overlooked, as they can be difficult to measure in practice. A range of tests is available including the Neale Analysis of Reading Ability (Neale, 1958) and the Graded Word Spelling Test (Vernon, 1977). Where a more broadly based screening test is required the Aston Index (Newton and Thompson, 1976) could be used. Designed for children aged 5–10 years it includes a vocabulary test, a draw-a-man test, a reading and a spelling test as well as memory, sound discrimination and sound blending tasks. Two profiles of the child's strengths and weaknesses in these skills can be drawn up from the results. It is a procedure that may be familiar to some teachers. Where possible the speech and language therapist should seek to work alongside the teacher and psychologist whenever assessing a child with written language problems.

It is also important to make a thorough investigation of reading and spelling strategies used by the child. Most children do develop strategies for overcoming current difficulties, even if it is a negative strategy like 'don't know'. Working with the child will reveal if any route is functional for the transposition of phonemes to graphemes (i.e., is the strategy predominantly based on visual memory, or is it phonetic?), what knowledge of errors the child has and what self-correction strategies, if any, are employed. It may be difficult to establish pre-trauma levels of language competence but it is important to look to see if there is any evidence of a family history of spelling difficulty or language problems. Clinical folklore abounds with stories about the numbers of HI children who were not very competent language users before injury or who come from a family of poor language users. This should not be taken as an indication that the child would have had some reading and writing difficulties anyway and that therefore nothing needs to be done. The combined effects of early developmental difficulty and further brain injury are likely to cause long-term problems and each child's needs must be individually assessed. The speech and language therapist should approach the management of written language difficulties alongside the child's teacher and educational psychologist. Together they should provide an appropriate remedial programme that is aimed at the child's educational needs and future language competence.

Overall, research reviewed by Yeates (2000) suggested that though 'overt aphasic disorders rarely persist following acute recovery (in children) ... subtle language difficulties often persist'. Chapman et al. (1995) argue that the complex relationship between linguistic and cognitive deficits within the context of each individual child means that our understanding would be better advanced by more careful case description. It is, after all, almost impossible to control all the possible variables when making an outcome study of HI in children. They give an example of two HI children responding to a story-recall task (like the story-telling tasks given in Appendix 2), one with left frontal and one with right frontal injuries. The child with the left frontal injury produces a sparse nonfluent account two years post-injury. The second child, with the right frontal injury, produces a fluent account with much perseveration and confabulation, three years post-injury. He also shows impaired sequencing and disruption to the story structure. These examples are similar to the differences in story-telling abilities observed in children with Benign Rolandic Epilepsy described in Chapter 10.

Rehabilitation of HI children

It should be clear that traumatic brain injury will lead to numerous potential difficulties for the child. The following impairments have all been reported from recent studies by Yeates (2000):

- Memory problems: children with severe HI show poorer learning and less retention over time compared to uninjured age peers.

- Executive functions: deficits in planning and execution of sequences are reported, though measuring these is problematic.
- Attention: reports of attention problems are common, though few of these use objective measures of attention. They are thought to be more pronounced among younger head-injured children compared to those children who were older at the time of injury.
- General intelligence: reduced intellectual functioning is commonly reported after HI. IQ score often continues to be depressed relative to pre-morbid level, particularly with the more severe injuries. However, prospective long-term studies suggest that children demonstrate significant recovery in intellectual functioning.

Add to this the background of the child's continuing development and it becomes clear that for her/his full learning potential to be maximized rehabilitation is properly a multidisciplinary concern. However, few rehabilitation centres exist to meet these needs. The child may be fortunate to spend the acute period in a children's ward of a specialist hospital where an acute rehabilitation team will implement an initial programme. Most often this will include physiotherapist, occupational therapist, psychologist, teacher and speech and language therapist alongside nursing and medical staff and the child's family. It will be important to begin to establish a daily routine for the child. The programme must be well understood by all concerned with carrying it out, and it must be reviewed regularly.

On discharge from hospital the majority of the 27 speech and language therapists responding to the 1986 questionnaire on the management of children with ACA said that between 60 and 100 per cent of the children they had seen continued to require speech and language therapy. However, many children will return to minimal provision and few will go on to placement in a specialized centre. Some will not even have begun to have their educational needs assessed at this stage. All too often clinical experience has shown that it is only years later, perhaps when legal claims for compensation are being dealt with, that some of these fundamental needs will be identified for the first time.

Once a child has a statement of educational need, placement is up to the local education authority. The availability of provision will vary but many children find themselves placed in schools for children with physical disabilities. Many of these schools, recognizing the challenges of meeting the needs of this group, are now arranging for local in-service training for their staff to provide them with information and skills for working with HI children. There is a growing network of local support groups under the guidance of the Child Brain Injury Trust and the National Head Injuries Association[2].

---

[2] Child Brain Injury Trust, Radcliffe Infirmary, Woodstock Road, Oxford OX2 6HE. Tel: 0845 601 4939, 01865 552467. National Head Injuries Association Ltd, 4 King Edward Court, King Edward Street, Nottingham NG1 1EW. Tel: 0115 924 0800.

Two particular aspects of the rehabilitation needs of HI children will be considered here: neuropsychology and neuropsychiatry, as these are not available in all areas. Johnson and Roethig-Johnson (1987) addressed some of the psychological needs of HI children. In the classroom, they described the HI child as one who 'becomes increasingly worried or frightened without really understanding why' and who gradually falls behind classmates. This is the beginning of what they termed the 'backward slide away from the peer group academically and socially'. They reported studies that suggest HI children find speeded tasks particularly difficult in comparison to their peers. It is the child's ability to integrate complex information and attend to tasks in a range of modalities that will determine whether or not they experience the backward slide. The neuropsychologist role will include assessing the various component skills used in a range of cognitive tasks of different complexity.

It is also recognized that the increasing number of children surviving HI has led to a growing need for neuropsychiatric services for this group (Parmelee and O'Shanick, 1987). A study by McCabe and Green (1987) is one of the few to date that has tried to understand the HI child's perspective. They reported three adolescents who had suffered severe HI and who displayed socially disinhibited behaviours. By the implementation of individually structured programmes they were able to effect some behavioural maturation, especially preparation for independent living. They also discussed the needs of families who have to cope with HI adolescents. Understandably, they reported a tendency for parents to develop 'an overprotective and lenient approach whereby limit-setting and appropriate challenge of the young person becomes reduced'. They discussed a number of components of a neuropsychiatric service to HI children which included: voluntary support systems, group psychotherapy, the appointment of a key worker, family support, the use of pharmacological therapies and, if necessary, the provision of secure hospital placement.

Examples of children with HI

It is not unusual for the claim to be made that a child with HI had developmental learning difficulties before their subsequent brain injury. This is always difficult to establish, unless the child already had special educational needs identified. Case 6 is a child about whom such concerns had been voiced but no specific provision had been made prior to his injury.

Case 6

This boy had a history of a mild general developmental and language delay. All his early milestones had been achieved at the low end of the normal range. His first words were at two and half years of age and he had one elder brother who attended a school for children with moderate learning difficulties. He sustained a severe closed head injury at the age of 5;3 years in a road traffic accident. He was admitted in an unconscious state. The right side responded to pain with flexion and the left with extension. He was given Mannitol, intubated and ventilated, and transferred to a neurosurgical unit. His pupils were small and reacting sluggishly to light. There were lacerations to his arm and tongue which were sutured, and abrasions to the skull, shoulders and right hand. A CT scan at this time showed moderate cerebral oedema and no intracranial bleeding. Five days post-onset he began to have generalized seizures and these were treated with anticonvulsants. Ten days post-trauma he was breathing independently and he was taken off the ventilator. Gastroscopy revealed stomach erosions and an acute duodenal ulcer that was also treated appropriately.

A repeat CT scan six weeks post-onset showed a degree of cerebral atrophy and enlarged lateral ventricles. He remained mute for five months. His first utterances were coprolalic, and this persisted for one month. At six months post-injury he was producing appropriate two-word phrases and some paraphasic errors (see Table 5.1). Nine months post-injury an assessment of general cognitive abilities was said to indicate a moderate degree of learning difficulty. There was a residual spastic weakness affecting the legs and the left arm, contractures and deformities in the lower limbs. He had a moderate mixed dysphasia. His hearing was normal. An assessment of special educational needs was made and he was placed in a school for children with physical and learning difficulties.

Table 5.1 Expressive language and naming errors during recovery for Case 6

Post-trauma (months)	Item	Response	Error type
8	Saucepan	Oven	Semantic paraphasia
9	Car	The car goes in the petrol	
12	Camel	Kangaroo	Semantic paraphasia
	Leaf	Flower	Semantic paraphasia
	Feather	Flower	Semantic paraphasia and perseveration
	Diver	Robot	Semantic paraphasia
16	Camel	Kangaroo/donkey	Semantic paraphasia
	Diver	Spaceman	Semantic paraphasia

Grammatical errors at the same assessment:

	It's getting dark	It's coming on night time
	It's a girl	It ain't a boy it's a her

Expressive language was nonfluent, as these two examples recorded one year post-injury demonstrate:

> Dog Story
> A dog ... who had meat...and he dropped it in the river...and the other dog ate it.

This conversation about a swimming trip (the interpretations in square brackets were provided by his father) shows how this child's expressive language was limited:

> It was Barbara's seaside [near where she lived]. It was a different pool. It was a blue pool [swimming pool]. Can I go home now?

However, to what extent inherited factors or the brain injury the boy sustained contributed differentially to this cannot be determined. All we can say is that it has been observed that both genetic factors and brain injury can lead to a pattern of reduced language skill. The overall pattern of his language recovery post injury is shown in Figure 5.1.

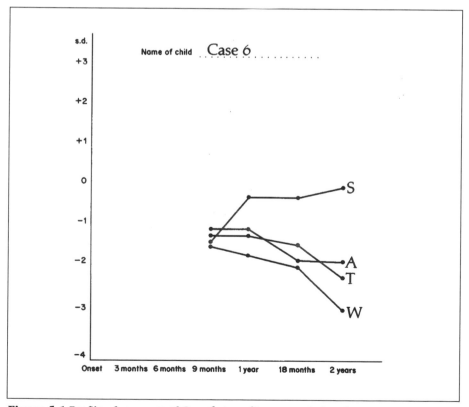

Figure 5.1 Profile of recovery of Case 6: A, auditory association; S, sentence repetition; T, TROG; W, Word Finding Vocabulary Test.

The considerable number of variables which influence the outcome of HI in childhood make it difficult to make specific predictions on the basis of, for example, age alone. Here two girls of about the same age who suffered HI are reported to demonstrate some of the potential variability of outcome that is more likely to be related to severity and extent of damage and to which the provision of different rehabilitation facilities may also have made a contribution.

Case 7

This girl (first reported by Lees and Urwin, 1991) had a normal developmental history until she was involved in a road traffic accident at the age of 12 years in which she sustained multiple injuries. She was admitted in an unconscious state with a severe head injury, ruptured spleen and haemorrhage, pneumothorax and chest injury, and fractures of the right clavicle and ankle. A Glasgow Coma Scale score of 5 was recorded at this stage. CT scan was reported to show subarachnoid blood over the right cerebellar hemisphere, within the vermis and the 4th ventricle and the right lateral ventricle. There were two dissociated intracerebral bleeds and virtually no oedema. This was described as a general cerebral contusion.

Due to the girl's deteriorating condition a repeat scan was carried out 24 hours later. It was unchanged. However, another one seven days later suggested that the haematomas were less dense, although there was little change in the size of the ventricles. She was nursed in intensive care for four weeks, the first week of which she was critically ill. Ultrasonic angiography at this stage showed no evidence of occlusion of the extracranial carotid arteries and middle cerebral artery flow was detected to be similar bilaterally. However there was a suggestion of increased and turbulent flow in the left jugular and possible obstruction in the right jugular.

Once out of the critical care stage she had evidence of a very severe motor disorder. There was spasticity in the right limbs and extra-pyramidal signs on the left side, including tremor. Six weeks post-trauma she began to show some awareness of her surroundings. At 10 weeks post-injury she was responding to being spoken to but had a severe receptive and expressive dysphasia. She still had a profound motor disorder. Twelve weeks post-injury the girl was making steady progress and marked improvements were noted in all skills; she was responsive, cooperative, cheerful and talking. There had been a great improvement in motor function. The right side was still worse than the left, but she had reasonable hand function on both sides, could sit independently and walk with support. She continued to make excellent progress from her severe head injury and was discharged to a weekly boarding placement for rehabilitation where she gained mobility to walk independently within one year. She continued to make good progress with language and learning, within this structured environment. Both education and therapy were well integrated, goal orientated and directed to specific deficits. Two years post-trauma she was transferred to another school for children with physical difficulties nearer her home, with only moderate residual motor problems and a slight dysarthria.

Table 5.2 Assessment of naming difficulties on the Word Finding Vocabulary Test and the Graded Naming Test during recovery of Case 7

Initial assessment	Item	Response	Error types
2 months post-onset	Cup	Cup	
	Table	Table	
	Boat	Sink	Semantic paraphasia
	Tree	Glass	Semantic paraphasia
	Window	Table	Semantic paraphasia
	Snake	Table	Perseveration
	Basket	Table	Perseveration
	Saw	Knife	Semantic paraphasia
	Clown	Dog	Semantic paraphasia
	Bear	Dog	Perseveration
	Moon	Pear	Semantic paraphasia
	Chimney	Chair	Semantic paraphasia
9 months post-onset	lighthouse	Windmill/ lightmill/ lighthouse	Self-corrected Semantic paraphasia
2 years post-onset	Buoy	Sandcastle	Semantic paraphasia
	Corkscrew	Screwdriver	Semantic paraphasia
	Turtle	Tortoise	Semantic paraphasia

Story telling demonstrated the generally nonfluent nature of her expressive language. There were frequent hesitations, some repetitions and false starts. The overall content of the story was well preserved:

The Dog Story (recorded six months post-onset)
The dog had a piece of meat he was taking home and on his way he had to cross a plank over ... over a pond. He looked down and ... there was ... his own reflection in the water and he thought there.... in the water was another dog ... with the piece of meat. He thought he'd have that piece of meat too ... So he snatched at the dog ... but as he opened his mouth ... the piece of meat fell into the pond and was never seen again.

Case 8

This girl (first reported by Lees and Urwin, 1991) had a normal developmental history. She was from a bilingual Italian/English family. She was admitted at the age of 11;6 years in an unconscious state, having been knocked down by a car on her way to school. She was unresponsive and her pupils were small. A CT scan performed urgently showed multiple contusions in the left anterior and the right posterior parts of the internal capsule, with possible blood in the right lateral ventricle. She also had a displaced fracture of the right tibia. She was admitted to the intensive care unit, ventilated and given intravenous Mannitol. The EEG was not abnormal. Brain stem and visual evoked responses showed increased latency. She was ventilated for 13 days, during which time she did not respond to commands and had marked dystonic movements, more on the left than on the right.

She remained unchanged for five weeks when she suddenly started responding to commands and became less restless. She was mobile, could understand simple requests, had single-word speech and was eating and drinking well. She also regained continence of urine and faeces within the same week. She was discharged six weeks later with a mild right upper motor neurone 7th nerve palsy, a tremor of the left hand which was worse on movement, a slightly broad-based gait and a moderate mixed dysphasia.

She returned to her previous mainstream secondary school but had considerable problems in language, learning and emotional stability. Within the large, mixed ability classes, in which it was difficult to give specific teaching help, she made very poor progress and became depressed. It was difficult for the family to attend local speech therapy appointments, even in the school holidays, and she therefore received little specific help. She had a dysphonia due to bilateral vocal cord weakness and also a significant word-finding problem. Two years post-trauma a statement of educational needs was eventually made by which she received extra teaching help of 0.2 w.t.e. She received some outpatient treatment from the department of child and adolescent psychiatry. She said she had few friends, felt isolated and found it difficult to communicate with her parents. Her responses on the Graded Naming Test (McKenna and Warrington, 1983) showed some of the difficulties she had with naming (Table 5.3).

The girl's progress with story telling showed that she was gradually becoming more fluent and was able to use longer sentences. These examples are from the Dog Story, the first one at six months post-onset:

> There was a dog walking with a piece of meat in his mouth. ... He saw another dog ... with another piece of meat in his mouth. The meat fell out of his mouth.

Table 5.3 Assessment of naming difficulties on the Word Finding Vocabulary Test and the Graded Naming Test during recovery of Case 8

Initial assessment	Item	Response	Error types
3 months	Camel	Giraffe	Semantic paraphasia.
	Goat	Giraffe	Perseveration
	Waterfall	Waterchute	Semantic paraphasia
9 months	Cup	Glass	Semantic paraphasia
21/2 years	Kangaroo	Giraffe	Semantic paraphasia
5 years	Buoy	Tambourine	Semantic paraphasia
	Thimble	Nimble	Phonemic paraphasia

Then again at 18 months post-onset:

> The dog was walking home with a piece of meat in his mouth ... and he crossed a plank ... and then saw a river and then saw his own reflection in the water and he thought it was another dog with another piece of meat in his mouth. ... and... and so er ... he ... he dropped the meat and it fell in the river and he never saw it again.

This written language sample revealed some of her feelings about her school placement and lack of friends. She complained of headaches and tiredness (common features of depression) and her description of her comprehension difficulties was consistent with her test results. The difficulties she had with her written language included spelling and punctuation errors as well as some sentence formulation difficulties. This piece was written one year post-injury.

> teachers sort of miss me in class, I have tried to ask to play but all of a sudden they give lies meant to hurt me. When I stay with Friend I (fel) stay happier to them and they think twice. When I'm in class and the teacher goes to Fast For me and I get mygrians and because of that I move about a lot and do the work wrong somet(h)imes. Work sheets I have to read over again and again until I get aroond to now what its (an) about. everyBody had a Friend to(e) go home with play with and do over things with. if it carrys on like this I with just (t go hom) leave.
> (self corrections in brackets, spelling and punctuation as original)

She left home at age 17 years to live with close relatives and was given a place on a youth training scheme. However, she found timekeeping difficult and was often late, or failed to attend at all. After a further period of neuropsychiatric treatment she took up a place on another scheme, as a trainee receptionist, and coped better. She recognized that she had continued difficulty with communication, saying 'I want to talk faster but it takes hours to come out, if I'm in a conversation it takes hours to get it out'.

She was particularly mindful of the reactions of others to her word-finding problems. As she said 'People think you're stupid. I change the subject but it doesn't always work and it won't stop people thinking I'm stupid.' Her hobbies included a particular interest in personal fitness in order to make the best of her disability. All in all her reactions to her HI are best summed up in her own words: 'I just feel like I missed a big gap in my life'.

The graphs of Figures 5.2 and 5.3 show the progress made by these two girls over the first two years after their head injuries. Case 7 made significantly better progress overall than Case 8. All the scores for the former child were within the normal range by the end of the first year. Case 8 continued to have z-scores in the range −1 to −2, and below, at two years post-trauma, which directly reflected the moderate to severe nature of her aphasia and reported significant problems five years post-trauma. In both cases the most consistent period of progress was during the first six months after injury, after which progress gradually tailed off.

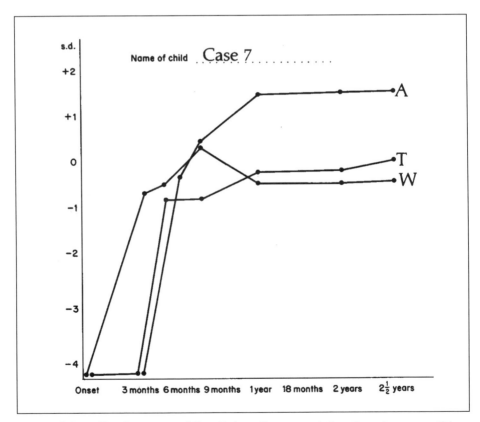

Figure 5.2 Profile of recovery of Case 7: A, auditory association; S, sentence repetition; T, TROG; W, Word Finding Vocabulary Test.

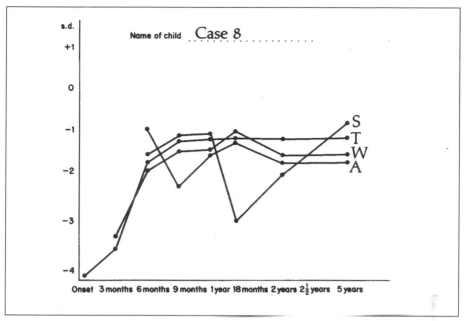

Figure 5.3 Profile of recovery of Case 8: A, auditory association; S, sentence repetition; T, TROG; W, Word Finding Vocabulary Test.

Conclusions

Only a minority of HI children present with the classic symptoms of ACA after HI (Chapman et al., 1995). Not all children who suffer severe HI will have severe residual aphasia or other communication difficulties. However, a complex range of speech and language problems are common sequelae to severe brain injury along with other motor, cognitive and psychiatric problems. Recent research does not uphold the generalization of a favourable prognosis for language skills following HI in childhood. Complex inter-related impairments are best dealt with by a multidisciplinary team within a dedicated rehabilitation situation. Only comprehensive assessment carried out over time will reveal the nature of the child's changing needs and allow for the appropriate management to be planned. Over time, subgroups of common language disturbances after HI may emerge as appropriate frameworks for assessment and remediation receive further attention. There has been little attempt to date to document the effects of rehabilitation for HI children in sufficient detail for firm conclusions to be drawn. This requires urgent attention if we are to plan for the needs of this increasingly large population. Detailed case studies of children placed in rehabilitation programmes would contribute to the present lack of information in this area.

Chapter 6
Cerebral neoplasm

Pathology

Cerebral tumour, or neoplasm, is defined as the abnormal new growth of tissue that may be benign or malignant. Intracranial or cerebral tumours are the terms used to identify these space-occupying lesions of the brain. They may arise from the abnormal and increased division of a number of different types of cells, which accounts for the variety of sites and the range of prognoses. The overall survival rate for children treated for the range of neoplastic conditions (including brain tumours and acute lymphoblastic leukaemia) has improved dramatically over the last three decades (Murdoch, 1999). Some cerebral tumours can be a cause of ACA, depending on the site of the lesion but, aside from recent work by Murdoch and his team in Queensland, Australia, there have been few detailed reports of specific cases in the literature.

Martins et al. (1987) reported a case of what they termed 'acquired crossed aphasia in a child'. This was a 15-year-old right-handed boy who was diagnosed as having a tumour in the right cerebral hemisphere, the localization of which was confirmed by CT scan and surgery. The tumour did not extend into the left hemisphere or involve the corpus callosum. He was severely aphasic and subsequently developed left focal seizures. Subsequent investigations, as the aphasia worsened, showed continued growth of the tumour and the child died three months after the initial diagnosis. As the boy was right-handed and all the cerebral damage was confined to the right hemisphere it was concluded that he had a crossed aphasia. He was only the second example of a child with a crossed aphasia in their larger series of 31 cases.

Agostini and Kremin (1986) reported a child with aphasia subsequent to a cerebral tumour. This boy, who was followed up for three years, had a slowly developing tumour, the exact location of which was not given. During that time it was possible to monitor his language. His expressive language was said to have progressively reduced but his verbal comprehension remained unaffected. He was described as anomic and the overall pattern was said to

86

be a transcortical motor aphasia. Of the two cases described by Paquier and Van Dongen (1991), one had a space-occupying lesion of the left temporo-parietal area that was removed surgically. She later developed a predominantly right-sided seizure disorder and was aphasic. She had a slight right hemiplegia and a right homonymous hemianopia. This 9-year-old girl demonstrated mild receptive comprehension deficits on the Token Test (Di Simoni, 1978) and severe jargon aphasia with neologisms, paraphasia and perseverations. The aphasia did show some improvement but was still evident as a mild disturbance two years later, and the epilepsy also persisted.

Posterior fossa tumours are a more prevalent type in childhood, according to Hudson (1990). Murdoch et al. (1999) state that they account for up to 70 per cent of all paediatric intracranial tumours. The implications of tumours of the cerebellum, fourth ventricle and brain stem for speech and language disorders in childhood has been considered in some detail by Hudson et al. (1989), Hudson (1990) and Murdoch (1999). The nature and severity of the speech and language difficulties reported in survivors are quite varied (Murdoch and Hudson, 1999). Ataxic dysarthria has been reported; however these authors also draw attention to ongoing language problems in children following treatment for posterior fossa tumours. Mutism has also been described as a common symptom post-operatively and this may last for several weeks (Catsman-Berrevoets et al., 1992; Van Dongen et al., 1994). These authors described several cases (three and 15 respectively). Where mutism does occur, it can be indicative of a poor speech prognosis. Problems in classifying dysarthrias presenting in childhood are highlighted by them.

Hudson et al. (1989) used the Frenchay Dysarthria Test to assess six children and found a wide range of motor speech problems. The retention of phonological immaturities was also observed in two of the children. The authors also proposed a link between the occurrence of long-term language disabilities and post-surgical radiotherapy. Language impairments were observed in four of the six children reported. The only two children not to have language problems had not received post-surgical radiotherapy. They concluded that 'although it is recognised that radiotherapy may be essential for the long-term survival of the children ... the medical team needs to be aware of the possible long-term effects that this treatment may have on language abilities'. Speech and language assessments reported to be useful in describing the impairments encountered include the Token Test for Children (Di Simoni, 1978) and the Clinical Evaluation of Language Fundamentals, for which there is a UK version (Wiig et al., 2000).

Hudson (1990) concluded that the speech and language therapist should take an active role in the management of children treated for brain tumours in both the long and short term 'even if intervention is not initially warranted or has been discontinued'. Murdoch et al. (1999) also review the effects of chemotherapy on subsequent speech and language development for children who have been treated for leukaemia and brain tumours. These treatments 'induce structural and functional changes in the brain' and it is these that lead to the long-term adverse consequences for speech and language (Murdoch et al., 1999). Amongst the factors influencing prognosis in recovery for children with cerebral tumours are:

- tumour type;
- the extent of surgical resection;
- the amount of radiation given;
- whether chemotherapy is part of the treatment.

Long-term follow-up of surviving children is important so that those with special needs, for both language and general learning, do not fail to be identified. It is important to use a suitable assessment protocol, as described in Chapter 2, and arrange to review the child at sensible intervals which may be monthly, six-monthly or annually depending on the situation. In general where the clinical picture is changing fast, more frequent reviews are indicated. Murdoch and Hudson (1999) advocate an active role for the speech and language therapist with this client group. They note that high-level language problems that undermine academic abilities may appear some time after initial treatment.

Where a child's speech and language needs have been recognized, any decisions about therapy will depend on a number of variables such as age, medical prognosis, and educational provision. It is possible that augmentative or alternative communication techniques will be needed by some children, both those with general motor problems and those with deteriorating conditions. Where a local specialist in this aspect of management is not available, referral to a communication aids centre is advised.

The importance of comprehensive assessment and multidisciplinary working must again be emphasized. We need to learn much more about the short- and long-term effects on speech and language in all of these subgroups. We also need more detailed description of the rehabilitation programmes that may benefit these children. An area that has attracted very little consideration is the construction of curricula specific to children with such multiple needs.

In the case example given here, ongoing epilepsy contributed to an evolving severe communication difficulty, after an early tumour had been identified and excised.

Case 9

A girl, the eldest of three female siblings, was a normal full-term delivery and subsequently appeared to make normal developmental progress. Her epilepsy began at 18 months with partial seizures, followed by developmental arrest and then regression, including speech and language. Investigations established a diagnosis of dysembryoplastic neuroepithelial tumour (DNET) in the right temporal lobe that was first operated at 24 months and again then at 48 months. After each operation there was a short-term increase in social and verbal behaviour, followed by further developmental arrest and subsequent regression. She produced no further speech after five years of age. When seen at 9 years of age she was walking with an ungainly gait, was not consistently able to deal with her own personal hygiene, but could feed herself, although occasional dribbling was reported, and she responded to some verbal commands. She had no verbal expression but would attempt to spell out words with her finger or write a few single words. She indicated 'yes' and 'no' by pointing at her knees. The girl had an alphabet board and a small communication aid for use at residential school for children with complex needs, where she had been placed for three years. An EEG showed slow and sharp wave complexes over the right temporal region and prolonged bursts of sharp spike and wave over the left temporal region.

SLT assessment before commencing treatment with antiepileptic drugs was difficult as Table 6.1 shows.

Table 6.1 Case 9: Initial assessment before treatment (A)

The girl was unable to respond consistently enough for assessment using TROG or any other formal standardized assessment task.

On a rhyming task, she generated the following responses to CVC spoken words using her alphabet board:

cat	nat
bed	head
meat	feet
lake	make
rail	bdspot
goat	coat
wish	fish

After six weeks treatment on an appropriate dose of sodium valproate the girl was reassessed. The details are in Table 6.2.

However, to establish the treatment effect the sodium valproate was withdrawn and a further assessment confirmed the changes in her communicative abilities, detailed in Table 6.3.

Having established a treatment effect with sodium valproate, the series of assessments was repeated for a second antiepileptic treatment, this time high dose corticosteroids.

Table 6.2 Case 9: Second assessment during first treatment (B)

A more consistent style of response meant she was able to:

Identify the nonsense word in a list of real versus nonsense CVC words 10/10
Identify the real word in a list of real versus nonsense CVC words 10/10
Rhyme real CVC words in a list 10/10
Identify the first sound of a list of CVC alliterated words 10/10

She would produce some Makaton signs appropriately: home, dinner; and was using the toilet consistently.

Table 6.3 Case 9: Observations after withdrawal of treatment (A1)

When the sodium valproate was withdrawn a regression in communication and social behaviour was seen once again: day-time wetting, withdrawn and not using signs or using communication board consistently. Although there were some signs that she still retained some auditory processing abilities as at A, responses were too inconsistent to access these.

Table 6.4 Case 9: Third assessment after second treatment (B1)

After six weeks on high dose corticosteroids she was able to:

Complete the TROG, passing 12 blocks, a z-score of –3.
Repeat all the auditory processing tasks at the same level of accuracy as at B.
Produce a wider range of Makaton signs, and initiate some communication: 'more ice cream'.

This ABAB treatment design is also referred to as a single case research design. It is a clinical experimental research design that allows the child to act as her own control in establishing whether or not a particular treatment does affect communicative abilities. This child was one of a series reported by Lees et al. (1998), using the ABA design.

Outcome

Eighteen months after her first evaluation, she was settled on a regime of sodium valproate and lamotrigine. She was able to deal consistently with her own personal hygiene needs, greet people using signs and appropriate facial expressions, also use signs or alphabet board, or electronic vocal output device for expressive communication. Whilst she clearly did have a complex range of learning, language and social communication problems, her skills were more accessible than previously. The range of drug trials had been monitored using language testing and general developmental observations. These had demonstrated that some of her skills were being hidden by 'state-dependant' epilepsy. However, the fact that she did not regain expressive speech with any of these treatments suggests that this was a 'permanent' loss earlier in her history although it is not possible to say whether this is due to the early lesion of the right hemisphere or the five years or so she spent with the undiagnosed sub-clinical 'spike and wave' over her left hemisphere, or a combination of the two.

This example demonstrates:

- the importance of using a structured approach to language testing in children with complex disorders; epilepsy may be related to 'reversible disability' (Neville, 1999) as part of a syndrome;
- the need to tailor-make assessment material in some of these situations where 'off-the-peg' assessments will not do in order to reveal the full range of individual impairments and skills;
- the combination of a variable auditory processing input disorder with a more permanent output disorder, with motor signs, in a complex situation with both developmental and acquired aspects.

Chapter 7
Cerebral infections

There are a number of different types of childhood infectious diseases of the CNS and they are an important cause of mortality and morbidity in infants and young children worldwide. These include bacterial and viral infections such as meningitis, encephalitis and meningoencephalitis (where both the meninges and the brain are infected), as well as cerebral malaria. These infections usually have a diffuse effect but focal infections can occur. In their review, Carter et al. (2003a) found that cognitive and motor impairments were the commonest persisting sequelae after CNS infections.

Meningitis

Meningitis is an infection of the meninges usually involving the subarachnoid space and the cerebrospinal fluid, and these are commonly bacterial in origin although viral and tuberculous meningitis infections can occur. Accurate diagnosis will require examination and culture of the cerebrospinal fluid. There are three ways in which these infections spread to the meninges: from the extension of a pre-existing infection usually of the sinuses or mastoid, from infection through the bloodstream, or after fracture of the skull. One variable in determining the prognosis is the effectiveness of the antibiotics used against the infection. In general these have greatly reduced the mortality rate amongst children with cerebral infections. However severe deficits of speech and language do still occur as can deafness, motor impairments and learning difficulties.

Cerebral abscess

Of the types of cerebral infection that can result in language impairment, intracranial abscess resulting in a focal lesion of the cortex of the left hemisphere is the most common. In early studies of ACA (Guttman, 1942; Collignon et al., 1968) children with aphasia after cerebral abscess, particularly of the left temporal lobe, were common. These usually arose as a complication of severe otitis media and mastoiditis (infection of the mastoid bone). They would then infect the middle to posterior portion of the temporal lobe. They are less common with the present use of antibiotics to treat otitis media.

Another area that is vulnerable to infection is the frontal lobes. Here an abscess may follow frontal sinusitis. Where the dominant hemisphere is involved, aphasia can be part of the presenting symptoms. Treatment usually involves surgical draining of the abscess and antibiotics for the infection. Cerebral abscess has not been a frequent contributor to cases of aphasia in recent series, although one of the five cases reported by Lees and Neville (1990) did present in this way. There was no evidence of more than cortical damage in this case and he had a mild aphasia.

Encephalitis

Encephalitis is the common name for viral infection of the brain. The number of viruses that are known to attack the central nervous system is large. They may be transmitted in a number of ways: by human contact, by insects or other animal contacts. Diagnosis will usually involve examination of the CSF. Mortality and morbidity are common sequelae. Commonly incomplete recovery results in a range of motor, sensory and cognitive deficits. These may range from mild to severe.

Cerebral malaria

One of the commonest infections in the world affecting 300–400 million each year, malaria kills over one million people, most of whom are children from sub-Saharan Africa (Carter et al., 2003a). Cerebral malaria (CM) is an acute encephalopathy in which patients present with impaired consciousness, and it is strongly linked with a fatal outcome. Seizures are reported in at least 80 per cent of children at the acute stage and are associated with subsequent death and with neurological impairments in survivors. Persisting neurological impairments, including speech and language deficits, have been reported in up to 24 per cent of children who survive, with epilepsy being reported in up to 10 per cent of children surviving cerebral malaria (Carter et al., 2003b).

The prevalence of neurological impairment following non-cerebral falciparum malaria (i.e., severe falciparum malaria without prolonged coma) is not known. Children often have complicated seizures (i.e., prolonged, multiple and focal), which in other contexts have been associated with neurological damage, particularly to the temporal lobe. Carter et al. (2003b) found that children surviving malaria and complicated seizures also had an increased risk of neurological impairments, including speech and language deficits, and that 12 per cent had epilepsy.

Carter (2002) study was the first to document significant language problems in children who survived cerebral malaria. These impairments were in higher-level language functions, lexical semantics and pragmatics. In children who survived malaria with complicated seizures phonology and pragmatics were the areas of significant impairment. Where children had epilepsy they were more likely to have difficulties with receptive language, receptive vocabulary, syntax, pragmatics and word-finding than those children who had not had epilepsy. Obviously these findings have a huge significance for the future planning of health, education and community services for children who survive cerebral and severe malaria in the resource-poor countries in which this condition is endemic. They should not be overlooked in children who arrive in the UK from such areas as refugees and asylum seekers.

Assessment of speech and language

Because of the possible co-presentation of speech and language disorders in these conditions, as well as other general learning and motor difficulties, the SLT needs to carry out a comprehensive assessment of both speech and language skills. The availability of assessment material will depend on context, and a number of tests commonly used in the UK have already been mentioned. However, malaria is endemic in sub-Saharan Africa and it is not a matter of merely translating assessment materials used in the UK for use in this context. Issues in developing appropriate speech and language assessment material for use in non-western cultures were addressed briefly in Chapter 2.

As a minimum, verbal comprehension and expressive language, both naming and spontaneous language, should be tested. As far as motor speech disorders are concerned a few studies have used the Frenchay Dysarthria Test (Enderby, 1983). This is actually designed for use with adults but may be used with cooperative children over the age of about 8 years. The Paediatric Oral Skill Package (Brindley et al., 1996) should provide an assessment that is more appropriate to the needs of children. It includes three different scales: observation, examination and performance. The former is particularly useful for young children, those very poorly or uncooperative. The examination scale is predominantly concerned with eating and drinking, and the performance scale with speech production and voluntary oral movements. The completed profile aims to assist therapists to set achievable goals in treatment planning for children with oral dysfunction.

Hearing loss is one of the reported complications after some types of meningitis, and occasionally other cerebral infections in childhood. Smyth et al. (1990) summarized more than one dozen infections known to cause hearing loss in childhood. They also discussed the recent changes in diagnostic audiology that have improved the detection of hearing loss in these children, especially the increased use of auditory brain stem responses.

All children who present with acquired aphasia should have a hearing test to establish audiological status. The competence of the auditory mechanism for effective language rehabilitation is just as important for children with developmental or acquired conditions.

The recovery of hearing loss associated with cerebral infection in children has been reported and is discussed by Smyth et al. (1990). They state that 'there appears to be no doubt that in some instances recovery (either complete or partial) of auditory function can occur following even profound hearing loss', and go on to say that such recovery can occur over a long time scale, even throughout childhood. Brookhouser et al. (1988) studied a group of 280 post-meningitic children. They reported that 31 per cent of the group had sensorineural hearing loss. They also documented changes in hearing threshold in some of these children over the three and a half years of their study.

From the reviews of this group of conditions it is clear that any child may have a wide range of needs: motor, cognitive, sensory and social as well as communication. The speech and language therapist working with the multiply impaired child needs to give particular attention to effective team working. S/he will need to liaise with a number of medical, educational and social services professionals as well as the family. These professionals may change at various times during the course of the child's problems due to the changing emphasis of the deficits in the acute or chronic stages. In the acute stage it is important that all the rehabilitation personnel meet to set goals which all members of the team understand, particularly the nursing staff and parents, who will probably be managing the child most of the time. Instructions for other staff should be discussed beforehand and demonstrated. Then a therapist should observe the other person carrying out the instructions to check for accuracy. Any written instructions should be clear and simple. Provide diagrams where possible, or better still photographs. A single-use or digital camera can do this quite cheaply and the photographs can be kept by the child's bed with the care plan for everyone to refer to. This technique can be used for general motor activities like posture and seating, for the use of a communication device or a feeding programme.

Examples of children with cerebral infections

Case 10: A child with a cerebral abscess

This boy (first described by Lees and Neville, 1990) presented with acute aphasia at 15 years of age, and a previous history of normal development. CT scan revealed frontal cortical damage following the anterior medial frontal lobe and laterally round to the centro-Sylvian region (i.e., involving the parietal lobe) secondary to a subdural abcess that was drained. There was no infarct and the damage would appear to have been purely cortical. Pure tone audiometry confirmed normal hearing. Pre-illness IQ (at age 11 years) was tested for educational placement and said to be above average on the WISC. This would appear to have been preserved as he returned to continue his education at the same school and achieved 11 passes at GCE 'O' level at the usual time. He received a period of speech and language therapy for 3 months beginning 6 months post-onset. At that time he was experiencing considerable difficulty in initiating some sounds and presented with a dysfluent speech pattern. However, this improved during the course of therapy and was more or less unnoticeable 1-year post-onset. He never had a significant comprehension problem nor did he produce paraphasias. Once the initial dysfluency problem was overcome his language soon returned to its former level, as this example of the Farmer Story recorded six months post-onset shows:

> There once was a farmer, who owned a stubborn donkey. The farmer wanted to get the donkey into the barn. First he pushed him, then he pulled him, but the donkey would not move. So he asked the dog to bark so he could frighten the donkey into the barn, but the lazy dog refused. So he asked the cat to make it bark. The cat was co-operative and scratched the dog. The dog barked and the barking frightened the donkey so that he jumped into the barn.

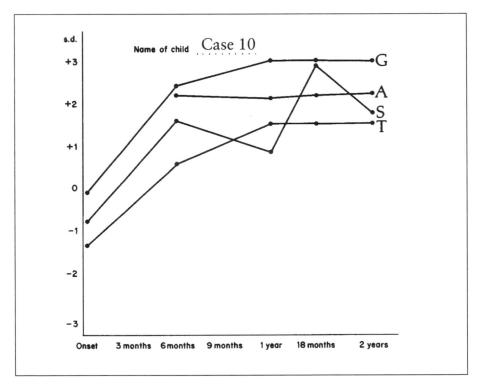

Figure 7.1 Profile of recovery of Case 10: A, auditory association; S, sentence repetition; T, TROG; W, Word Finding Vocabulary Test.

Case 11: A child with meningitis

This girl had a history of normal development until the age of 15;7 years when she was admitted in coma. She had had a fever for a few days that had been followed by a severe headache, vomiting and drowsiness. A diagnosis of meningococcal meningitis was confirmed by examination of the CSF. She was treated with penicillin and chloramphenicol for ten days. On examination there was a right-sided motor disorder and problems with both comprehension and expressive language. There was a papilloedema, right more than left, minimal right-sided weakness of the face and arm and a high tone hearing loss of 45dB bilaterally.

One-week post-onset her TROG raw score was 9 blocks passed (a z-score of −6) and her sentence repetition score was 5 (a z-score of −7.4). Expressive language at the same stage revealed both naming and grammatical errors. She produced yes and no responses appropriately as well as some single-word paraphasias (for example: brother = 'boyfriend' and tin opener = 'cantin'). Perseveration was also observed, particularly with the word 'oranges' being used as a persistent verbal error response. Grammar was telegrammatic, omitting prepositions and determiners such that only the main objects in action pictures were described. For example, a picture of a man drinking was described as 'man and cup'. She had a tendency to reverse passive sentences to make them active and made errors with personal pronouns.

Two weeks post-onset she was still omitting main verbs or using incorrect verbs in short sentences, often making errors with verb endings or the pronouns. Word order difficulties were also observed including reversal (for example: 'the girl is giving the dog a bone' was transformed to 'the girl is give the bone a dog').

A CT scan performed 5 weeks after onset showed some widening of the sulci on the left in the parietal region only and no abnormality of cerebral substance. She had a mild residual right facial weakness. She was almost at school-leaving age at the time of her illness and chose to leave school at the first opportunity. She found employment as a trainee hairdresser.

Case 12: A child with a viral encephalopathy

This girl had a normal developmental history until the age of 6 years when she presented with an obscure illness characterized by vomiting and generalized fever followed by neck stiffness and an increase in tone. An EEG performed at the time showed a generalized high voltage slow activity abnormality, but no focal features. An initial CT scan and carotid and vertebral angiograms were normal. A repeat CT scan one month later showed low attenuation in both thalami spreading out on the left to involve the posterior internal capsule and further out to the external capsule but not involving the cortex. This also extended down to the mid brain. A further CT scan one month later revealed progressive widening of the cerebral sulci. She had a series of tests for infection and metabolic abnormalities without any specific diagnosis being made. On the premise that she might have non-specific cerebritis she was started on a course of steroids and thereafter made a steady improvement. Pure tone audiometry confirmed normal hearing. She continued on steroids for one year, over which period she appeared to make an excellent recovery. Three years later her full scale IQ (WISC-R) was 92, with verbal IQ at 98 and performance IQ at 88.

Although her general level of ability was within the normal range she continued to find it difficult to learn in mainstream school and made slow progress particularly with reading. At the age of 8;1 years her Neale Analysis of Reading Ability (Neale, 1958) was an age equivalent of 8;0 years for accuracy but 7;3 years for comprehension. Samples of written language produced 20 months post-onset show some of her persisting difficulties with written language (self-corrected errors are in brackets):

> The dog tried to chasing the cat and the cat tried to chasing the dog and wad day the cat and dog sed to each other lets be(e) friends.

> It was snowing before going to school and it was very cold out side because was (ter) snowing and after lunch we(v) coom home and it was time to amegng the birds wes seeds and bread and cheese.

Expressive language samples 15 months post-onset using the Farmer Story show some mild difficulties:

> There was a farmer. The farmer wanted to put the donkey in the barn. First he pushed him but it was still. Then he pulled him but it did not move. So he asked the dog to woof at the donkey. But he stayed still. So he asked the cat to scratch him. The cat scratched him. The dog started woofing. The donkey was frightened and ran in the barn.

34 months post-onset:

> There was a donkey, a very very naughty donkey. One day the farmer wanted the donkey to go in the barn. First of all he pushed him. Then he pulled him and he didn't ... and the lazy donkey fused to move. So then he asked the dog to bark at the ... at the ... at the donkey. But he didn't fuse so he got the cat to scratch the dog. The cat scratched the dog. The dog barked and made the donkey go in the barn.

44 months post-onset:

> There was a ... a lazy donkey who w...who wouldn't go into the barn. The farmer tried to push the donkey but then he tried to pull him into the barn. He tried to

ask the cat (hesitation) the dog to bark at the .... bark at the donkey but the dog didn't want to. So instead he asked the cat to scratch the dog which might frighten the donkey in to the barn. So the cat /srækt/ scratched the dog and the dog barked at the donkey and then the um... donkey jumped into the barn.

Summary

As with all the subtypes of ACA, those that begin with cerebral infections can be at best puzzling and often quite devastating for both the individual and family. For some, like cerebral malaria, it is difficult to say that we are dealing with a true 'acquired' disorder, as the child may be infected several times from the first year of life onwards. Thus development will have been compromised from an early age.

Simon Hattenstone (1998), now a journalist, has written about his own experience of surviving encephalitis. As he puts it, 'The lunatic is in my head', saying 'You shout and no one seems to hear'. The account, which includes some words from his mother's perspective, is one of few that give an insider's view on such experiences. The Encephalitis Support Group[3] has been set up to support individuals and families facing such situations.

[3] Encephalitis Society, Encephalitis Resource Centre, 7b Saville Street, Malton YO17 7LL. Tel:/Fax: 01653 699599.

Chapter 8
Cerebral anoxia and prolonged coma

Cerebral anoxia

Normal brain function depends on an adequate, continuous supply of oxygen. Anoxia is defined as a condition in which the oxygen level in the body tissues falls below the level required to maintain normal function. This may be due to a complete absence of oxygen or a deficiency in its supply. There are two factors that regulate the supply of oxygen to the brain. These are the cerebral blood flow and the oxygen content of the blood. Cerebral anoxia may result from a drop in cerebral blood flow or the level of oxygen in the blood, which may have a number of causes, including near-drowning and suffocation as well as cardiac and respiratory arrest. The results of cerebral anoxia will depend to a large extent on the amount of time the oxygen level has been reduced. Deficits may range from mild to severe and in extreme cases, death can be the result. Where oxygen levels are restored to normal within one to two minutes, there are unlikely to be any long-term effects.

Murdoch and Ozanne (1990) reviewed the literature on cerebral anoxia in children and subsequent speech and language deficits. They stated that both the grey and white matter of the brain may be damaged in cerebral anoxia and further that anoxic lesions of the cerebral cortex are usually bilateral, although they may be asymmetrical. Equally, damage to the cerebellum was reported as a common finding in all types of cerebral anoxia. In respect of the brain stem nuclei they reported that damage here has been said to be more severe in children than in adults.

There are few specific reports of children presenting with speech and language deficits subsequent to cerebral anoxia. Murdoch and Ozanne (1990) reviewed two papers that discussed a total of five children, one of whom continued to have major learning difficulties five years after the trauma and four others with subcortical lesions who had reading problems (Aram et al., 1983 and Aram et al., 1989). A number of other language symptoms reported by Aram et al. (1989) included auditory comprehension, word retrieval and expressive syntax problems. Slow articulation and poor verbal memory was also reported in one child. Murdoch and Ozanne (1990) concluded that children were at risk for potential acute and chronic speech and language problems following anoxic episodes in childhood. As with all types of ACA, the deficits may be subtle and only comprehensive assessment will reveal their true nature and extent to allow for the planning of appropriate remediation.

Prolonged coma in childhood

There are a number of causes of coma in childhood including traumatic brain injury, infectious diseases of the CNS and cerebral anoxia. A child may also fall into a coma as a result of prolonged convulsive status, but this group will be considered in Chapter 10. The long-term recovery of children after coma has been poorly documented. Few studies have used adequate measures of cognitive and language skills and compared these with information available during the acute stage to allow for a discussion about prognosis for recovery after prolonged coma (coma of more than 24 hours duration) in childhood. In practical terms, the satisfactory educational placement of survivors of coma in childhood requires a comprehensive understanding of the child's cognitive and language skills.

A study by Kirkham et al. (1990) aimed to assess the proportion of children surviving prolonged coma who suffered cognitive and/or language deficits (either permanent or transient), motor problems, psychiatric problems and other neurological deficits. They were also concerned to establish whether there were any factors that were predictive for outcome including the severity of the coma, its aetiology and the age of the child at the time of insult, as well as some of the measures taken in the acute stage including cerebral perfusion pressure. The ultimate aim of the study was to define useful predictors of long-term cognitive/linguistic outcome during the acute stage. A five-year retrospective study of childhood survivors of coma was reported. Thirty-five children (aged between 4 and 16 years at the time of testing) participated in the study. They were designated to one of three groups depending on the severity of their coma, defined by its length in days. In the first group were children who had a coma of one day or less. The second group were those with a coma of more than one day and less than or equal to one week. Those in group three were in a coma for over a week but less than 60 days. The aetiology of the coma in these groups included cardiac arrest, encephalitis, head injury and other traumatic causes.

All of the children were cared for intensively during the coma and measures of cerebral perfusion pressure and intracranial pressure were available in relation to length and depth of coma as well as outcome. Individual psychometric assessment was carried out on all the children up to five years after the end of the period of coma using the tests listed in Table 8.1.

Table 8.1 Tests used by Kirkham et al. (1990)

1. The Weschler Intelligence Scale for Children (Wechsler, 1974) or the Griffiths Scale of Mental Ability (Griffiths, 1954, 1970), depending on age.
2. Neale Analysis of Reading (Neale, 1958) and Vernon Graded Word Spelling Test (Vernon, 1977) for those of school age.
3. The Test for Reception of Grammar (Bishop, 1983) for verbal comprehension of language.
4. Measures of memory, behaviour and motor impairment.

Results indicated a significant relationship between severity of coma and cognitive performance; between aetiology of coma and coma length, and between clinical measures of cerebral perfusion pressure, etc., and cognitive ability ($p = 0.01$ or 0.02 level) (see Table 8.2). Therefore the lower the cerebral perfusion pressure in the acute stage the greater the likelihood of learning, motor and language difficulties. A trend was also observed between length of coma and motor ability ($p = 0.02$).

Table 8.2 Results from Kirkham, Edwards and Lees (1990) for 34 children surviving coma

Learning difficulties
    57% of children who survived coma were experiencing learning difficulties 5 years later (full-scale IQ less than 80)
    31% of these had severe learning difficulties

Special education
    42.5% of the children had special educational needs (1981 Education Act)
    34% of these attended special schools
    25% were in residential care (at least during the week)
    8.5% were receiving special help within mainstream education
    A further 8.5% were referred to an educational psychologist as a direct result of this study

Other problems
    57% of the children had motor difficulties
    34% of the children had epilepsy
    Two children had been referred for help with behavioural problems

Kirkham et al. (1990) concluded that cerebral perfusion pressure is a useful predictor of potential recovery from coma in childhood. Children who survive prolonged coma in childhood require detailed assessment of cognitive and language skills to plan for their educational needs, as a significant proportion of the children have special educational needs as a result of cognitive and language problems. In their view, this indicates the need for future larger, probably multi-centre, multidisciplinary studies to validate their findings. In addition, the learning potential of children who have survived coma and their response to intervention needs to be studied so that effective education and therapy can be planned for them.

The role of the speech and language therapist

Because of the possible co-presentation of speech and language disorders in these conditions, as well as other general learning and motor difficulties, the speech and language therapist needs to carry out comprehensive assessment of both speech and language skills. A number of tests were mentioned in Chapter 2. As a minimum, verbal comprehension and expressive language (both naming and spontaneous language) should be tested. As far as motor speech disorders are concerned a few studies have used the Frenchay Dysarthria Test (Enderby, 1983). This is actually designed for use with adults but may be used with cooperative children over the age of about 8 years. The Paediatric Oral Skill Package (Brindley et al., 1996) should provide an assessment that is more appropriate to the needs of children. It includes three different scales: observation, examination and performance. The former is particularly useful for young children, those very poorly or uncooperative. The examination scale is predominantly concerned with eating and drinking, and the performance scale with speech production and voluntary oral movements. The completed profile aims to assist therapists to set achievable goals in treatment planning for children with oral dysfunction.

From the reviews of this group of conditions it is clear that any child may have a wide range of needs: motor, cognitive, sensory and social as well as communicative. The SLT working with the multiply impaired child needs to give particular attention to effective team working. Liaison with a number of medical, educational and social services professionals as well as the family will be vital. The professionals involved may change at various times during the course of the child's problems due to the changing emphasis of the deficits in the acute or chronic stages. In the acute stage it is important that all the rehabilitation personnel meet to set goals which all members of the team understand, especially the nursing staff and parents, who will probably be managing the child most of the time. Instructions for other staff should be discussed beforehand and demonstrated. Then a therapist should observe the other person carrying out the instructions to check for accuracy. Any written instructions should be clear and simple. Provide diagrams where possible, or better still, photographs. A single use or digital camera can do this quite cheaply and the photographs can be kept by the child's bed with the care plan for everyone to refer to. This technique can be used for general motor activities like posture and seating, for the use of a communication device or a feeding programme.

In such a varied group as this, there can be few general conclusions. Once again a number of variables seem to be operating and without larger studies, probably using pooled data, it is difficult to determine how they interact. However there are a number of guidelines that can be used in the management of these children:

1. Older children will not necessarily have more severe or longer-term problems than younger ones. Check the severity of the aphasia over time and do not forget to follow up younger children beyond the age of learning of written language to see if this has been affected.
2. Where the child has a history of coma of more than 24 hours duration be aware that an assessment of special educational needs may be indicated.

Summary

Advances in neuro-paediatric intensive care mean that we will see more child survivors of coma. Ethical questions concerning the management of children in long-term coma will continue to be raised. It will be important to document the recovery or otherwise of children in detail as a contribution to these debates. After acquired brain injury it is often the case that children have difficulty with new learning, as well as the re-learning of lost skills. It is this difficulty with new learning that can mean that children who make an otherwise good recovery continue to fall further and further behind their peers. This presents a significant challenge in educational placement. A support group called Acquire[4] aims to help children and young people who have acquired brain injuries and experience learning difficulties as a result.

---

[4] Acquire, Manor Farm House, Wendlebury, Bicester, Oxon. Tel: 01869 324339. Fax: 01869 234683.

Chapter 9
Landau-Kleffner syndrome

Pathology

Landau-Kleffner syndrome (LKS) must be the most puzzling language disorder of childhood. It is probably the least common and many paediatric speech therapists will never have seen a case. First described by Landau and Kleffner in 1957, it has a number of other names, including acquired aphasia with convulsive disorder and acquired receptive aphasia. These names refer to the co-occurring neurological disorder and the predominantly receptive language difficulty. There has been some confusion with the Worster-Drought syndrome after Worster-Drought described a series of cases with what he called 'an unusual form of acquired aphasia in childhood' (Worster-Drought, 1971). These are taken to be examples of epileptic aphasia of the Landau-Kleffner type rather than the condition which is usually referred to as Worster-Drought syndrome, which is a motor speech disorder also called congenital suprabulbar paresis (Worster-Drought, 1956).

In general terms the pattern of presentation in the Landau-Kleffner syndrome is that language regresses after a period of normal language development, usually with an accompanying seizure disorder. Beaumanoir (1985) described the two major symptoms as 'an acquired aphasia and a paroxysmal electroencephalographic recording with spikes and waves, mostly multifocal and unstable in the course of evolution', which may be associated with behaviour disturbances and epilepsy. The pathological basis of the disorder is not known, although numerous hypotheses have been advanced. Dulac et al. (1983) summarized these. First, the 'hypothese lesionelle' (lesional hypothesis) states that the EEG abnormalities and the language problems are the product of the same pathology, an inflammatory process in the cortex. Cerebral biopsies have failed to provide direct evidence of this. The alternative 'hypothese functionelle' (functional hypothesis) suggests that the bilateral discharges lead to a functional exclusion of the language centres in which even the possible remedial function of the minor hemipshere is cut off by the abnormal discharges. Dulac et al. (1983) concluded that the aphasia was the result of 'functional disorganization of the language centres due to important intercortical EEG abnormalities', which they described as being like a Todd's paralysis of language. Worster-Drought (1971) considered it likely that the pathological agent was a slow-working encephalitic virus and reported that a similar condition, commonly known as 'hard pad', occurred in dogs. It must be said that the debate in respect of the pathology of the condition remains unresolved.

In the first description by Landau and Kleffner in 1957 there were six children aged 5–9 years at onset, who presented with receptive aphasia in association with a range of epileptic symptoms. However, as Lees and Neville (1990) pointed out, a range of pathological mechanisms were implicated in the original paper. Of the five children described, the first had several periods of seizures, which were associated with positive motor phenomena on the right side, and evidence of family history of various seizure disorders. The second case was in fact a sibling of the first. This child's history included two minor head injuries in short succession. There are few studies of the effects of minor head trauma on a child's development. Even so it is interesting to note that minor head injury was also mentioned in case four. Generalized convulsions were also late sequelae in the second child. Grand mal seizures occurred in case three, as well as localized seizures of the left face. The fifth child's language regression began about one month after mumps. A later sequela was a grand mal seizure. Three of the children had a history of more than one period of aphasia and their condition appeared to have a fluctuating course. This summary demonstrates some of the difficulties of separating LKS from other epileptic aphasias. This later group will be discussed in Chapter 10.

There is still considerable debate as to what does and what does not constitute a case of LKS. For Lees and Neville (1990) the neuropathology of LKS was due to 'an organic event occurring with epilepsy' that did not fulfil the other criteria for epileptic aphasias. Clearly this definition by exclusion requires further work. However, it is important to try to distinguish between LKS and other convulsive aphasias. Neuropathology has implications for natural history, management and prognosis. In the summary of previous studies presented here we must accept that in some series, there is a mix of the two groups. Some, like Hirsch et al. (1995), want to call all epileptic aphasias LKS. They proposed that the term LKS should be extended to 'acquired deterioration of *any* higher cerebral function occurring in children' (their italics) who display:

- paroxysmal EEG abnormalities that are increased during sleep;
- epileptic seizures;
- developmental regression.

Other authors, like Lees and Neville (1990), will make some distinction between groups on the basis of possible pathology, in order to provide greater clarity about treatment and prognosis.

The exact relationship between the aphasia and the convulsive disorder in LKS has not been established. Dulac et al.'s (1983) suggestion that paroxysmal discharges act in some way to block access to the language areas of the cortex bears some relation to the phenomenon of aphasic arrest described by Penfield and Rasmussen (1950) in their studies of adults undergoing electrical stimulation of the cortex during neurosurgery for intractable epilepsy. This view has recently been reinforced by the adoption of surgical techniques, including multiple subpial transaction, to manage severe cases of LKS (Smith et al., 1989; Morrell et al., 1989), and this will be discussed later.

Bishop (1985) reviewed 45 cases from the literature in order to discuss the variable of age of onset in relation to outcome. She agreed with the widely held clinical view that the older the child at onset the better the prognosis. This is the opposite of the position in children with aphasia from unilateral cerebral lesions in whom prognosis for recovery is poorer with increasing age. Although LKS is not a common condition, the number of new cases published since 1978 has significantly increased (Beaumanoir, 1985). Bishop's statement that 'familial and personal medical history are irrelevant and there are no associated neurological signs' is not upheld by a careful analysis of either the original series (Landau and Kleffner, 1957) or subsequent reports.

According to Klein et al. (2000), the level of language development and behavioural stability before regression are more predictive of language recovery than the presence and persistence of clinical seizures. Whereas Robinson et al. (2001) concluded that the length of ESES (electrical status epilepticus in sleep) was the strongest predictor of outcome. Full recovery of language was only seen in those children who had ESES for less than three years.

Natural history

The literature includes single case studies, small group studies and retrospective analysis of previously reported cases. There is little general agreement about the course and prognosis of LKS. Landau and Kleffner (1957) optimistically declared that the prognosis for their children was good, although little objective data was available for their group. More recent studies have attempted to provide this information, although most series, particularly with long-term follow-up, are small.

Three stages of the condition are now recognized:

- stage one: acute deterioration in receptive language, and often in speech, with relative preservation of nonverbal IQ;

- stage two: chronic aphasia persists and may develop into mutism, and behaviour and attention problems increase;
- stage three: gradual improvement of skills: reacquisition of language and improving behaviour (Robinson et al., 2001).

Worster-Drought (1971) described 14 children: nine of them showed considerable improvement and in five a severe degree of receptive aphasia persisted after many years. It was an inability to describe a uniform clinical picture for LKS in both reviewing cases in the literature and in six cases of their own that led Deonna et al. (1977) to postulate that it was a heterogeneous syndrome with at least three courses. The first group, with the best prognosis, had a rapid onset and a rapid recovery of the aphasia. The second group showed progressive worsening of the aphasia after repeated seizures, and there were subsequent aphasic episodes. The third group also showed a progressive receptive aphasia, but there were no clinical seizures and recovery was variable. This study was not the first to mention fluctuating aphasic episodes (the original paper by Landau and Kleffner also does) but they were the first to see this group as presenting a slightly different course and prognosis. Only further research will determine whether these three subgroups do exist, have the same underlying pathology and therefore really are variations of the LKS.

The length of time reported cases of LKS have been followed up varies considerably between studies. This is an important consideration in terms of our understanding of the natural history of the condition. Van Harskamp et al. (1978), in describing a case that they followed up for seven years post-onset, stated that although the seizures had been medically controlled and EEG abnormalities improved, there had not been a parallel improvement in the child's aphasia. This girl was followed up annually until 18 years of age and later reported by Van Dongen et al. (1989), at which time subtle language deficits were still apparent and her EEG still showed mild abnormalities.

Mantovani and Landau (1980), in following up the six cases originally described by Landau and Kleffner and three new cases, found that in five of them there was a good recovery resulting in essentially normal language by adulthood. Their statement that 'the variability in outcome of similarly affected children remains one of the most puzzling features of this disorder' is echoed by most researchers in their attempts to find common denominators. They often review many of the previously reported cases in an attempt to do this.

Bishop (1985) suggested that one of the variables which might be expected to relate to eventual outcome was the age at onset of the disorder. She reviewed 45 cases of LKS which had been reported in the literature and followed up to at least 12 years of age. She reported a strong relationship to suggest that in LKS the older the child at onset the better the prognosis for recovery of aphasia, which is opposite to the accepted prognosis in relation to age at onset for traumatic aphasias (poorer prognosis of recovery of aphasia with increasing age). Once again, long-term follow-up of affected children is required to substantiate outcome.

Ripley and Lea (1984) attempted to provide such data in their follow-up study of ex-pupils of a school for children with speech and language disorders who had severe receptive language problems (it is worth noting that this was the same school from which Robinson (1991) later took his epidemiological data concerning speech and language disorders mentioned at the beginning of this book). Of the 14 children discussed 10 would appear, from case histories supplied, to have an acquired basis for their disorder. Neuropathology was as potentially varied as the Landau and Kleffner (1957) series and included evidence of mild head trauma, epilepsy and cerebral infection. Information about socio-economic status and achievements since leaving school shows that two were married and all were in full-time paid employment. Only two of the ex-pupils had ongoing health problems: one had migraine and another had epilepsy. At best they all had limited verbal communication, and a majority continued to rely on sign language to communicate.

The variable clinical picture has led to some debate on the core features of the condition, the typical course and the most effective management. It has been suggested that such a wide range of possibilities is hardly likely to represent one syndrome. Moreover, because the condition has rarely been comprehensively described from the language point of view, equally wide-ranging reports about the possible presenting language symptoms exist.

There would appear to be increasing recognition that only multi-centre longitudinal studies will help to further our understanding of the course and prognosis of LKS. Dugas et al. (1991) pointed out that most studies have approached the subject from one of three different objectives: to describe the condition and its various patterns and allow them to be distinguished, to consider the influence of the various variables like age of onset in respect of the pathology and nature of the primary disorder and thirdly to consider the early effects of rehabilitation and pharmacological therapies (therapeutic objectives). In order to further discuss the natural history, course and prognosis of LKS they selected 33 cases from 156 published cases between 1957 and 1989. These cases were selected on the following criteria:

• regression of language after a period of normal development;
• existence of epileptic seizures and/or paroxysmal EEG abnormalities;
• sufficient information for a multidimensional approach to prognosis;
• minimum follow-up to the age of 14 years.

The age of onset of these cases varied from 2 to 10 years with the majority being between 4 and 6 years. They defined four outcome groups:

1. Very unfavourable outcome (4 cases), in which there was no social or professional independence, almost total comprehension deficit and no oral expression.
2. Unfavourable outcome (11 cases), in which there was some degree of socio-professional skill and a severe communication disability in which oral language was unintelligible or significantly reduced.
3. Favourable outcome (11 cases), in which they gained good socio-professional skills and where the persistence of oral and/or written language difficulties did not impede communication.
4. Very favourable outcome (7 cases), in which they all lived independently without difficulty and there was no observable communication difficulty, oral or written.

Dugas et al. (1991) presented a detailed account of the symptoms of language disturbances seen in these groups and concluded by asking 'whether the length of the follow-up influences the rating of the prognosis'.

Two decades of seeing children with this syndrome in clinical practice has resulted in data from a highly varied group of children (some of which was reported in Lees, 1989; Lees and Neville, 1990; Lees, 1997). They have ranged in age from 2 to 14 years at onset. Some have presented acutely and in others there has been a period of language deterioration lasting between several weeks and several months. Those with the longer period of deterioration seem to have poorer prognosis. Complete verbal auditory agnosia has been seen in a number of cases. However, this is not always the major presenting symptom. The receptive language component may fluctuate. In others verbal language is absent or considerably reduced. Older children may present with a rather pedantic conversational style with inappropriate prosody. Data from Lees (1989) suggests that children who do not make progress to within 2 sd in verbal comprehension within six months of onset are in the poor outcome group. Most of these children required special educational provision within a specialized teaching environment in which visual methods of teaching language (signing and reading) were backed up with an emphasis on functional communication for everyday life.

Speech and language impairments in LKS

The characteristic language problem of LKS is a severe receptive aphasia. This has been variously described. Cooper and Ferry (1978) preferred to call it verbal auditory agnosia rather than aphasia. This suggests a view that LKS is not a primary language disorder but rather an auditory processing disorder. Indeed, many of the children are initially thought to be deaf, but on examination peripheral hearing is normal. In order to investigate whether the comprehension problems of children with Landau-Kleffner syndrome were restricted to the auditory modality, Bishop, (1982) set up a study using three forms of a test for the comprehension of grammatical structures (later called the Test for Reception of Grammar, Bishop 1983). Three groups of children, one with Landau-Kleffner syndrome, one with developmental language disorder of an expressive type, and normal controls, were tested with spoken, written and signed presentation of the test. Results confirmed that the children with Landau-Kleffner syndrome had deviant comprehension of language, in auditory, signed and written presentation. However a subsequent experiment with deaf children demonstrated that they had a very similar profile of difficulty in comprehension of language to the Landau-Kleffner children. Bishop suggests that this similarity is the result of an auditory processing difficulty in the Landau-Kleffner syndrome that then forces the children to rely on the visual modality to learn the grammar of the language, as deaf children do.

Reported language problems are not confined to receptive language. Case histories can reveal pre-existing difficulties in language acquisition, as in one child reported by Ripley and Lea (1984). Dugas et al. (1976) reported word-finding difficulty, perseveration, phonemic and semantic paraphasias in the verbal language of the 9-year-old girl they described. These were also observed to a lesser degree in her written language. Fewer papers concentrate on the expressive language problems in LKS, and none have tried to explain their occurrence, although it seems less likely that they could be accounted for by the 'auditory deprivation' model that has been suggested by Bishop (1982) to account for the receptive problems.

Van der Sandt-Koenderman et al. (1985) also reported a child who produced paraphasias and neologisms. They found that the frequency of these in spontaneous speech was a very sensitive indication of language breakdown as well as recovery. Beaumanoir (1985) supported the view that when the onset of aphasia is after the child has acquired written language (and if this ability is still retained), then there is a better prognosis for educational attainment.

Speech and language therapy

There are still few studies in which the speech and language therapy and educational rehabilitation of children with LKS is presented in detail. One exception is the detailed case study of a child who presented with slow deterioration in language beginning at 3;6 years, and which lasted for over eight months, by Vance (1991). He was first introduced to signing through the Makaton Vocabulary (Walker, 1980) and later the Paget Gorman Sign System (Paget et al., 1976), producing strings of seven or more signs by the age of 7 years. Other specific therapeutic methods used included the introduction of Cued Articulation (Passy, 1990), a series of hand shapes that identify each English consonant. These methods were used in individual therapy and in the classroom, where other educational techniques included a daily picture diary to help develop the concept of time and a colour pattern scheme for literacy skills (Lea, 1970). Other communication skills taught included auditory training and interaction skills. This boy went on to attend a partially hearing unit where signing was used. He was later followed up and further therapy offered to correct some residual phonological processing problems. A psycholinguistic framework was applied as the basis for the therapy (Vance, 1997).

In their discussion of speech and language therapy for LKS, Gerard et al. (1991) stated that the 'choice between alternative systems and a reconstruction of oral language seems ... an oversimplified approach to the discussion'. They reviewed the management of 18 children, of whom five received no speech therapy. Because of a difficulty in obtaining details of the treatment given in the other cases, most of their information is rather general. Of nine children who received therapy, the following methods were reported to be used at some stage: auditory therapy, phonemic analysis, modelling verbal expression, written language, symbols, signs. However, where Vance (1991) was able to give some indication of how specific methods were introduced for her one case, Gerard et al. (1991) were only able to give some indication of the duration of speech and language therapy in 13 cases. This ranged between three months and ten years. They did report one case in detail and proposed a therapeutic model based on a neuropsychological approach. Gerard et al. (1991) concluded that, when the limitations of speech and language therapy were taken into account, therapy should always aim to build on the residual language abilities of children with LKS. They went on to say 'when these are too insufficient, or when the intellectual potential does not allow one to be compelled to systematic, associative learning, creating a potential for lexical representation, then no more can be expected of sign language'. In such cases they advocated the use of 'minimal systems of communication using gesture, iconic or pictographic symbols', preferring the latter for their flexibility.

In 1997, Vance reported a follow-up to her 1991 paper, the case of the boy with LKS, using a psycholinguistic framework to remediate his residual auditory processing and phonological difficulties. At this stage of his rehabilitation, some five years after the onset of LKS, the child was making good progress in a unit for hearing impaired children attached to a mainstream school. However he continued to produce many words inaccurately, making both consistent and idiosyncratic sound substitutions and omissions in words, and some vowels were distorted. SLT assessment revealed a varied language profile across a number of tests with age equivalent scores from 4;06 to 6;09 years depending on the tests used, at the age of ten years. His auditory and phonological processing was further investigated using the psycholinguistic framework outlined by Stackhouse and Wells (1997). As a result, a therapy hypothesis was developed which stated that 'Therapy targeted at developing more accurate phonological representations should lead to a reduction in speech output errors' (Vance, 1997), and four aims for therapy were drawn up. Details of the therapy programme, including the further use of Cued Articulation (Passy, 1990) are given. Vance concluded that the use of the psycholinguistic framework allowed the source of the child's speech errors to be identified, and also identified the strengths and weaknesses in his speech processing skills.

These were then used to provide a clear rationale for therapy that could be fully evaluated as it progressed.

Educational strategies

De Wijngaert (1991) also recognized that there was little information in the literature concerning language therapy or educational methods for children with LKS. His preferred approach for these children is one in which speech and language therapy is integrated into the classroom programme to provide a comprehensive programme for educational needs. It is essentially an oral programme and is based on nine years of work with six children with LKS. The programme is based on creating the right environment for learning for these children and for de Wijngaert this means creating enthusiasm. He provided some indications of the ways in which oral and written language skills are taught and advocated that this should be done in stages. The Colour Pattern Scheme (Lea, 1970) was also used with these children. Unfortunately no specific details were provided about how children progressed with this programme.

Van Slyke (2002) described the classroom instruction of four children with LKS, two after surgery and two who had pharmacological treatment. Her 'qualitative case study reports' provided a description of the educational strategies used with each child in reading, mathematics and the general curriculum. She concluded that children with LKS learn best in a small language-based classroom with the following features:

- a highly supportive teaching environment including one-to-one work;
- intensive speech and language therapy;
- sign language;
- a functional approach to communication;
- language teaching in a developmental framework;
- visual methods including pictures, colour coding and a picture diary;
- computer programs.

These strategies might be useful for any language impaired children. However, the evidence Van Slyke provided and the descriptions given of these strategies is insufficient for replication in anything other than a quite general way.

This summary should serve to emphasize what a lot of further work is required concerning the speech and language rehabilitation of children with LKS. Unlike Landau (1991) I cannot agree that the use of single-case studies represents what he called 'a stupid level of speculation'. The use of single-case design ABA is possible, although not without significant administrative challenges. I do believe that small numbers make multi-centre collaboration essential, but like Vance (1991), Gerard et al. (1991) and de Wijngaert (1991), I also believe that carefully constructed programmes in which therapy and education work together, probably along a neuropsychological/psycholinguistic model, would be a sensible place to begin to provide some of the details which are now required.

Other aspects of the management of LKS

It is obvious from the literature reviewed so far that the complex nature of LKS has meant that it has attracted interest from a wide range of professionals. In clinical practice, the proper management of children with LKS requires a multidisciplinary team. Because of the nature of the condition this may mean liaison between more than one centre and will certainly require collaboration between health and educational services. This kind of working can be difficult and communication between the various professionals, and also between professionals and the family, can break down. If this is to be avoided it can be helpful to appoint a key worker for each child who will be responsible for coordinating information between the professionals and also to the family. Which professional carries out this role will depend on the child's situation, and may need to change if the educational placement changes or if the family moves. Whilst it has been traditional for those in the medical professions to head teams along rather hierarchical lines, there is some evidence to suggest that this may slowly be changing. A team of professional equals in which one member is chosen as key worker according to the child's needs at that time is to be preferred. Where the child is in special education this may be a teacher or educational psychologist whereas in the preschool period a therapist or health visitor may be more appropriate. The family should be fully involved in the choice of key worker where possible and the development of a good relationship between family and key worker should be a matter of priority.

Alongside the speech and language therapist and educational staff, those involved in the management of children with LKS are likely to include the audiologist and the paediatric neurologist. It will be important in the early stages of diagnosis to establish the child's audiological status. Children with LKS are often initially thought to be hearing impaired. The high incidence of conductive hearing loss in childhood, most often secondary to otitis media, means that it is important to rule out this cause of deterioration in language skills. Equally, even after a diagnosis of LKS is made, a child's hearing will require regular monitoring to ensure that it remains as stable as possible and that any treatable conditions are dealt with promptly, as fluctuating hearing in addition to the language problem can lead to further problems with both communication and behaviour.

Antiepileptic drugs

Two other aspects of the management of LKS warrant careful review: the use of antiepileptic medication and, more recently, surgical intervention. A number of papers have reported the successful use of a range of antiepileptic drugs with small numbers of children with LKS. McKinney and McGreal (1974) reported good results using steriods with six patients. Dugas et al. (1976) used phenobarbital in one case and claimed 'spectacular regression of the aphasia', although no formal measures of language function were given.

Marescaux et al. (1990) reported five children with LKS and also reviewed some previously published reports. They stated that pheno-barbital, carbamazepine and phenytoin were ineffective or worsened the EEG and neuropsychological symptoms, whereas valproate, ethosuximide and benzodiazepines were 'partially or transiently efficacious'. Dextro-amphetamine was said to produce a dramatic but transient improvement in EEG abnormalities in one of two children but had no effect on language disturbance. By contrast corticosteroid treatment resulted in both improvement of speech and normalization of EEGs in three children. They therefore concluded, from their own experience and from the literature, that 'corticosteroids should be given in high doses as soon as the diagnosis is firmly established' and should be continued 'for several months or years'. Although EEGs are included in the test, formal language test scores are not reported. It should be noted that the cases described in this chapter were treated with a wide range of anticonvulsants and that variable effects are reported. Careful monitoring of language is recommended when antiepileptic drugs are being used.

Surgery for LKS

Multiple subpial transection (MST) was first described by Morrell et al. (1989) when it was 'a new approach to the surgical treatment of focal epilepsy'. They recommended its use in those patients whose epileptogenic lesions lie in the regions of the cerebral cortex controlling speech, movement, primary sensation or memory. The procedure selectively severs certain horizontal intercortical neural fibres but preserves vertical ones with the aim of reducing 'the likelihood of occurrence of synchronized cell discharge and to do so in a manner which does not impair the major functional capacity of the tissue'. They reported ten patients in whom this procedure had been carried out directly to Broca's or Wernicke's areas, all of whom continued to be verbal language users post-surgery. In their evaluation of recovery no formal measures of language function were reported. This technique has been used with children with LKS since the 1990s.

It was not until 1995 that Morrell reported the effects of MST on 14 children in his series, all of whom had had LKS. They defined LKS as 'an acquired aphasia secondary to a focal epileptogenic lesion affecting the speech cortex and unassociated with signs of diffuse of generalized brain damage or autism'. They described a number of tests used to establish grounds for surgery including EEG and MRI. They claimed recovery in 11 of the 14 children treated, and described the recovery process as gradual. It would be about 12 weeks after surgery before the child regained single-word expression and most had made substantial improvement by six months. Seven went on to regain age appropriate speech and language and to return to mainstream school without the need for ongoing SLT input. Four others showed 'marked improvements' in verbal language. Thus, 11 of the 14 who had not used verbal language to communicate for at least two years were able to do so post-surgery. Amongst those who did not improve, one had chronic encephalitis and two had a progressive dementing disorder (one of these was thought not to have had normal language before the onset of aphasia).

It is interesting to note that the child reported by Morrell et al. (1995) to have had chronic encephalitis was seen by this author at age 16 years for advice about further educational placement. She continued to be aphasic, presenting with a nonfluent aphasia. Her communication was characterized by short spoken phrases augmented with sign and body language. She had word-finding difficulties but was a persistent communicator who had good eye contact and social skills. Her cognitive profile was in the low normal range. She went on to a further education placement in a specialist setting for children with epilepsy and communication difficulties.

Grote et al. (1999) further reported 14 children who had had MST for LKS. Their study included pre- and post-operative test data for receptive and expressive vocabulary with 11 children demonstrating significant improvements.

Six years of experience using MST in the UK with a small group of children with LKS led to a paper by Irwin et al. (2001). They reported results from five children who had undergone MST for LKS and its effect on the language, cognitive abilities, behaviour, seizures and EEG abnormalities of the children. Pre- and post-operative assessment data was reported. Both behaviour and seizure activity showed significant improvements after surgery in all of the children. Although language skills also showed improvement in the whole group, none of the children improved to age-appropriate levels. Whilst they claimed that these results indicated that MST was an important treatment option in LKS, they acknowledged that the long-term effect on language is still under investigation.

Managing behaviour difficulties

In their original defining paper, Landau and Kleffner (1957) included some reports of the behaviour impairments observed in their five cases. Neville et al. (2000) consider these to have been 'under reported'. Furthermore, descriptions like 'was hard to manage' (case 4, Landau and Kleffner, 1957) cannot be quantified. In a specialist assessment service seeing children with LKS and other types of complex epilepsy, the team noted that active behaviour problems were a major management issue. These included:

- attention-deficit hyperactivity disorder (ADHD), which may be so marked as to 'compromise the child's ability to engage meaningfully with his/her environment' (Neville et al., 2000);
- behaviour typically seen in autistic spectrum disorders including repetitive play, ritualistic behaviours and obsessions;
- sleep disorder such that many children have long periods of wakefulness, preventing normal sleep patterns;
- aggression and rage attacks that are 'quite out of proportion to the scale of the response, and end abruptly' (Neville et al., 2000);
- apathy and global regression which is behaviour of the other extreme such that the child may become completely adynamic (Neville et al., 2000).

Clearly, these behaviours present a significant burden of care for families and may lead to children being excluded from educational and social settings, further limiting their opportunities. It is therefore vital that multidisciplinary management includes skilled psychiatric and psychological help where indicated.

Examples of children with LKS

Case 13: A child with an acute onset, rapid recovery and good prognosis

This boy (first described in Lees and Neville, 1990) had a history of normal development when he presented with an acute aphasia at age 12;7 years. He reported a feeling of discomfort in his right arm that he described as 'like an electric shock'. EEG revealed bilateral temporal spikes and the sensations suggest a persisting dysrhythmic element. CT scan was normal. There was no other pathological evidence and a diagnosis of Landau-Kleffner syndrome was therefore reached. Initially he presented with a severe receptive and expressive aphasia. This gradually resolved, but not without some fluctuations in verbal comprehension. Pure tone audiometry confirmed normal hearing. Expressive language contained both jargon and paraphasias. He received no further speech and language therapy after his discharge from hospital. Apart from the reported mild fluctuations in verbal comprehension, the course of recovery from aphasia was unremarkable. There were no seizures. Within the two-year follow-up his language test scores returned to the normal range. He continued to make reasonable progress with his peers in a mainstream comprehensive school. Figure 9.1 records his progress on language assessments during the two years of follow-up.

Results from the story-telling test at onset confirmed a jargon aphasia characterized by inappropriate unfinished sentences:

Dog Story (initial assessment)
Is it the middle bit ? He the thing in. The thing was up really.

However, this resolved quite quickly to a more nonfluent pattern as subsequent story telling examples demonstrate:

Farmer Story (3 months post-onset)
A old farmer had a lazy donkey. The farmer wanted to put the donkey in the barn. He pushed him, then he pulled him but the donkey didn't move. So he asked the lazy dog to bark at the donkey. The dog refused. So the co-operative cat scratched the dog. The dog began to bark and the donkey jumped into the barn.

Farmer Story (12 months post-onset)
There was an old farmer who had a stubborn donkey. The farmer wants to get the donkey into the barn. First he pushed him but the donkey wouldn't move. Then he pulled him but the donkey still wouldn't move. The farmer thought he could frighten the donkey so he tried to get the dog to bark ... to frighten the donkey. But it ... refused. So he got the cat to scratch the dog to make the dog bark. That, that didn't work er ... er ... The dog barked. The donkey went in.

He made a small number of paraphasic errors on confrontational naming tests, all of which gradually decreased during the two-year follow-up period as Table 9.1 shows.

Written language was never more than moderately affected, as this example of spontaneous writing soon after onset of the disorder shows: (spelling and punctuation as original, brackets mark self-corrected errors in the original).

Table 9.1 Paraphasic errors on tests of confrontational naming for Case 13

Date from onset	Item	Response	Error type
Onset	Sling	Slung	Phonemic paraphasia
	Crutch	Clutch	Phonemic paraphasia
	Watering can	Bucket	Semantic paraphasia
	Lighthouse	Lightbulb	Semantic paraphasia
6 months	Corkscrew	Screwdriver	Semantic paraphasia
9 months	Sporran	Spirren	Phonemic paraphasia
18 months	Handcuffs	Cufflinks	Semantic paraphasia

One Harvest Monday I was combining my feild when I came across this mole, I didn't want to run him down so I picked him up and took him in the cab. I decided to call him a name 'Fred'. I took him everywhere I went.

One morning I had a (fo) phone call saying I had to go to a meeting a long way a way, so I couldn't take 'fred' with me. So I asked a freind to look after him for me. The freind was a busy person too who just this once he thought he would let him loose in the garden. 5 minutes later the friend looked around and saw the mole was squashed on the road.

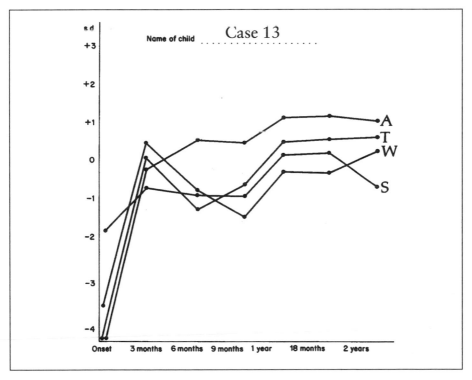

Figure 9.1 Profile of recovery of Case 13: A, auditory association; S, sentence repetition; T, TROG; W, Word Finding Vocabulary Test.

Case 14: A child with repeated seizures and gradual worsening of the aphasia, with subsequent aphasic periods and good recovery

This boy had a history of early feeding difficulties and delay in speech and motor development. He was said by his parents to be slightly slower than his older sister, but this did not give cause for more specific concern. At the age of 4;9 years he was reported to have had a left-sided focal attack progressing to grand mal with transient left-sided weakness afterwards. He was treated with phenytoin. There was a further episode at the age of 7 years; shaking in the left arm spreading to the left leg and lasting for approximately 20 minutes and followed by transient left-sided weakness. An EEG at the age of 7;6 years showed a right mid-temporal and fronto-parietal focus. At the age of 9 years his school performance deteriorated. There was noticeable pausing in his speech. He was dropping things from his left hand and there were episodes of eye blinking. The phenytoin was increased. An IQ assessment at this time showed a low average intelligence and there was some gradual improvement recorded when he was re-tested a year later. At this time some mild ataxia of his left arm was noticed, and he was having episodes of dribbling, jerking and apparent deafness. He was treated with sodium valproate. At the age of 10 years it was clear that he did not understand what was said to him and he was admitted for investigations. Treatment with a ketogenic diet produced a possible transient improvement. Corticosteroids were ineffective. He continued to be treated with phenytoin to the age of 14 years. It was observed both at school and home that phenytoin in the upper end of the therapeutic range had some significant effect on his comprehension, and informal clinical observation confirmed that there was some evidence of this.

CT scan at 11 years of age was normal, as were brain stem evoked auditory responses. An EEG performed around the same time showed a background rhythm that was rather slower than the previous record. The left temporal abnormality was much more marked. There were sharp waves in the Rolandic areas, predominantly on the right side. In addition there was a focal sharp and slow wave abnormality in the left temporo-parietal region suggesting a focal abnormality. It was quite difficult to maintain the correct phenytoin dose in the top end of the range and there were signs associated with mild phenytoin toxicity from time to time. There was no persisting physical deficit and his overt fits were fully controlled by the age of 11 years.

He was admitted to a school for speech and language disordered children at the age of 12 years. His performance IQ on the WISC was 92. His hearing was confirmed as within the normal range for speech. He made good progress in language although high-level auditory-verbal processing problems did persist. At 13;7 years his Schonell spelling score was an age equivalent of 11;6. At the same time his Neale Reading score was an age equivalent of 11;9 years for accuracy and 11;2 years for comprehension. He was transferred back to a mainstream comprehensive school at 14 years where he passed four GCSEs. He went on, at 17 years, to attend further education to train in furniture- and cabinet-making. At 19 he completed his course and won a five-year apprenticeship with a furniture-making company.

It is often difficult to establish the pre-aphasic language abilities of children with ACA. This boy's expressive language was taped by his family when he was 6 years old. Family audio and videotapes can provide a useful source for information about previous language abilities.

> One day the old man planted a seed ... a turnip seed and ... um the old man ... one day ... he said 'Grow strong, grow strong, grow, grow'. So the turnip did grow strong and grow ... and ... the um ... one day when he came out to pick it the old m ... man ... he pulled and he pulled but he couldn't get it up.
> He got the old woman. The old woman pulled the man. The man pulled the turnip, but it still wouldn't come up. So the old lady got the granddaughter and the granddaughter pulled the ... u, ... the old lady. The lady began to pull the old man. The old man began to pull the turnip but it still wouldn't come up. So the um ... granddaughter got the dog. The dog pulled the granddaughter. The granddaughter pulled the ... old lady. The old lady pulled the old man. The old man pulled the turnip but it still wouldn't come up. So the dog collected the cat and the cat pulled the dog and the dog pulled the granddaughter. The granddaughter pulled the old lady. The old lady pulled the man and ... and the old lady pulled the man and the man pulled the turnip ... but it still wouldn't come up. So old man ... um ... um ... um pulled the turnip but he still couldn't get it up.

And this example of pre-aphasic written language was taken from schoolwork at age 9 years:

> If I drove the London bus it would be very bumpy and uncomfortable, and when it rains the people who sit at the top will get quite wet. When it's sunny the people downstairs would get hot. To start the bus you have to wind up a handle and the bus is washed every week. So it is in good condition. If someone leaned over the top of the bus it might be dangerous. I would like to have a bus of my own.

These examples of story telling were recorded during follow-up, 2;2 years and 3;9 years post-onset respectively:

> Farmer Story (2;2 years post-onset)
> There was a very stubborn and very lazy donkey. The farmer wanted him to go in the barn. He pushed him and he didn't move. He pulled him too. The farmer had a good idea to frighten the donkey. He asked the dog to bark at the donkey but he refused to. So he asked the cat to scratch him. The cat scratched the dog. The dog began to bark loudly. The barking frightened the donkey and he went in the barn.

> Farmer Story (3;9 years post-onset)
> There was an old farmer who wanted to put his donkey in the barn. But the donkey would not move because he was stubborn. First he pushed him, then he

pulled him but he still wouldn't move. So he asked the dog to bark at him but the lazy dog refused. So he asked the co-operative cat to scratch the dog to get the dog to bark. The cat scratched the dog and the dog barked and the donkey went in the barn (13 episodes).

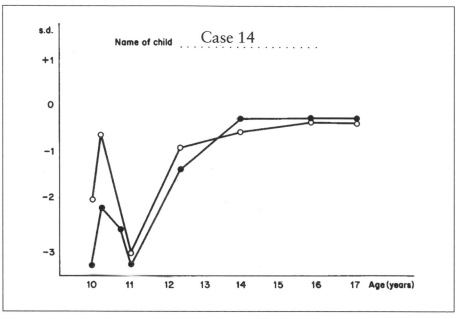

Figure 9.2 Profile of recovery of Case 14: (o) receptive language; (•) expressive language.

Case 15: A child with progressively deteriorating language, no seizures and little recovery

This boy's developmental history was described as normal, although there was some language delay, with first words at 18 months and phrases at 4 years. This was first diagnosed by an SLT who saw him at the age of 4 years. He had speech and language therapy for one year. Six months after the commencement of speech and language therapy, a conductive hearing loss of 30–40dB bilaterally was diagnosed. Myringotomies and adenoidectomy were performed a year later. At that time his speech began to deteriorate and this was confirmed by the local speech and language therapist. At the age of 5;7 years his score on the Reynell Developmental Language Scales for verbal comprehension was below the 2 years level. However he began in normal school and his teacher suspected that he had a hearing problem. By age 9 years his verbal comprehension was nil except for some slight situational understanding. An EEG performed at the age of 6 years showed an epileptic pattern but there were no overt fits. His IQ, measured on the Leiter International Scale at the same age, was recorded as 80. At the age of 7;3 years it was measured again as 75.

At the age of 9 years his motor function and dexterity were assessed as being below the 5 years level and he was described as markedly dyspraxic. He was left-handed. His hearing was at 40dB for most frequencies, and at 65–70dB for 250Hz. EEG was repeated at the age of 10;4 years and was also described as 'markedly epileptic'. He never had an overt fit, although there were one or two suspicious episodes. He had been receiving phenytoin as an anticonvulsant since age 6 years. This was gradually and successfully withdrawn from the age of 13 years. His acquired receptive aphasia was described as one preceded by a period of near-normal language development and followed by a fade-out of receptive skills. He finished his education at a school for the deaf as he relied entirely on signed language for communication. His language assessment scores are given in Table 9.2.

Table 9.2 Case 15: Language assessment scores

Onset of aphasia at age 6;6 years.
Three months post-onset RDLS verbal comprehension was below 2-year level.
Three and a half year later RDLS verbal comprehension was nil, but using Paget Gorman Signs a 3-year level was recorded.

Assessed at the age 14 years his score on the Test for Reception of Grammar was 2, a z-score of -10. When the same test was presented so that he could read the sentences his score improved to 16.

Case 16: A child with progressively deteriorating language, later development of seizures and variable recovery

This girl (first described by Lees and Urwin, 1991) presented at age 6;9 years with a history of a slow deterioration in language skills that had begun nine months previously. Prior to this she had been developing normally and had attended a mainstream infant school. There was no family history of speech and language problems. She had no history of epilepsy. Initially the problem had been thought of as a fluctuating hearing loss but all audiological investigations were normal. By the time she was referred for this assessment, she was only able to comprehend simple phrases in situational context. Her expressive language was also reduced to simple stereotyped phrases. The school reported that her behaviour was difficult to manage. Neurological examination was normal throughout, as was a CT scan. EEG revealed a focus of abnormal activity in the left temporal lobe but there were no overt fits. She did complain of not sleeping well and a pain in her left ear but nothing could be found to explain this. Her IQ on the WISC(R) was full scale 71, performance 91 and verbal 55. She passed two blocks on the TROG, comprehending single nouns and single verbs only. She produced a number of naming errors on the WFVT, which were often irrelevant stereotypes or requests for her mother to respond on her behalf. The changes in these test scores over two and a half years are shown in Figure 9.3. A trial of carbamazepine was begun to see if verbal comprehension would improve, but it was unchanged six weeks later. A trial of corticosteroids was introduced instead and discontinued six weeks later when verbal comprehension remained unchanged, although behaviour deteriorated further. After this all anticonvulsants were withdrawn without further effect.

It was clear from observations of her at school and home that this girl understood very little. Her deteriorating behaviour was directly related to her failure to comprehend. She was reluctant to be parted from her mother and relied heavily on her for 'translation' of what was happening or being said. She would turn her mother's face towards her when she wanted such an explanation and also used the same technique if she was trying to tell her mother something. This behaviour is fairly common in young language disordered children with severe comprehension problems. A statement of educational need was drawn up and she was placed in a language unit at age 7;4 years. Her verbal comprehension remained unchanged over the course of the following six months.

A system of language teaching through reading based on the Colour Pattern Scheme (Lea, 1970) was used to work on visual comprehension of language structure. She was also taught the Makaton Vocabulary (Walker, 1980) but was reluctant to use more than a few single signs. Listening and attention work were also encouraged, as was basic sentence construction work. Her expressive language was essentially nonfluent and telegrammatic with both phonemic and semantic paraphasias and neologisms as well as perseverations. Some examples of these impairments are given in Table 9.3, taken from responses to the Renfrew Action Picture Test and the Word Finding Vocabulary Test (Renfrew, 1988 and 1977a) (see Table 9.3). With no change in her verbal comprehension it was clear that she was likely to require long-term placement in a school for children with speech and language disorders. At the age of 9;3 years, two and a half years post-onset, she was referred for a neurosurgical assessment to see if she would be a suitable candidate for multiple subpial transaction (as described by Morrell et al., 1995).

The operation was carried out when the girl was ten years old. Immediately after this some gradual improvement was seen. Her behaviour, sleeping and concentration were all described as better by her parents. However, she was completely mute in the post-operative period. Within two weeks of the surgery her verbal comprehension began to show some improvement and she was able to respond to environmental sounds, like the telephone ringing and birds singing, that she had not done for several years. She did understand short verbal instructions, although these often had to be repeated. Expressive language also began to appear, and she was heard using

Table 9.3 Expressive language and naming for Case 16

From the Action Picture Test at age 9;3 years:

1. A girl sitting ... cuddle (+ Makaton sign for teddy).
2. The girl ... the mum ... put shoe in.
3. The dog ... the man stay in ... the dog stuck.
4. The horse ... jumping under.
5. The cat ... eating the mouse.
6. The girl up ... the girl down ... running on the floor ... she broke her eyes (+ gesture for glasses).
7. The mum ... a girl is boy up (+ gesture for stamp) is in.
8. The man ... going up the house ... the man... trying to get the cat.
9. The boy ... the boy ... the shoe ... the dog eat and the boy crying.
10. The mum ... and the bag ... ball ... a lot ... and the boy drop it on the floor.

From the Word Finding Vocabulary Test at age 9;3 years:

Item	Response	Comment
Cup	Cup	+ Makaton sign
Table	Table	+ Makaton sign
Boat	Boat	+ Makaton sign
Tree	Tree	+ Makaton sign
Key	Like a door key	+ Makaton sign
Knife	Dinner	Semantic paraphasia
Window	Glass	Semantic paraphasia
Finger	Hand	Semantic paraphasia
Duck	Bird	Semantic paraphasia
Snake	Snake	
Basket	Bag	Semantic paraphasia + gesture
Saw	Cut	
Pear	*Unintelligible*	Neologism
Clown	Queen	Semantic paraphasia
Case	Bag ... go work	
Bear	Bag ... bear	Self-corrected
Moon	In the dark ... when you sleep	
Chimney	House	Semantic paraphasia
Kangaroo	/kærə/	Neologism
Kite	/kærə/ you hold up	Perseverated neologism
Camel	/kærə/ sometimes two	Perseverated neologism
Squirrel	Squirrel	
Leaf	A tree one	
Owl	Dark ... a bird dark	
Snail		Gesture

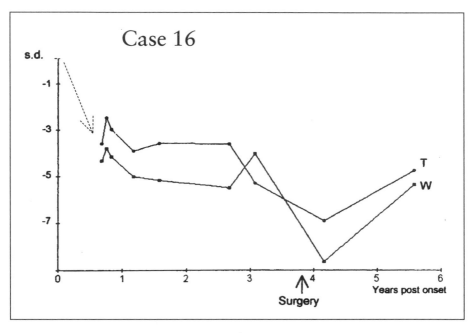

Figure 9.3 Language profile graph of Case 16. T = TROG; S, sentence repetition; W, word findings; ------- marks presumed course of deterioration.

new sounds on a regular basis. For communication she continued to use a combination of signs, verbal language in short phrases and single words and mime.

She was educated through to 16 at a residential school for children with severe speech and language disorders, where the change in her aphasia was noted. Before surgery she had had a fluent aphasia with many stereotyped phrases. After surgery her expressive language was more nonfluent, with some signs of motor speech impairment, dyspraxic features and inconsistencies in phonemic production. She had no further seizures and her AEDs were discontinued nine months after surgery.

At age 18 years she went on to a further education placement at another specialist school. Her communication had not changed a great deal. She was a sociable girl who liked to discuss the usual sort of topics: pop, fashion. She used both her verbal and nonverbal communication effectively.

Summary

Some of the variability of LKS has been presented here. These included cases of acute and prolonged onset as well as those with variable and fluctuating course, good and poor recovery. These include recent studies of the use of anticonvulsants and neurosurgery in the management of LKS. Unfortunately difficulties associated with the diagnosis and management of this syndrome continue to be encountered even in specialist medical settings. Overall it is clear that more long-term detailed studies of LKS are required to improve our understanding of the management of these children.

The evidence suggests that a number of variables interact to influence the course and prognosis of the disorder. Indeed, we may go on to discover that Landau-Kleffner syndrome is really a number of related conditions that include different neuropathologies. Meanwhile, continued confusion about this disorder points to the need for multi-centre studies using an agreed protocol for both short-term monitoring of management with antiepileptic drugs or to determine the outcome of surgery as well as clearly presented detailed case studies of long-term follow-up of the effects of language remediation and education.

The distressing effect that the relentless course of this rare disorder can have on both child and family points to the need for support for those with this condition. This should include the cooperation of the voluntary sector where appropriate, as the burden of care can be very heavy. A national charity called Friends of Landau-Kleffner Syndrome (FOLKS)[5] operates for this purpose in the UK. It is managed by parents and carers and runs a telephone helpline, provides an information pack and has also held a number of family activity days. Its online service is well used by families across the globe.

---

[5] FOLKS, 3 Stone Buildings (Ground Floor), Lincoln's Inn, London WC2A 3XL. Tel: 0870 847 0707. Fax: 01302 752662. http://www.bobjanet.demon.co.uk/lks/fws.htm

Chapter 10
Other epileptic aphasias

Pathology and natural history

For those unfamiliar with epileptic aphasias then this chapter may introduce a number of previously unconsidered ideas. It is reasonable to ask what is the underlying cause of the seizure activity with which a child presents. It is because of a previous failure to identify the possible mechanisms underlying epileptic aphasias that confusions about diagnosis have arisen.

The division of the epileptic group of aphasias into Landau-Kleffner syndrome and other epileptic aphasias poses a number of problems. The neuropathological mechanism underlying Landau-Kleffner syndrome has not been fully identified, but its place as a subdivision of epileptic aphasias is supported by the belief that, whatever the mechanism, it is related to seizure activity, particularly continuous spike and wave in slow sleep (CSWSS). Previous reports of epileptic aphasias in childhood in the literature further complicate the problem because in many the descriptions make it difficult to separate possible cases of Landau-Kleffner syndrome from other epileptic aphasias. Indeed, in the original paper by Landau and Kleffner (1957) first describing the syndrome, a whole host of different possible mechanisms can be identified including minor head trauma and convulsive status. It is certainly possible that there are reports in the literature of Landau-Kleffner syndrome that are other types of epileptic aphasia and reports of epileptic aphasia which might be called Landau-Kleffner syndrome by other writers. Some researchers dismiss this problem, including Dugas et al. (1991), who said that 'authors who have been involved with the question of the evolution of LK syndrome have generally been cautious in using restrictive criteria of inclusion'. Deonna (1991) has emphasized the common ground between all the epileptic aphasias of childhood that he calls 'a particular form of resistant epilepsy'.

Part of the reason for this confusion is, as already mentioned, a failure to look in detail at the possible mechanisms that can be identified as underlying epileptic aphasias. Lees and Neville (1990) proposed a classification of epileptic aphasias that identified a number of potential mechanisms. They said:

The convulsive group could include children who lose language comprehension by a number of different mechanisms:

1. As a consequence of convulsive status.
2. As a post-ictal phenomenon (a Todd's paresis).
3. As a consequence of the primary pathology, e.g. temporal lobe inflammatory or malignant disease.
4. As a feature of minor epileptic status.
5. As a psychological reaction to epilepsy.
6. As an organic event occurring with epilepsy but not fulfilling the criteria 1–5.

Of course these categories required further definition in that the original cause of the seizure disorder would require comprehensive investigation. However, for Lees and Neville (1990), Landau-Kleffner syndrome was the sixth category (these children were described in the last chapter). This chapter is concerned with the first five proposed groups, recognizing that we are still some way from understanding this group in depth. As far as the author is aware no previous studies of epileptic aphasia have discussed this possible framework and this provisional categorization.

'Aphasic arrest' is a phenomenon in which speech production is stopped when certain areas of the cerebral cortex are stimulated electrically. It was described by Penfield and Rassmussen (1950) in their neurosurgical work for intractable epilepsy. Figure 10.1 shows a diagram of the cerebral cortex according to this model.

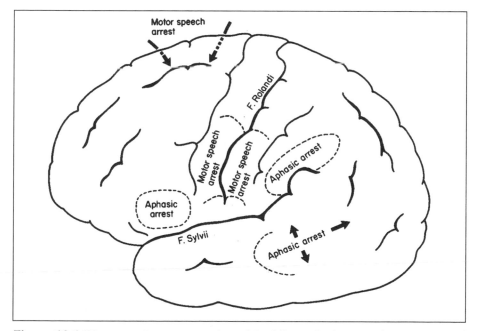

Figure 10.1 Diagrammatic representation of the left cerebral cortex showing areas of aphasic and motor speech arrest.

More recent work has identified other aspects of aphasic arrest including the interference of comprehension by the electrical stimulation of Wernicke's area (Lesser et al., 1986). These observations make it clear that language comprehension and production can be interfered with by artificial electrical stimulation. They are the basis of the hypothesis that abnormal electrical discharges of the cerebral cortex that occur in seizure disorders can produce aphasias.

Epilepsy is known to co-exist or develop as a sequela to a range of childhood conditions in which there is CNS involvement. Corbett (1985) gives figures of an incidence of six per cent (in children with IQ 50–70) to nearly 50 per cent (in those of IQ below 20) prevalence. For children with specific language difficulties Robinson (1987 and 1991) reported 21 per cent with definite history of seizures and a further 11 per cent where the history was 'questionable' in respect of seizures. In the 1991 paper he stated that this was 'an unexpectedly high frequency of previous seizures' when compared with the five to seven per cent in the general population and proposed three hypotheses to account for this. Firstly, that 'the seizures themselves might cause the language disorder by interfering with brain function'. Against this hypothesis he said that the 'great majority of children with epilepsy do not have specific language disorders'. Whilst such children are not the subjects of this book I would suggest that the extent to which the language of children with epilepsy has previously been described through rigorous and systematic linguistic investigation is limited. Secondly, he proposed that 'genetic factors that predispose to specific developmental language disorder might also lead independently to epilepsy'. Against this his data on children with a family history of language disorder showed a negative trend towards the development of epilepsy. His third hypothesis was 'that seizures may indicate abnormal brain development or damage' and, in favour of this, his data demonstrated a correlation between a history of seizures and antecedent abnormalities which might cause language disorder. This hypothesis implies that language disorders in childhood are not isolated abnormalities but 'associated with other kinds of cerebral abnormality or dysfunction'.

Furthermore there are some epilepsy syndromes in which language disturbance has recently been reported. One of these, Benign Rolandic Epilepsy (BRE), deserves more detailed consideration.

Benign Rolandic Epilepsy

The widely held distinction between benign and malignant epilepsies in childhood has been clinically useful in both clinical management and research (Scott and Neville, 1998). However, recent studies of a condition previously considered benign in respect of its effect on language development, Rolandic epilepsy (Staden et al., 1998), have shown that this is far from the whole picture. When developmental arrest and disorder do occur in association with epilepsy, particularly in respect of language, the long-term consequences are increasingly reported and command attention. It has still to be demonstrated whether or not earlier more aggressive treatments can remedy such impairments. Cognitive disorders, including language, may be categorized as 'permanent' or 'state-dependant', with the latter being considered potentially reversible or treatable. The possibility that continued long-term state-dependant deficits may lead to permanent ones has been supported with evidence from BRE but also LKS and CSWSS.

BRE usually begins between 4 and 10 years of age. It is characterized by partial sensori-motor seizures that produce mid-temporal spikes on EEG. These seizures often occur at night and are generally considered easy to control with AEDs. Although classified as benign, more recent research has confirmed a range of neuropsychological deficits including speech and language impairments such as auditory processing and discrimination difficulties, verbal memory deficits, expressive grammar difficulties, and problems with written language. Sometimes general learning difficulties and oro-motor dysfunction are reported (Staden et al., 1998).

Four core questions relating to speech and language development in epilepsy syndromes like BRE have been the subject of ongoing research:

1. What kind of language problems do we observe in children with these types of epilepsy? That this question still needs to be asked at all is the product of two issues related to service delivery: the extent to which specialized assessment of language impairments is limited to 'centres of excellence' and the resource-driven nature of health and education services. Both of these factors mean that children with these conditions and their families can still have difficulty in obtaining full recognition of their complex needs.
2. Are these language impairments permanent or reversible in nature? This question requires careful assessment and long-term follow-up of a target population.
3. How can these be measured? Assessment, as we have seen, is a complex issue that may require the development of specific tools and techniques. It is important that a clear and comprehensive assessment framework is adopted.
4. How does such measurement affect management and outcome? In a clinical service many variables operate. The role of language assessment in the total management of children with these types of epilepsy will depend on the presence of a multidisciplinary team in which a range of researcher/practitioners collaborate not just to 'fix' some parts of a disordered or aberrant system but to maximize total quality of life for children and families.

It might be reasonable to assume that the language impairments in a single epileptic syndrome would be the same. According to this assumption all children who have a diagnosis of BRE would have the same or similar language profile. This is not the case and will be illustrated here with reference to some expressive language samples obtained from a story telling task in a follow-up study of children with BRE.

Narrative is an important later developing language skill in which the form, content and use of language are integrated (Nippold, 1988). The development of competence in narrative is one of the ways in which language impaired children can be distinguished from their unimpaired peers (Bishop and Edmundson, 1987). For children with language impairments related to epilepsy, the use of a narrative task like story telling in language assessment provides a simple, quick and easy procedure which has real communicative validity. Longitudinal use of story telling provides insights where fluctuations in language abilities are still being reported, as these may be readily observed through story telling and residual impairments can also be noted by long-term follow-up (Lees and Neville, 1990). We have been using story-telling tasks in language assessment with children who have epilepsy and language impairments for 20 years (and many examples accompany the cases described in this book). Given that narrative skills develop between the end of the first decade of life and on into the second, it may be reasonable to assume that such skills might be at risk in a condition like BRE that is likely to be active during this age period.

Of the 20 children with BRE reported by Staden et al. (1998), 12 completed a follow-up programme three years later, when they were aged 9 to 16 years. Using the 'form, content, use' model of Bloom and Lahey (1978), and based on the assessments used in the first battery, a number of language assessments were carried out. A questionnaire about school performance and further EEG were also used.

The main findings of the follow-up were as follows:

- 7 out of 10 children classified as having language dysfunction in the original study were no longer classified as language impaired by the follow-up;
- 2 of the 5 children not found to be language impaired in the first study did demonstrate language impairment at follow-up;
- only 2 children scored within normal limits on all measures;
- all 7 children still taking AEDs at the time of follow-up had language difficulties;
- there were no specific connections between such variables as age at first seizure, or time since onset of BRE, but there was a tendency to improvement of language function over time;

- auditory-verbal learning, one of the five specific areas of language impairment identified in the original study, showed the most significant improvement between the two studies.

Whilst the language impairments detected in the follow-up were subtle in nature they have important educational and social implications. They were largely confined to complex language skills such as:

- defining words;
- formulating sentences;
- recalling narrative;
- basic literacy skills.

That these difficulties had educational implications was endorsed by the data from the school questionnaires. Teachers identified the children with BRE as being high risk for literacy difficulties. Similar high-level language problems have also been reported in the long-term follow-up of children with other types of acquired language problems (Lees, 1997).

In respect of language impairments, no single characteristic language profile was shown to account for all of the subjects. Whilst BRE may be considered a homogeneous syndrome the linguistic profile is varied. The story-telling results demonstrate some of the different language problems the children still experience.

The story telling task involves recalling a simple story of 11 episodes (referred to as The Dog Story, see Appendix 2). Across the group, scores ranged from 9.5 to 2.5 with a mean of around 7 episodes recalled. However, it is an examination of the narratives themselves that provides evidence of different kinds of language difficulties (see Tables 10.1, 10.2 and 10.3). The commonest pattern of difficulty to emerge from the narratives is a nonfluent delivery; this was seen in six of the responses. This is characterized by hesitation, false starts and rewording of episodes.

A child can score very low and produce a nonfluent narrative or can score well and still have a nonfluent response. Here are three examples of stories by children from the BRE follow-up study showing different degrees of language impairment, narrative fluency and episodes recalled. The second example, in Table 10.2, also shows some of the phonological processing problems that can occur (some unintelligible utterances).

Not all children with low episode scores were nonfluent. One child's response is characteristic of the 'fluent' type of narrative impairment. This is characterized by over-embellishment of the narrative, and additional episodes not present in the original.

The fluent type of narrative impairment is often overlooked, given that the child seems to produce a lot of language. Even so, when the child has

Table 10.1 Nonfluent narrative scores 9.5 episodes (overall mild high-level language impairment), aged 14 years.

1. walking in the walking back home a dog carrying a piece of meat
2. crossed over a stream via a footbridge um
3. he peered down into the water
   which was crystal clear
4. and saw his reflection
5. thinking this was (the reflection) was another dog he er er he er saw the meat in his reflection's mouth
6. and he er er wanted to have that piece of meat as well as his own
7. as he tried to er bite the er meat from his reflection
8. er er he er opened his mouth and his piece of meat fell out of his mouth
9. and er dropped into the stream
   that piece of meat was never seen again.

Table 10. 2 Nonfluent narrative scores 3 episodes, with neologisms (overall significant language impairment), aged 13 years.

   there was a
1. there was a dog who had a piece of meat in his mouth
2. and um he walked home
   and um he went to the um [*unintelligible*] the water
   and and he saw his [*unintelligible*]
   no he thought he um saw another [*unintelligible*] of a dog
   but it was him and when he um when he looked down [*unintelligible*]
3. then it fell out of his mouth
   and never saw it again.

Table 10.3 Fluent narrative scores 2.5 episodes (overall moderate language impairment), 12 years.

   a dog called Peter was walking down the street
   he decided to go to the dustbin so he went to the dustbin and he found a scrap of meat
   he thought 'oh this is good'
   so then he ran back home
   he ran over the bridge and over the um and into the woods
   he ran past the woods until he reached the lake
   where he looked in the lake because he was thirsty
1. he looked in the lake and saw a reflection
2. he didn't know it was a reflection
3. but he could see this dog that was full of which had meat in its mouth
4. and he decided that he was going to have that bit of meat
   so he leant in and tried to get that bit of meat
   but he fell in
   I can't remember the rest what happens at the end.

difficulty keeping to the point or maintaining structure these can have an effect on language use both educationally and socially.

We are not yet able to confirm that these children have permanent language difficulties as a result of BRE. However, the evidence so far shows that:

- More children with BRE have language impairments than in the general population;
- These language difficulties have educational and social implications during the first two decades of life;
- There is no one language impairment profile associated with BRE;
- Children with BRE require appropriate long-term language assessment and, where indicated, educational support.

There follows a discussion of epileptic aphasias based on clinical observations. The five categories groups described by Lees and Neville (1990) are discussed separately.

Convulsive status

Convulsive status may occur in children with a number of types of seizures: tonic/clonic, simple and complex partial and myoclonic (Brown and Hussain, 1991). Major convulsive status is a continuous state of epilepsy, with major convulsions lasting 30 minutes and no recovery of consciousness between seizures. The condition is more common in children, particularly those under five years of age, but no sex bias has been reported.

The epileptic discharge creates an increased demand for glucose and oxygen in that part of the brain. PET scanning has confirmed that there is an increase in cerebral metabolic rate, blood flow, oxygen consumption and glucose uptake by the human brain during seizure activity. Brown and Hussain (1991) summarized the stages of convulsive status and the metabolic changes that take place in the brain when this lasts for more than 30 minutes. In children various areas of the brain are highly susceptible to damage. Death may also result. Possible deficits include post-convulsive hemiplegia, which may occur when the child convulses for two hours or more. Unlike the Todd's paralysis which may occur with seizures of shorter duration and which will recover, this form of post-convulsive hemiplegia is permanent. Brown and Hussain give figures of 11 per cent of children with acquired hemiplegia having convulsive status as the cause. Unilateral cerebral atrophy has also been reported on CT scans and temporal lobe damage is also common.

Deonna (1991) states that children may become permanently aphasic after convulsive status. He goes on to say that 'this situation is analogous to the persistent hemiplegia developing sometimes in the course of severe focal motor epilepsy'. However, he further observes that its pathophysiology is not understood.

Where convulsive status is followed by prolonged coma then the child may recover with a range of deficits including speech and language problems. These may be associated with other cognitive, motor and behaviour deficits. The rate of recovery of speech and language after convulsive status has not been reported but is probably dependant on a number of variables including the extent of the cerebral damage and the control of further seizures. Control of the epilepsy will be an important factor in prognosis as repeated convulsive status and subsequent coma is likely to add to such deficits.

Post-ictal phenomenon

The occurrence of a transient motor weakness after an epileptic attack is one of a possible range of post-ictal phenomena. Such a weakness may last for a few hours or a few days and is known as a Todd's paralysis. Other kinds of post-ictal phenomena are known, including a transient motor speech difficulty, or other language disturbance (Deonna, 1991). The essential feature of a post-ictal phenomenon is that it follows seizures, and that the deficit is not permanent. Thus a post-ictal hemiplegia can be separated from a convulsive hemiplegia by its transitory nature. Where speech or language disturbance occurs as a post-ictal phenomenon then it is important to establish the child's baseline language ability between attacks and to ensure that no significant communication or learning difficulties persist. In some children with only evidence for the post-ictal phenomenon might be an increase in paraphasic naming errors (see cases 3 and 25). Even such transient deficits can have a traumatic effect on the child and s/he will require sensitive support. Other kinds of speech and language disturbances have been reported in children including stereotyped and perseverated utterances, neologisms and dysarthria (McKeever et al., 1983).

As a consequence of primary pathology

Few of the studies of traumatic aphasia have considered the implications of the occurrence of seizures. Aicardi (1990) reviewed the data on epilepsy in brain-injured children and recognized that a wide range of epileptic syndromes can occur secondary to cerebral injury. O'Brien and Cheeseburgh (2000) state that epilepsy is not uncommon after HI in childhood but still only affects 'a quite small minority' of around 5 per cent, although this rises to 9 per cent in younger children. The incidence of epilepsy after head injury in childhood is not as well documented as in adults but Ross et al. (1980) found at least four cases from 64 with epilepsy in the National Child Development Study follow-up data. After HI both early and late post-traumatic epilepsy can occur. Early post-traumatic epilepsy occurs in the first week of the trauma and late at any time after that. This accounts for up to 20 per cent of those children who will develop epilepsy after HI. Aicardi (1986) stated that the incidence of early seizures in children was probably higher than in adults and that at least 50 per cent of cases occurred within the first 24 hours. The majority of these are focal, usually partial motor attacks. However, he also reported that convulsive status was much more common following head injury in children than adults and was highest in children under five years old. Most post-traumatic epilepsy develops in the first year after injury. Late post-traumatic epilepsy, appearing up to four years later, accounts for 20–30 per cent of children affected by epilepsy after HI (O'Brien and Cheeseburgh, 2000).

The presence of cerebral tumour can also be a cause of epilepsy. Cases in which epilepsy starts after the removal of a cerebral tumour have also been reported. Similarly cerebrovascular abnormalities may lead to epilepsy or epilepsy may develop subsequent to haemorrhage of an AVM. Aicardi (1990) stated that 'the relationship between anatomical brain lesion and the functional phenomenon of epileptic seizures is poorly understood and extremely complex'. There have been various hypotheses concerning chemical changes, both at the cellular level and in the cerebral metabolism. Cerebral damage is usually increased where there is epilepsy. However, generally, suppression of epilepsy may be obtained with either AEDs and/or neurosurgery depending on the case.

A number of the children reported in this volume have presented either initially with seizures or later developed seizures as a result of primary pathology (see particularly cases 3, 18, 19 and 21). In some of them (cases 3 and 21) an increase in paraphasic errors in expressive language and some fluctuations in receptive language have been noted in association with episodes of seizures. In all of them appropriate management of the epilepsy was an important part of their overall management.

As a feature of minor epileptic status

Whilst convulsive status is a life-threatening condition in which overt seizures are easily identified, minor epileptic status is often a hidden condition. Children may have periods of minor status for many years before they are diagnosed as the seizures themselves can be difficult to see. They may occur at night while the child is sleeping. When they occur during waking hours it may be thought that the child is not attending, not listening, has poor hearing or that the child's fluctuating behaviour is 'just one of those things'.

The way in which minor epileptic status acts to cause cerebral damage is not clearly understood. It is recognized that a range of cognitive, behavioural and language deficits may occur. Usually these are fluctuating in nature. Where these persist for some time without being diagnosed they may be dismissed as part of the child's background condition or even the child's fault. Where there is a high variability in some skills, particularly receptive language, which is not explained by hearing loss or general cognitive problems, then the possibility of minor epileptic status should be considered. If a series of formal language assessment results are available for a period of one to two years previously then these should be looked at carefully to see if they confirm the suggestion of a fluctuating disorder.

There should be a clear distinction, however, between those children with a long-term cognitive deficit associated with CSWSS and the typical picture of waking minor epileptic (electrical) status with minute to minute variation in attention; often a 'groggy affect', continued myoclonic jerks and after this a variable motor disorder particularly involving bulbar movements.

As a psychological reaction to epilepsy

Little has been reported about the psychological effects of acute loss of communicative ability in children. One of the cases reported here (case 10) clearly demonstrated a psychological reaction to his acute aphasia. When discharged home after one week in hospital for the treatment of cerebral abscess and mild aphasia he was readmitted 48 hours later with complete loss of expressive speech. He was only communicating through writing. This was not the same pattern of presentation as his acute episode and led to further investigations on the supposition that he might have suffered a cerebrovascular accident subsequent to neurosurgery. However all investigations were normal. Over the course of three days, through intensive support from the speech and language therapist, it became clear that he had many anxieties about returning to school. Three days after admission he began speaking again and confirmed that he had not had aphasia but rather an elective mutism. He had thought he would be unable to cope back at school and had preferred readmission to hospital. With counselling and further support for communication skills he did return, successfully, to his former school two weeks later.

It seems possible that if this kind of reaction to illness can occur in a child with a mild traumatic aphasia then it is also possible in other situations, including as a reaction to epilepsy. The emotional support available to children who require it will vary greatly from family to family and from school to school. A sensitive awareness of the stress suffered by children who experience speech and language loss is important for all team and family members. Children need to feel there are people they can turn to for support in traumatic situations like the one described here.

Role of the speech and language therapist

The assessment of speech and language in a child with epileptic aphasia will depend to some extent on the duration of the problem. Where there is a post-ictal aphasia the language disturbance may be passed before formal assessment can be arranged and only informal observations will be available. However, in such children it is important to carry out comprehensive assessment to see that residual language disturbances have not been overlooked and to provide a baseline for assessment after any subsequent episodes. Similarly in other epileptic aphasias a number of baseline assessments will be helpful in determining any subsequent deterioration or in monitoring the effects of anticonvulsant medication.

As a minimum an assessment of auditory verbal comprehension, naming and expressive language should be carried out. Where repeated assessments are required ensure that this is within the bounds of test validity. If not, then a repeated series of informal observations, as carefully controlled as possible, may be used. An informal examination for use in these circumstances might include naming a set of pictures, selection of pictures to verbal command, and story telling. The series of pictures should be large enough (i.e.; over 30) to help rule out a memory component in subsequent reassessment.

A study by Caplan et al. (2002) of the social communication skills of children with epilepsy showed that children who had complex partial seizures were more likely to have such impairments by comparison to their normal peers. Characteristically these impairments meant that the narratives the children produced were less cohesive, often illogical in thought order and contained extraneous comments or information. Furthermore, ongoing primary generalized epilepsy was found to have a more persistent effect on social communication development than had previously been thought. These findings point to the need to include social communication assessments as part of the speech and language assessment of children with epilepsy, particularly in long-term monitoring. There have been no studies to date that have investigated whether or not such deficits are remediable.

Other aspects of the management of epileptic aphasias

In the diagnosis of epileptic disorders the use of EEGs plays an important part. An EEG may be recorded while the child is awake, or asleep, or even while the child is active over 24 hours or so, depending on the situation. Some seizure disorders produce characteristic EEG patterns. In other cases it should be possible to identify whether the abnormality is bilateral or unilateral, symmetrical or asymmetrical, focal or diffuse. An analysis of these variables will contribute to the paediatric neurologist's management of the child.

The main aim of the treatment of epilepsy is to control seizures. Aicardi and Chevrie (1986) stated that 'complete suppression of fits is obtainable in a majority of the childhood epilepsies' and further that a significant proportion will remit before adulthood. They reviewed a wide range of AEDs and their side effects. They recommended the use of a single drug (monotherapy) wherever possible as this is simple for the child and family and also avoids interactive effects. Where a child is maintained on AEDs for some years then s/he should be monitored regularly. Where a child with epileptic aphasia is being monitored then reassessment of speech and language should form part of that review procedure. It has been established that in some children the use of AEDs may improve their aphasia (see cases 13 and 19 particularly). Equally the level of AEDs needs to be carefully monitored to ensure that the dose remains at the right level for the particular child. This is done with a simple blood test.

There are other non-drug treatments for childhood epilepsy. The ketogenic diet is based on the suggestion that ketosis and acidosis produced by a special diet may help to control some types of seizures. The use of the diet requires daily urine testing and skilled dietetic support. The most obvious non-drug treatment for epilepsy is neurosurgery that may aim either to remove the origin of the seizures or to stop the discharges from spreading. Pre-surgery an extensive range of psychological, speech, language and behavioural measures are carried out in order to predict as much as possible the effects of surgery on specific functions.

The schooling of children with epilepsy will depend on their educational needs. Many children will be well placed in a mainstream school. Others will require special educational placement, but not necessarily just because they have epilepsy. Similarly social activities need not always be restricted. The team managing the child's epilepsy should be consulted in respect of any specific concerns about activities either at school or at home.

Examples of children with epileptic aphasias

Case 17: A child with aphasia after convulsive status

This boy had a normal developmental history until he was admitted at the age of 8;3 years with a sudden onset of generalized grand mal convulsions. He was unconscious, but there were no focal neurological signs. He responded to pain and not speech. CSF was clear and the white cell count was not raised. He had further fits and these were treated with rectal and intravenous diazepam. He was an only child, and his paternal uncle also had epilepsy. CT scan was normal. He went into convulsive status and was transferred to intensive care. He was treated with intravenous diazepam, phenytoin, heminevrin and intramuscular paraldehyde, all of which failed to control his fitting. Mannitol was given and he was ventilated. Thiopentone finally controlled the fits. An intracranial pressure monitor was inserted but the pressure was not elevated. A repeat CT scan was again normal. He passed a stormy two days in intensive care. Extubation was attempted but it was clear from the stridor that he had a lot of laryngeal ulceration and tracheostomy was performed.

There were further periods of seizures over the next five days as he gradually became more stable. However, he was withdrawn, made little eye contact, was unwilling to speak, had a weakness of the right arm and walked with a shuffling gait. His speech returned as a fluent aphasia; very long monologues irrelevant to time and place, interrupted with bursts of coprolalia. He had a severe receptive aphasia and was unable to localize sound, although brain stem evoked auditory potentials were normal. He made a good gradual recovery and was discharged home on carbamazepine and phenytoin. Before this episode of aphasia he was right-handed but since the episode he has been left-handed. His expressive language continued to include paraphasic errors (see Table 10.4). He received home tuition and continued to make progress with no further episodes of convulsive status. His major residual problems have been behavioural, particularly aggression, although he did eventually return to his previous school.

Table 10.4 Examples of paraphasia errors from the Word Finding Vocabulary Test* for Case 17

Assessment	Item	Response	Error type
2 months post-onset	Tree	Hat	Semantic paraphasia
	Knife	Nail	Semantic paraphasia
	Finger	Hand	Semantic paraphasia
	Snake	Snail	Semantic paraphasia
	Pear	Apple	Semantic paraphasia.
	Bear	House/cow	Semantic paraphasia
	Chimney	Tree	Semantic paraphasia
	Kangaroo	Rabbit – not a rabbit	Self-correction
1 month later	Table	Chair	Semantic paraphasia
	Moon	Sun	Semantic paraphasia.
	Snail	Snake/worm	Semantic paraphasia
	Coat hanger	Coat peg	Semantic paraphasia
	Feather	Leaf	Semantic paraphasia
	Goat	Cow	Semantic paraphasia
	Lighthouse	Windmill	Semantic paraphasia
	Anchor	Hook	Semantic paraphasia
	Parachute	Balloon	Semantic paraphasia
	Sleeve	Bat	Semantic paraphasia

*Renfrew (1977a).

An example of his spontaneous language at the initial assessment, one month post-onset, shows his jargon aphasia that contained many neologisms and was highly unintelligible (from a monologue while playing with toy cars):

> Leave me alone [*unintelligible*] eating [*unintelligible*] I don't know what [*unintelligible*] eat [*unintelligible*] I don't know what.
> I don't feel like that. I don't know. I feel sick. I'm barking, I know. The white [*unintelligible*] the same [*unintelligible*]. Your pandas, white pandas. That hand you like, it's the same. It's the same as the white pandas. I said about the … [*hesitation*] oh ! Lead pandas. Up, up, yes, hot me. Hot boy. Really hold it. But I won't [*unintelligible*].

However, by three months post-onset this had resolved as the following example of the Dog Story shows:

> There was a little dog, carrying a piece of meat. He walked over the bridge. Looked over the bridge and saw his reflection. He thought he wanted that piece so he opened his mouth and dropped the fish and never saw it again.

There have been no subsequent episodes of convulsive status or aphasia.

Case 18: A child with aphasia as a post-ictal phenomenon

This boy was induced at term for Rhesus incompatibility, and had an illness associated with seizures at three weeks of age. At 2;6 years he presented again with a generalized febrile convulsion. A CT scan at that time was normal. Focal seizures beginning on the right developed over the following two weeks and an EEG at that time showed a left occipital focus. He was treated with clomazepam. Over a period of two years this was withdrawn and there were no further fits. There was a recurrence of right focal fits at the age of 5;6 years that were diagnosed as myoclonic absences and focal attacks. These were associated with brief aphasic episodes and a deterioration in behaviour. His score on the TROG within 24 hours of one episode gave a z-score of -2 and he produced semantic paraphasias in expressive language. The episode lasted for less than 48 hours. He was treated with carbamazepine. An EEG at that time showed a bilateral abnormality. His hearing was normal. He was making little progress at school and was placed in a unit for children with behavioural difficulties at age 6 years. There have been no further episodes of aphasia, although his behaviour is still described as 'difficult' at school.

Case 19: A child with aphasia after seizures during recovery from neuro-surgical treatment to remove a cerebellar tumour

This boy had a normal developmental history until admitted at the age of 10;10 years with a history suggestive of a mass lesion in the cerebellum. This was confirmed on CT scan as a mixed density mass and obstructive hydrocephalus. He underwent neurosurgery, ventriculo-peritoneal shunting and resection of what proved to be a cerebellar astrocytoma, all of which was successful. He did well initially but on the third post-operative day he had a short series of right focal fits of unknown aetiology. A repeat CT scan showed no evidence of mass effect or bleeding. However this incident left him with an acute aphasia and a degree of cortical visual loss. The latter was characterized by a transposition of some images, either back to front or upside down. He showed little awareness of the visual loss. His vision gradually resolved so that two months post-onset it was 20/100. His hearing was normal. The major feature of his aphasia was a severe word-finding difficulty with some paraphasias as his responses on the Graded Naming Test illustrate (see Table 10.5), and very little expressive language. Six months post-onset he had made good progress in all areas of skills and his recovery is shown in Figure 10.2. However, his Neale Analysis of Reading Ability was still below the six-year level and his rate of response on all tests was slow. He remained in mainstream school until secondary age when he was transferred to a placement for children with complex needs.

Table 10.5 Examples of naming errors from the Graded Naming Test* for Case 19

Post-onset	Item	Response	Error type
3 months	Turtle	Tortoise	Semantic paraphasia
	Trampoline	Tortoise	Perseveration
6 months	Kangaroo	Dog	Semantic paraphasia
	Buoy	Bucket	Semantic paraphasia
18 months	Buoy	Sandcastle	Semantic paraphasia
	Tweezers	Knife	Semantic paraphasia

*McKenna and Warrington (1983).

A sample of expressive language three months post-onset shows his nonfluent aphasia (from a description of a radio controlled car):

> Well it goes quite fast and um ... it goes left and right and forwards and backwards and it can go above ground.
> Well I actually have it on one of the school fields. When the school isn't [*unintelligible*] you know when there's nobody there.
> Well it's um ... a radio controlled um ... well, sort of, well it's called a 'lunch box'.
> Well it's a um ... yellow van and its um ... shaped like a lunch box ... sort of thing.

Results from the Story Telling test also show the same characteristics of a nonfluent aphasia and the graph of his recovery is shown in Figure 10.2.

Dog Story (6 months post-onset)

The dog was carrying a piece of meat and he got to a pond and um ... he looked down and saw his reflection and he thought it was another dog and w...w...w...with a piece of meat and um ... and he wanted that piece of meat which the dog was carrying as well. So he opened his mouth and he dropped the piece of meat into the pond.

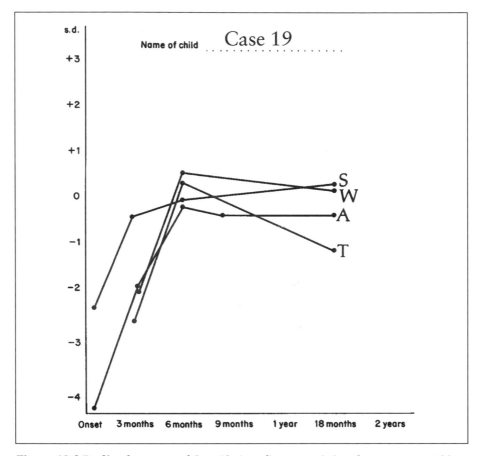

Figure 10.2 Profile of recovery of Case 19: A, auditory association; S, sentence repetition; T, TROG; W, Word Finding Vocabulary Test.

Two children with aphasia and minor epileptic status:

Case 20

This boy (first reported in Lees and Urwin, 1991) was referred at the age of 8 years for further investigations as there was some concern that his language skills, particularly his verbal comprehension, might be fluctuating. He had a congenital left hemiplegia arising from a large infarct in the region of the right middle cerebral artery and affecting a major part of the right motor cortex (confirmed by CT scan). He had no history of epilepsy or other developmental problems. He had first been seen by a speech and language therapist at the age of two and a half years for concern about his speech and language development. Although he had made some progress with this he continued to have a severe language problem and had been placed in a language unit since five years of age.

His mother said that she had often been concerned about his hearing in the past and that he often appeared not to hear. However, all hearing tests were, and always had been, normal. Test scores of receptive language obtained since the age of 2;11 years using the RDLS and later the TROG consistently gave standard scores below -2. Apart from the motor signs on the left consistent with the hemiplegia there were no other neurological signs. An EEG revealed an epileptic focus in the left temporal lobe, the region associated with the auditory association cortex and Wernicke's area. Anticonvulsant medication (carbamazepine) was begun and gradually increased until blood tests confirmed a level within the recommended therapeutic range. Repeat language testing did suggest an improvement in receptive language as shown in Figure 10.3.

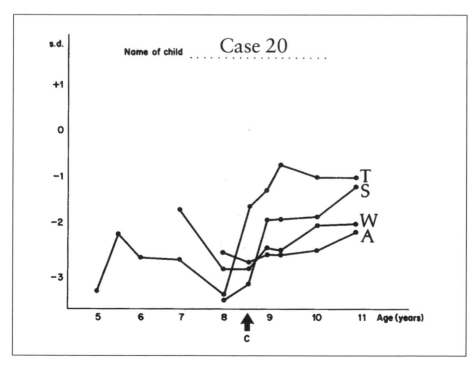

Figure 10.3 Profile of recovery of Case 20: A, auditory association; C, anticonvulsants started; S, sentence repetition; T, TROG; W, Word Finding Vocabulary Test.

Case 21

This girl, the youngest of a family of three, was born after a full-term pregnancy, during which there had been some intrauterine pains from 37 weeks onwards. Birth and early development were considered to be normal. Birth weight was 4 kg. She walked at 14 months. Her first words were at 2 years. There was a strong family history of migraine and allergies in both siblings. She began in mainstream school at five years and at that time speech and language did not cause any concern, although she was described as 'shy' and 'often on her own'. The school had open-plan classrooms and she did not appear to make any progress there, wandered around and often seemed distracted. It was at this stage that teachers and parents first began to ask questions about her comprehension and hearing. However, her hearing was normal when tested with pure tone audiometry.

At 7;4 years a significant problem with verbal comprehension and expressive language was confirmed and she began speech and language therapy. Within a year she had been transferred to a school for children with speech and language disorders. Speech and language assessment from 7 to 10 years of age all commented on the variability of her verbal comprehension and auditory–verbal processing skills, particularly memory. She would sometimes score within the normal range on tests used and on other occasions there would be a drop of one or two standard deviations below the mean. There were no difficulties in articulation but language was described as short telegrammatic utterances. On other occasions she would use quite long phrases. Her expressive language was described as empty and immature but there were few grammatical errors. She was a good mechanical reader but comprehension was always poorer. At 8 years of age her handedness was not clearly established. She was very slow to learn verbal concepts, like time, and other aspects of more abstract language. Despite frequent mention of her variable performance in speech and language tasks, auditory verbal memory tasks and even in general responsiveness, it was not until nearly three years later that she was investigated further.

At the age of 10 it was noted that she was usually groggy on waking in the mornings. She had problems with fine motor function that made dressing difficult and on some days even basic washing and self care seemed to take a long time and could be quite clumsy and disorganized. However, there was never any nocturnal incontinence. Her comprehension seemed to vary from day to day and she had particular difficulty with conversations with more than one other person. Otherwise a physical and neurological examination was normal. Her full scale WISC(R) IQ was 80, with verbal IQ at 95 and performance IQ at 68. An EEG recording at this time showed bilateral abnormalities with episodes of poly-spike and wave and sporadic spike and wave over both hemispheres with no clear focus. It was concluded that the bilateral atypical spike and wave activity was suggestive of minor epilepsy that could well have been affecting her behaviour. She had a course of carbamazepine that had no effect and then phenytoin, which did lead to some improvement.

She was placed in a secondary school for children with speech and language disorders at 11 years of age. The same kind of variability in receptive language and other auditory processing skills was also noted from time to time. Her language profile was rather patchy across expressive language skills with good scores for grammar but poor scores on semantic tasks.

Some examples from both written and verbal language show how these were affected:

At age 8 years
Written language
I am seven yeurs old. I have Blue Eyes. I like wriTing and Drawing. When I grow up I will Be a nurse. I like going To school. a friend come to play. I like to make Things at school.

Verbal language (The Bus Story Test, Renfrew 1977b)
Blew his whistle ... trying to say stop ...but he just wouldn't stop ... nearly ran over a few people.

At age 10 years
Written language
I am ten. long time from now I atopped being a Brownie. my eyes are blue. my best thing on a Saturday is watching neighbours. I hate getting stuck in sums. But I like doing seins and I like doing writing. my packed lunch is milk greek yogat pate roll. When I grow up I will be a zoo keeper looking after the Animals. I quite like Wednesday because there is swimming every Wendesday.

Verbal language (Dog story)
There was a dog ... who found a piece of meat. He went home to eat it. He went into the water and saw ... a flection ... a reflection ... and ... and ... when he saw that he thought that the other dog wanted his piece of meat. So he got his jaw open and tried to go for the reflection ... but ... but his bone fell in the water and was never seen again.

Summary

The group of children with epileptic aphasias is potentially a very mixed one. Only careful consideration of each case including an understanding of the possible underlying mechanisms will establish if the child is presenting with an epileptic aphasia of the Landau-Kleffner type or another form of epileptic aphasia. However, clinical experience with a number of children with epileptic aphasia has led to the observation that some professionals call any epileptic aphasia Landau-Kleffner syndrome, and parents may adopt this label in a quest to gain further understanding of the child's problem. More detailed case studies are required for better understanding of the subgroup of children with epileptic aphasias.

This group is also one in which we need more detailed longitudinal studies to evaluate speech and language outcome in respect of the management of the epilepsy as well as the provision of education and therapy and long-term prognosis. Clearly some children do experience an improvement in their aphasia when their epilepsy is treated with AEDs. However, no clear pattern relating to specific seizure disorders and particular AEDs has yet clearly emerged. Where a child with aphasia is going to be treated with AEDs, assessments to monitor speech and language are important. In other children AEDs may suppress the epilepsy but speech and language will remain impaired. Such children need careful assessment to define their strengths and needs so that a programme can be drawn up to maximize communicative potential, alongside their educational programme. Where epilepsy continues uncontrolled it will be important to monitor any further effects this may have on speech and language and/or any response to other forms of intervention, including neurosurgery.

Chapter 11
Other deteriorating conditions of childhood affecting speech and language

Clearly, acquired childhood aphasia is a rare disorder and, equally, children all have a unique potential, although general developmental trends are recognized. It is not therefore surprising to find that it can be difficult to make generalizations about children with ACA. This is especially true of a subgroup of children with what could be termed 'anomalous aphasias'. They are 'anomalous' in the sense that they do not easily fit the traumatic/epileptic division that was outlined in Chapter 1. Indeed, it is the very existence of this group which points to our ultimate need to develop a method of classifying ACA which is more satisfactory, not only in coping with unusual causes but which includes more of the linguistic perspective. Because of the individual nature of these cases, it is not possible to discuss neuropathology and natural history in a general sense across the group. The cases will therefore be presented first and then the neuropathology and management implication of each one will be discussed.

When language regression remains unexplained

Case 22

This boy was born at term from a pregnancy complicated by bleeding from 10 weeks onwards. However, his birth weight was 3.3 kg, and he was healthy and thrived with normal sucking and, later, chewing. His developmental milestones were initially normal: sitting at six months and 2 words with meaning at 14 months. He was just beginning to walk at this age. He had his measles immunization and was ill for two weeks. He stopped walking and communicating. For six months he was described by his parents as 'a different child'. He lost his previous communication skills, the words and gestures and seemed not to understand what was said to him. In other respects he seemed normal, including symbolic play. His attention was poor and it was difficult to tell whether he was not attending or not hearing at times. However, when tested his hearing was normal.

He did not walk again until 18 months of age at which time he was still described as uncommunicative with poor attention. At the age of 3;4 years both his receptive and expressive language were moderately impaired with standard scores of -1.5 and -1.8 respectively on the Reynell Developmental Language Scales (revised) (Reynell, 1985). Once again his hearing was questioned in view of his variable attention but it was again normal. In view of the history of regression of language skills and the persisting communication impairment he was investigated for the Landau-Kleffner syndrome. An EEG and CT scan were both normal and he has never had any seizures. He received regular speech and language therapy in a small group for a year twice weekly and individual therapy once weekly. At the age of 5 years he went into a mainstream primary class without additional support. Six months later he was said to be holding his own. His scores on formal language assessments were within the normal range for both receptive and expressive language. He was cooperative and had adequate attention although his school report stated that 'he can still present as being shy and timid'.

This child demonstrates some of the difficulties in diagnosing acquired language problems in childhood. His normal EEG and CT scan ruled out any significant cerebral pathology. However, he did undergo a marked change in behaviour and regression of communication skills that took over three years to resolve. When taking a detailed case history of any child presenting for speech and language assessment the clinician should be alert for a history of unexplained periods of language regression. It is possible that, as in case 22, these will remain unexplained. However, such children require careful monitoring to ensure that long-term problems do not persist.

Other conditions and syndromes where loss or deterioration of communication skills may be a factor

Children may present with a history of loss of language skills and upon further investigation it becomes clear that more than just language has been affected. The loss of language or a more general deterioration in communicative ability in a very young child can be the first sign of a more pervasive disintegrative disorder. When taking a case history in a older child with an acquired disorder it may be observed that a reduction in communicative intent or the loss of recently acquired first words were noted early in the onset of the disorder. Reviews of studies of the effects of early brain damage in previous chapters have highlighted the vulnerability of language development in children with cerebral dysfunction. It is not therefore too surprising that children presenting with complex CNS dysfunction should also first show signs of loss of language. The importance of comprehensive multidisciplinary assessment to establish the range and extent of the child's problems and needs must be emphasized. Two such conditions are Late Onset Autism and Rett's Syndrome.

Late onset autism

There is continued debate about this condition. The syndrome Infantile Autism was first described by Kanner in 1943. He presented a series of eleven cases (eight boys and three girls) and commented on five particular aspects of the development of these children. These were:

- an inability to relate to other people as an early developmental difficulty;
- failure to develop normal communication skills;
- a range of abnormal responses to things in the child's environment (objects and events) which appeared to be governed by an obsessive desire for sameness;
- some advanced cognitive abilities, particularly with rote learning, memory and form boards;
- normal physical development.

The syndrome was further defined by Rutter (1978a). He emphasized the distinction between general mental retardation and autism and recommended the adoption of four criteria for the diagnosis of autism in children under 5 years. These were:

- onset of the disorder was before 30 months of age;
- a specific impairment of social development not consistent with intellectual development;
- the pattern of disordered language development was also inconsistent with intellectual development;
- an obsession for sameness demonstrated by stereotyped play, a resistance to change and unusual preoccupations.

It was his insistence that the onset of infantile autism could be anything up to 30 months of age that led to some dispute about the existence of late onset autism. However, more recent research has advanced the case for separate recognition of such a syndrome.

Late onset autism or disintegrative disorder was defined by Volkmar and Cohen (1989) as 'a type of pervasive developmental disorder characterized by a period of clearly normal development before age 2 followed by the onset of a marked loss of previously acquired social and communicative skills'. They stated that the typical course of the disorder was that the child's 'communication skills profoundly regress or virtually disappear and that 'there is a marked deterioration of social and other skills', disinterest in the environment, and stereotyped movements', with motor skills and toileting being less consistently affected. The extent to which this late onset or disintegrative condition accounts for individuals with autistic spectrum disorders is not clear but Kurita (1985) claims that it may have been up to one-third in one series.

There is 'no known unitary brain pathology common to all autism cases' (Gillberg, 1988) and the neurobiological basis of late onset autism has not been identified. A number of mechanisms have been proposed, the most popular of which has been cerebral infection. Gillberg (1986) reported a girl who developed autism after herpes simplex encephalitis at the age of 14 years. Robinson (1988) reported 25 cases of children with 'acute disintegrative psychosis' who were investigated using auditory evoked potentials, CT scan and EEG. Of these, 22 children, aged two to five years, had EEGs. In five of these the record was normal. Of the remainder the abnormalities localized to the mid-temporal region in 10 cases, temporo-parietal in three and fronto-parietal in four others. In all but four children there was some evidence of involvement of the other hemisphere with either contra-lateral spikes or generalized discharges. In five of the children the EEG abnormalities were left-sided and in six they were right-sided or bilateral. Robinson found no correlation between sex, laterality of handedness, age at onset or side of EEG abnormality but admitted that the small numbers made this difficult.

As far as prognosis is concerned, Volkmar and Cohen (1989) idenitified 10 cases with 'late onset' from a larger sample of 165 children who met the behavioural criteria for autism, and stated that they made at best only a limited recovery. These ten cases, 6 per cent of their total sample, were compared with two groups, autism of onset under 24 months and autism identified after 24 months but no evidence of regression (i.e., a 'late identified' group). The 'late onset' group had the lowest mean IQ. Differences in sex ratio and the presence of seizure disorder were not significant between the three groups. They concluded that once the condition was established it was behaviourally indistinguishable from other cases of autism.

This of course raises the question of whether there is any advantage in identifying these children as a distinctive group. Volkmar and Cohen (1989) agree that the distinction may be less important at the practical clinical level than in research studies. In the latter situation such cases may provide insights into the pathology of autistic disorders in the future.

The characteristics of the communication of these children have not been described in detail. The language disorders of 22 children with late onset autism, aged two to five years at the time of examination, were described by Lees (1988) (these 22 children were also reported by Robinson, 1988). The language of the children could only be assessed using informal observations due to the severity of the communication, cognitive and social deficits. Results indicated that 14 of the children had no auditory verbal comprehension, that 10 had auditory verbal comprehension for single words only and that one (who was the eldest at onset) could comprehend two-word phrases. In respect of expressive language, 14 had no expressive language, 10 others used single words occasionally and one used occasional two word phrases and some echolalia. One of these children is described in case 23.

Case 23

This boy was the only child of well, unrelated parents and had a history of a normal pregnancy, birth and delivery. He was said to have been developing normally, although first words might have been a little slow at 18 months of age. However this might be accounted for by his bilingual Spanish/English background. At 2;6 years he was reported to use 2-3 word phrases in Spanish. At the age of 3;4 years concern was expressed by his parents and his nursery teacher that his development seemed to be slowing down. He gradually became uncommunicative and his behaviour regressed such that he became very difficult to manage, and engaged in repetitive behaviours. He was diagnosed as autistic. Nine months later his comprehension was at a single-word level and his expressive language consisted of a few echoed and stereotyped phrases. The deterioration in language continued so that 14 months post-onset he had variable comprehension for single words and some echolalia. At this stage an EEG showed phase reversing sharp waves in the left temporo-parietal region. He did not have overt fits and his CT scan was normal. His behaviour remained difficult to control and there was no evidence of new learning in any modality.

By 18 months post-onset the boy had comprehension for common objects only and almost no expressive language. By 22 months post-onset he appeared to have no verbal comprehension or expressive language. He scored at a 21-month level on the Symbolic Play Test (Lowe and Costello, 1976). An EEG at this time revealed phase reversing sharp waves in both parietal regions, but more often on the right, and he was treated with carbamazepine. By two years post-onset he had no verbal comprehension or expressive language and his Symbolic Play had fallen to a score equivalent to a 14-month level. He was then treated with a course of corticosteroids. Two months later he had improved so that he had situational comprehension and engaged in some brief symbolic activities with a symbolic play score at the 21-month level. However, there was no further improvement and former levels were not regained.

In many ways this child presented very like a case of Landau-Kleffner syndrome with the additional loss of cognitive and social skills. Bishop and Rosenbloom (1987) recognized that 'differentiation between the Landau-Kleffner syndrome and infantile autism is ocassionally problematic' and stated that while the majority of children with LKS have normal social behaviour some children do react badly to the experience of loss of communicative abilities. However they are clear that 'these emotional disturbances are typically quite unlike the aloofness and avoidance of eye-contact found in autistic children'. The grey areas which appear between syndromes and disorders or the sense in which there seems to be some overlap has been a feature of the author's clinical experience of children presenting with both acquired and developmental language problems. The distinction made by Bishop and Rosenbloom (1987) between LKS and autism stresses the need for multidisciplinary assessment of children presenting with deteriorating conditions, so that a comprehensive profile of cognitive, social and linguistic abilities can be prepared to enhance the accuracy of differential diagnosis.

Rett's syndrome

First described by Rett (1966, 1969), this syndrome is a severe form of learning disorder, the onset of which is between one and two years of age. Diagnostic criteria include: female sex (there are no known male cases), early regression of behaviour, social and cognitive development such that skills gained appear to be lost, signs of dementia, loss of hand skills and the development of hand-wringing stereotypes, the appearance of an ataxic gait and the deceleration of head growth. The most common misdiagnosis is with infantile autism where difficulties of social and cognitive development are also seen, as are motor stereotypes like hand-wringing. Children with Rett's syndrome do have stereotypical movements of the hands and poor social interaction. Gillberg (1988) pointed to the differentiation of Rett's syndrome as 'a striking clinical illustration of how the "autistic syndrome" will eventually turn out to consist of a number of syndromes with varying aeitiology'. Evidence that the two syndromes, Rett's and infantile autism, can occur in one family was reported by Gillberg et al. (1990). In an extended family there were three female relatives with severe developmental disorders with onset in infancy: two with infantile autism and one with Rett's syndrome.

The usual course of the condition is that it follows a fairly normal first year of life, although motor milestones may be slightly delayed. Cognitive development is usually normal for the first nine months, and then slows down before regressing in the second year. One of the most characteristic features of Rett's syndrome are the hand-wringing movements and that the children also frequently put the fingers or hands in the mouth. Objects may also be mouthed persistently. A change from hypotonicity to hypertonicity in oral motor tone has been reported. This is said to be directly related to postural changes, fasciculating tongue movements and tongue deviation (more often to the left than the right) (Budden et al., 1990). These authors also assessed the communication development in 20 girls, aged 3–19 years, none of whom demonstrated a level above 20 months. The resulting clinical picture was of profound learning difficulties.

A study of the feeding difficulties of 20 children with Rett's syndrome was reported by Morton et al. (1997). They identified reduced tongue movements in the middle and posterior parts of the tongue and delayed pharyngeal swallow, using videofluoroscopy. The tendency for girls with Rett's syndrome to be malnourished as a consequence of feeding problems is a further issue in the management of these children. The burden of care is high and families that need support may find the Rett's Syndrome Association[6] helpful. They provide a telephone support service and a network of local support groups.

Case 24

This girl was born after a normal pregnancy and delivery at a birth weight of 2.8 kg. She was healthy and thrived. She was considered to be developing normally for the first six months of her life, although hindsight might suggest that she always reached motor milestones at the lower end of the normal age range. By the end of the first year she could feed herself with her fingers, could pull herself up to standing and cruise around the furniture. She would babble and had two or three clear words. At the time of her first birthday her development began to show a marked decline. She had periods of screaming and stopped using the few words she had learned. She gradually withdrew from social contact. She stopped babbling and was unable to feed herself. After about six months she was able to use her hands less and less and stopped playing. She began to wring her hands almost continually and seemed to have them or toys always in her mouth, which became sore, and she dribbled. By the time she was two she had ceased to engage in any constructive activity. Her communication was reduced to basic moaning and screaming. She was not mobile, continent, or capable of any self-care. Neither did she learn any new skills. It is likely that she will remain severely communication- and learning-impaired.

There are other congenital syndromes that may predispose a child to an acute episode in which skills may be lost. One of these is the Sturge-Weber syndrome.

Sturge-Weber syndrome

The Sturge-Weber syndrome is a capillary-venous malformation on the surface of the cerebral cortex and usually occurs in association with a facial naevus (port wine stain). These malformations are congenital in origin and consist of a large mass of enlarged and twisted vessels that are supplied by one or more of

[6] Rett's Syndrome Association UK, 113 Friern Barnet Road, London N11 3EU. Tel: 0870 770 3266. Fax: 0870 770 3265.

the large cerebral arteries and drained by abnormal large cerebral veins. They most commonly occur supplied by the middle cerebral artery and arise from a failure in the embryonic development of the cerebral circulation. In the most severe cases, the naevus may be quite large and extend from the face down the neck and arm. Epilepsy is commonly associated with this syndrome and the child may have a range of learning difficulties. Isler (1971) reported the considerable variability of the syndrome, from children with developmental abilities within the normal range to those with severe impairments in general learning or specific impairments of language.

Case 25

This boy (first described by Lees and Neville, 1990) had a history of seizures from the age of 22 months. He had a congenital arteriovenous malformation of the left cerebral hemisphere in association with a capillary naevus on the left side of his face (his angiogram is Figure 4.1, page 52). He had no evidence of large arterial disease. There was progressive hemiatrophy over the period of observation as revealed by subsequent CT scans. However, none of these scans showed evidence of cerebral infarction. The association of seizures and the absence of completed infarct all suggest that the likely pathology was small arterial cortical ischaemia. No further anatomical localization was possible.

He was treated with anticoagulants. This was associated with a suppression of major episodes but not with complete suppression of epilepsy. Attempted withdrawal of anticoagulation on two occasions was associated with a relapse. Pure tone audiometry confirmed normal hearing. He was six years old at the onset of an acute aphasia, with a right hemiplegia that resolved over three days. Aphasia persisted for five days and the return of language was characterized by a severe deficit of auditory verbal comprehension and jargon in expressive language as well as some neologisms in naming tasks. This gradually improved and he did not receive speech and language therapy after discharge from hospital. He continued to make occasional paraphasic errors in naming tasks. Although he continued to make reasonable progress in his mainstream primary school he did have particular difficulty with reading. A statement of educational need was made to include additional teaching (0.2 w.t.e.), provided by the LEA. Three years after the acute episode described here he did experience some further episodes of disturbance in comprehension and expressive language that were characterized by a difficulty of auditory verbal processing and increased phonemic paraphasias, but they were all under 24 hours in duration.

Story telling data from the Farmer Story shows how his expressive language improved over the first year of recovery from the initial aphasic episode to a rather nonfluent pattern. The overall course of his aphasia is shown in Figure 11.1.

Farmer Story: 3 months post-onset
Scratched the dog, barked at the donkey and frightened.

6 months post-onset

He had a farmer and he had a donkey and he had ... He was trying to put the donkey in the b ... barn and he said he thought and then he said. He was um ... he thought a minute then he said if the dog bark the donkey go in the barn and he didn't. So he asked the tat ... cat to frighten him into the the um ... barn and he didn't. He asked the dog to bark. Then the cat frightened the um ... into the barn.

9 months post-onset:

There there was an old farmer right and he had a donkey and he thought he could make him jump into the barn. So the dog bark and he and he didn't jump into the barn. Um ... so the cat miaowed and then it still didn't jump into the barn. So so the farmer thought if if the cr ... the cat scratched the dog and and the cat and then the dog barked and then the donkey jumped into the barn.

12 months post-onset

There was an old farmer and an old donkey and um ... um ... pushed him and pulled him. And he said the dog might have frightened him so he had a bark but he didn't move. So he asked the dog ... the cat to as ... asked the cat to scratch the dog and ... then he said woof woof and he went into the barn.

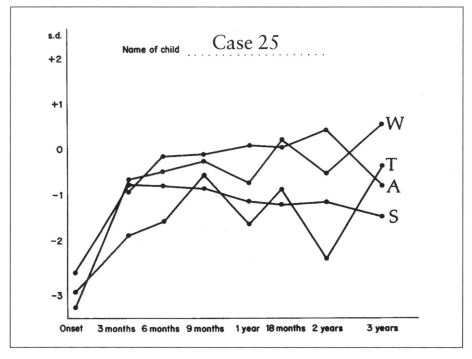

Figure 11.1 Profile of recovery of Case 25: A, auditory association; S, sentence repetition; T, TROG; W, Word Finding Vocabulary Test.

At age 11 years this boy transferred to a mainstream secondary school, but did not really settle there. Within six months he was moved to a small school for children with learning difficulties. He passed two GCSEs in Art and Drama at age 16, and then continued his education through a vocational studies programme at his local further education college. He continued to experience language and learning difficulties.

The child described here was atypical by the way in which language disturbance occurred in association with the withdrawal of anticoagulants, thought to signify further episodes of cerebral dysfunction. These episodes appeared to have no effect on general learning and his IQ remained unchanged, in the lower part of the normal range. The episodes were all quite small and were well controlled as long as both anticonvulsants and anticoagulants were given. In this case it is difficult to determine what separate contributions the vascular and convulsive disorders were making to the overall neuropathology. Rather, it was possible only to observe the combined effect.

Vargha-Khadem et al. (1997) have described another child with SWS who failed to develop speech in early childhood. He was able to understand single words and simple commands, and his language development was around a 3–4 year level. Because of intractable epilepsy, he underwent hemispherectomy at age 8;5 years, followed by withdrawal of AEDs by 9 years of age. What was remarkable about this case was that the boy then began to acquire speech and language. He made good progress in speech and language and in the acquisition of other cognitive skills between the ages of 9 and 15 years. In the first three months of his recovery, his mother reported around 50 words that he was using for the first time, among them nouns, verbs, adjectives and prepositions. By his mid-teens his receptive and expressive language scores on a range of tests were the equivalent of 8–10 years. The authors argued that his case appeared 'to challenge the widely held view that early childhood is a particularly critical period of acquisition of speech and language'. He demonstrated that language 'could be acquired for the first time as late as age 9 years with the right hemisphere alone'. However, it is not clear whether the 8–10 year level was the final ceiling on his language acquisition skills, and what, if anything, he managed to acquire of the later language skills described by Nippold (1988).

Summary

These children point to the need to establish a comprehensive protocol for children with acquired disorders. Our classification systems rarely account for all the cases we see. At present, our understanding of language impairments in childhood, while progressing, calls for further research, the basis of which is often clinical observation, particularly of children with atypical conditions. If we are to learn from such children we need to develop and use a comprehensive assessment/investigation protocol that will at least mean that cases are reported consistently. This would help to facilitate comparisons between children as well as providing a clear way of monitoring a child's long-term progress.

Because of the individuality of the children reported here, no conclusions about the course, prognosis and recovery of the group can be advanced. After all, it is not one group; rather a collection of subgroups and anomalous individuals. However, in general it can be said that where children present with regressive disorders, late onset disorders or atypical acquired disorders in childhood then those in whom the most skills are lost and in whom severe and uncontrolled epilepsy is a concomitant disorder probably have the poorest prognosis.

Chapter 12
Conclusions

'It's a very heavy stone to carry' said the parent of three children, all with LKS, in recent correspondence to a support group. Of her twins, one male and one female, the boy had developed LKS first, his sister a couple of years later. The third child, also a girl, was just beginning to show the first signs of loss of verbal comprehension. Although she lived in Europe, not far from a large city, it was difficult to get consistent access to services that helped her manage the day-to-day burden, let alone bring about any improvement in the children's condition. Whilst three children with LKS in one family may not be that common, other familial cases are known and some are reported in the literature (including two siblings in Landau and Kleffner, 1957).

However, this mother's problem with access to consistent services is not unique. The list server used by parents in the FOLKS network has global uptake. Whilst it may seem reasonable to expect that families in less developed countries might have this experience, it would not appear to be confined to such contexts. Neither is it true that LKS is the only form of acquired childhood aphasia in which families experience such variability, or even inconsistency, of services.

In the ten years since the first edition of this book, more cases of ACA have been reported in the literature, and some ways of managing the conditions from which these arise have been subjected to some research and evaluation. But too few of the techniques that aim to improve the quality of daily life, the rehabilitation and education, the social and therapeutic services, have undergone very rigorous examinations. It is still too common for parents to face significant struggles with education and social services in respect of a decent level of provision for their child's educational or social needs. Such battles often leave families feeling powerless, perhaps even deeply depressed and with little sense of hope for the present, let alone the future, for their children.

Whilst this book is primarily addressed to a professional audience, it is written with the aim that the management of children with ACA should become more of a level playing field in respect of both the parents' role in the process, and the resources that might be mobilized to meet the needs.

There are few publications of this size devoted to the acquired aphasias of childhood from the perspective of a speech and language therapist. By now some of the reasons for that should be clear. It is a rare disorder and one that has attracted more attention from neurologists and psychologists than speech and language specialists in the recent past. Yet the speech and language therapist will potentially be called upon to work with more of these children. This author has seen a steady increase in the number of enquiries about cases of ACA over the last two decades. It is hoped that the discussion and cases presented here will help the clinician in the quest for 'How to know what to do' (Coombes, 1987).

There is, undoubtedly, a lot more we need to know, particularly about the relationship between developmental and acquired language disorders in childhood, the way in which improvement in function should be interpreted, and the relationships between neuropathology and language disorder subtypes. Most of all we need to know what kinds of rehabilitation, education and therapy are the most effective at promoting a language for life for children with ACA.

What follows here is a summary of what is currently understood about ACA that might constitute acceptable standards for SLTs working with children with these conditions. They are based on guidelines published by the Royal College of Speech and Language Therapists (Communicating Quality 2, RCSLT, 1996).

Definition and description of ACA

The child with ACA is one who has a language disorder secondary to cerebral dysfunction, but appearing after a period of normal language development. The cerebral dysfunction may be the result of:

1. a focal lesion of one of the cerebral hemispheres or other area primary for language processing.
2. a diffuse lesion of the CNS above the level of the brain stem secondary to head injury or cerebral infection.
3. or related to epileptic activity: either as a consequence of convulsive status, a post-ictal phenomenon (a Todd's paresis), as a consequence of primary pathology (e.g. malignant disease), as a feature of minor epileptic status or as a psychological reaction to epilepsy.
4. unknown aetiology as in the Landau-Kleffner syndrome.

This definition aims to be inclusive of all known causes of ACA, both traumatic and epileptic. Furthermore, for the purposes of this definition, a language disorder is defined as a language profile which deviates from the normally expected profile of the child's peers in one or more areas; i.e., phonology, grammar, semantics, pragmatics, such that the child is disadvantaged in relation to their communication potential. It is therefore based on the premise that specific language deficits can be identified.

Aims and principles of the work of the speech and language therapist

It should be noted that:

- the child with ACA enters the social and educational context at a disadvantage due to the loss of previously held skills and abilities.
- whilst the usually understood model of ongoing development throughout childhood is still pertinent to this group it must be viewed against a background of specific cerebral damage leading to significant impairments that may make a long-term contribution to a lack of progress in specific skills.
- the complex nature of cerebral damage in ACA means that these children's needs are best served in a multidisciplinary, child-focused, family friendly setting.
- the child with ACA is a potentially different child to the one the family have always known and the therapist should seek to support and encourage appropriate communication within the family.

The rate of recovery of a child with ACA will vary depending on a number of variables, including the severity of the initial damage and the stage of recovery which child has reached, as well as the child's age and background. Therefore, the therapist's aims and objectives will require constant review, and ongoing longitudinal assessment will be vital for appropriate placement and progress. Even though the child may recover to a remarkable extent, present knowledge does not allow us to believe that complete long-term recovery to previously held levels is likely for the majority. The clinician must continually be aware of current research developments in this field and seek to relate these to her/his practice.

Referral to a speech and language therapist

There are a number of things a speech and language therapist needs to know in order to deal competently with a referral:

1. the neurological background of the child;

2. the child's developmental history, family history and history of previous educational attainment, where relevant;
3. any change since the onset of the condition;
4. where the referral is taken from another speech and language therapist, the previous history in respect of speech and language therapy should be provided;
5. all the relevant members of the multidisciplinary team, educational, social, medical, therapeutic, psychological, but primarily the parents, should be informed of the therapist's conclusions in respect of the referral.

For the future, the SLT should aim towards developing a comprehensive referral system for all children with complex brain injury.

Assessment by a speech and language therapist

In each chapter some specific aspects of assessment have been addressed. General conclusions that can be drawn about speech and language assessment for children with ACA are that:

1. Few specific assessment techniques arc available for this client group. This means that the clinician needs to be informed about the use of the most appropriate ones for the child's age, background and needs.
2. A complex association of motor, cognitive, perceptual, emotional and communication problems can arise from brain injury in childhood and these make demands on the assessment procedure. This means the assessment process should be flexible to fit the needs of the child.
3. The impairments encountered in ACA are likely to require different assessment techniques, both during the initial stages of often rapid improvement as well as for long-term residual problems when the child's progress has reached a plateau.
4. These problems are uncommon and potentially complex. This may mean that the clinician will need to refer to a specialist colleague for advice during any stage of the management of the child.
5. It is important that an appropriate longitudinal reassessment protocol is used to map change; either spontaneous recovery or as a response to treatment.
6. Assessment should seek to establish a comprehensive profile of the child's speech and language skills in a wide range of situations both formal and informal, including observations of the child in his/her environment and family setting.

Assessment of communication skills should include the following:

Language
- auditory-verbal comprehension
- expressive language including
- word-finding ability,

and should monitor the presence of jargon aphasia, phonemic and semantic paraphasias, the presence of errors including perseveration.

Speech
- motor speech skills
- oro-motor competence including swallowing.

Pragmatics and nonverbal communication should also be assessed.

In respect of the timing of assessments, during the first three months of recovery assessment should be more or less continuous. During the remainder of the first year of recovery, assessments should be carried out regularly and at least every three months. After the first year of recovery long-term assessment plans should be between six months and annually until the child leaves school or recovery is thought to have maximized. Research suggests that a few severely impaired children can show marked change in the long term yet equally few recover fully, so speech and language assessment needs to identify and document both change and residual impairments as appropriate.

Intervention by a speech and language therapist

There are a number of general principles of speech and language therapy in ACA:

- remember to function as a member of a multidisciplinary team;
- be aware of the child's impairments.
- always seek to maximize the child's communication skills by working through the child's strengths in an atmosphere of success.
- avoid unnecessary, prolonged and ineffective strategies which concentrate on the child's weaknesses such that the child's experience of failure is reinforced.
- during the acute stage of recovery, concentrate on assessing the direction of change in communication skills, and where possible, building on residual skills, encourage the child to widen her/his communication.
- during rehabilitation, be aware of the range of contexts in which therapy needs to be presented in order to achieve a well balanced, diverse and relevant programme.

- do not ignore any long-term residual problems, which may be at a high level and which require practical and functionally based therapy.

These children usually have complex educational needs that change during the course of recovery. The SLT should seek to represent the child's changing communication needs in the educational context and work within this setting in partnership with other professionals. In doing so, be aware that with the more limited flexibility in learning after brain damage, the child's communication needs are best served by a broadly functional approach which extends through all the child's learning contexts. Therapy of whatever sort should not be seen as additional, but as an integral part of the child's education.

Discharge from speech and language therapy

Although few children may make full recovery to previously held levels, where the child needs to be discharged from the service, there are a number of principles the SLT should remember:

- the changing nature of ACA warrants continued long-term review rather than premature discharge;
- there should be an open re-referral system for those discharged.

Working with other professionals

For the child with ACA, it is essential that professionals work together due to the complex nature of their difficulties and the way in which these need to be managed by medical, educational and social services. Not every therapist works within an integrated multidisciplinary team but it is essential to good speech and language therapy to be able to communicate with other professionals. Every therapist should seek appropriate ways of doing this and show awareness of the contribution of other professionals to the needs of the child with ACA.

Because paediatric SLTs deal predominantly with clients who have developmental disorders they often find themselves poorly prepared to deal with the needs of the child with ACA. Where they are unfamiliar with the client group they should liaise with a more experienced therapist. Where such a specialist does not exist within the locality the national network of advisors and special interest groups of the Royal College of Speech and Language Therapists should be approached for advice.

A specialist speech and language therapist, for these purposes, should have had a period of experience with children with other special needs, both those with language disorder and physical disabilities, and be aware of the current state of research in this area, where they have no direct previous experience with ACA. The Royal College of Speech and Language Therapists also provides a network of relevant local or specific interest groups for those who want support and/or seek to learn more. Because of the paucity of information specific to ACA and the way in which it overlaps with other areas, clinicians should be prepared to liaise with those working in relevant areas including adult aphasia, augmentative communication, special education, developmental language disorder and physical disability.

Other aspects of the study of ACA

Amongst the things that must be finalized before completing this discussion of ACA, one outstanding matter, mentioned in the introduction, is that of classification. The question of what to call the various subtypes of aphasic syndromes encountered in ACA is unresolved. It was concluded that neither the Goodglass and Kaplan (1972) or the Rapin and Allen (1987) categories accounted for the majority of children presenting with acquired aphasias (Lees 1992). Yet many continue to use these categories and will do so until other more satisfactory systems are proposed.

In this respect it is proposed here that the speech and language characteristics of children presenting with acquired aphasias should be reported as objectively as possible so that it can be demonstrated how severe or mild is any aspect of their presenting disorder. If the author of such a report claims that this child does, or does not, have any specifically named aphasic syndrome, according to whichever classification, then the reader can weigh up the evidence and agree or disagree. Where the child clearly does fit the criteria for any aphasic subtype then this should be demonstrated in the report. Where the child fails to meet any criteria this should also be clear. By strict reporting we should arrive at a more satisfactory understanding of the aphasic syndromes in childhood and the extent to which they can or cannot be categorized with present systems.

Lastly we must address the problem of the evaluation of speech and language therapy in ACA. There have been no studies to date that have presented RCT data in respect of the efficacy of speech and language therapy for these children. There have been a small number of single-case studies of different types of treatment (Vance 1991 and 1997; Gerard et al., 1991; Lees et al., 1998). Most studies that have said anything about the speech and language therapy the children have received have provided insufficient details to draw any conclusions about its efficacy. Whilst not supporting Landau (1991) in his wish to see large numbers of randomized control trials in ACA, it is clear that we do need to address the efficacy issue.

There are a number of ways of evaluating outcome but most will require much more detail about intervention than has previously been provided.

Whurr et al. (1992), in a paper which analysed a large number of studies into the efficacy of speech and language therapy with adult aphasics using a method of meta-analysis, concluded that in this client group insufficient details were provided in most reported studies. They proposed some minimal criteria that are required of future research if outcome measures are to be properly evaluated. These included specifications about the subjects, details of assessment, treatment and outcome. It is with future studies of ACA that we now need to be concerned. Some types of language impairment in childhood have been the subject of systematic literature reviews. This has yet to happen for ACA. For the sake of each child who can say 'I just feel like I missed a big gap in my life' we must improve the way in which we study acquired childhood aphasia. I hope that this commitment will be the impetus of future clinical work and research.

Appendix 1
Norms for the Graded Naming Test (McKenna and Warrington, 1983)

This test was developed for the clinical assessment of adults with naming difficulties. Unlike many other tests the items are not confined to common objects to ensure similar vocabulary for all subjects. It is well established that less frequently used names are more vulnerable to naming difficulties than the more frequently used and practised ones. Thus this test attempts to include some items that might be less commonly used in general vocabulary in an attempt to take into account some individual pre-morbid differences and look at items on the fringes of the individual's naming capacity that might be more difficult to recall. In the original study with adults the standardization sample was prepared from 100 subjects ranging from 20 to 76 years of age.

This test is commonly available to speech and language therapists, is easily administered, presented and scored. Some of the vocabulary items were not thought to be well known by teenagers. However, it was thought to be a useful test of naming ability for the population 11 to 16 years and so preliminary measures of standardization were sought.

The subjects for the standardization were taken from two mixed comprehensive schools and two mixed junior schools in the south of England. All were state schools with classes of mixed sex, ability, race and socio-economic status. One of each type of school was situated in a city area and in a new town. A total of 88 children were tested and their age groups are detailed in Table A.1.

The mean scores, standard deviation and range of scores for the age groups were calculated and are shown in Table A.2.

Whilst this data requires supplementing, particularly at the higher age range, it does serve as a basis for using this test with teenagers who have specific naming problems. Observations from the responses of this normal sample which have proved useful when seeing aphasic teenagers include:

Table A.1 Children tested on the Graded Naming Test*

Age range (years)	Girls	Boys	Total
11;0–11;11	14	14	28
12;0–12;11	13	9	22
13;0–13;11	11	11	22
14;0–14;11	8	8	16

*McKenna and Warrington (1983).

Table A.2 Mean scores, standard deviation and range of scores for 88 children tested on the Graded Naming Test*

Age range (years)	Mean score	Standard deviation	Range of scores
11;0–1 l;11	9.6	5	3–19
12;0–12;11	10.5	2.72	6–15
13;0–13;11	14.4	3.2	10–20
14;0–14;11	12.2	4.8	3–22

*McKenna and Warrington (1983).

Order of difficulty of test items for normal children

McKenna and Warrington (1983) discuss the order of difficulty of the items in the test in respect of their normal adult population. The test is arranged in order of difficulty for normal adults. It is therefore interesting to note that this order of difficulty was not the same for the normal children in this sample. They found items like 'trampoline' (item number 17), 'shuttlecock' (19) and 'leotard' (23) much easier to recall than 'persicope'(12), 'blinkers' (14) and 'monocle' (15). These appear easier for adults according to the test manual. There was one item almost unknown to all the children: 'sporran' (8). These observations are thought likely to be related to the children's experience of these items.

Cueing techniques used by normal children

Most of the children found the test situation quite demanding, although all were happy to comply. However, almost all of them showed evidence of word-finding difficulty under the stress of the test situation. This could be described as the 'tip of the tongue' phenomenon. When this occurred they used a range of self-cueing strategies that are arranged here in order of frequency of use:

- gestural cue: making a movement indicative of the item.
- verbal description cue: using a phrase or sentence to describe the item.
- negative statement: saying 'it's not a .....'.
- phonemic cue: saying 'it begins with .....'.

These observations are of interest in respect of therapy with aphasic children as the teaching of such strategies often forms the cornerstone of therapy for children with word-finding problems.

Naming errors in the normal children

McKenna and Warrington (1983) also discuss the naming errors found in their normal sample. They are very like those observed from this normal sample of teenagers. The children differed from the aphasic children in respect of the errors they made in that only one child in the normal group produced a paraphasic error ('cuttleshock' for 'shuttlecock') which she was unable to self correct. Uncorrected paraphasias were the main persisting errors in the naming of the aphasic children.

Appendix 2
Story telling

In order to make judgements about a child's expressive language abilities including sentence structure, word order errors and fluency of expressive language, a language sample is required. In view of the difficulty of eliciting expressive language from children with acquired aphasia, a story-telling task has been used in a number of the studies reported by the author (Lees and Neville, 1990; Lees, 1997), according to the method recommended by Mandler and Johnson (1977). The two stories used were the Dog Story (11 episodes) and the Farmer Story (16 episodes). The complete texts are given here (and may also be found at the end of Lees and Neville, 1990; Lees and Urwin, 1991 and 1997). Unfortunately norms are not yet available. However, the technique can be used successfully with most children of six years and over to elicit a short expressive language sample. The episode numbers refer to the major components of each story. A ratio of episode numbers (e.g. 8 out of 11) could be used to give an indication of how much of the story was accurately recalled. The stories should be told at an even pace, without any undue emphasis, but in as natural a manner as possible. The child should then be asked to retell the story and can be cued if necessary. It is recommended that the child's response is tape recorded for later transcription and any cues given should be marked. These stories can form a useful point of departure for subsequent conversation, particularly if the child was initially reluctant to converse spontaneously.

Complete Dog Story

Episode number:

1. There was a dog who had a piece of meat
2. and he was carrying it home in his mouth.
3. On the way home he had to cross a bridge across a stream.

4. As he crossed he looked down
5. and saw his reflection in the water.
6. He thought it was another dog with another piece of meat
7. and he wanted to have that piece as well.
8. So he tried to bite the reflection
9. but as he opened his mouth his piece of meat fell out,
10. dropped into the water,
11. and was never seen again.

Complete Farmer Story

Episode number:

1. Once there was an old farmer
2. who owned a very stubborn donkey.
3. One evening, the farmer wanted to put his donkey into the barn.
4. First he pushed him,
5. But the donkey would not move.
6. Then he pulled him.
7. But the donkey still would not move.
8. Next the farmer thought he could frighten the donkey into the barn.
9. So he asked the dog to bark at the donkey,
10. but the lazy dog refused.
11. Then the farmer thought that the cat could get the dog to bark.
12. So he asked the cat to scratch the dog.
13. The co-operative cat scratched the dog.
14. The dog immediately began to bark.
15. The barking so frightened the donkey
16. that he jumped into the barn.

References

Agostini M De, Kremin H (1986) Homogeneity of the syndrome of acquired aphasia in childhood revisited: Case study of a child with transcortical aphasia. Journal of Neurolinguistics 2: 179-87.

Aicardi J (1986) Post-traumatic epilepsy. In J Aicardi (ed) Epilepsy in Children. New York: Raven Press.

Aicardi J (1990) Epilepsy in brain injured children. Developmental Medicine and Child Neurology 32: 191-202.

Aicardi J, Chevrie JJ (1986) Children with Epilepsy. In N Gordon, I McKinlay (eds) Neurologically Handicapped Children: Treatment and Management. Oxford: Blackwell.

Alajouanine T, Lhermitte F (1965) Acquired aphasia in children. Brain 88(4): 653-662.

Anderson C (2001) Children with feeding difficulties. In M Kersner, JA Wright (eds) Speech and Language Therapy: the decision making process when working with children. London: David Fulton Publishers.

Aram D (1991a) Test battery for language and speech assessment. In IP Martins, A Castro-Caldas, HR Van Dongen, A Van Hout (1991) (eds) Acquired Aphasia in Children: Acquisition and Breakdown of Language in the Developing Brain. Dordrecht: Kluwer Academic Publications (in cooperation with NATO Scientific Affairs Division).

Aram D (1991b) Scholastic achievement after early brain lesions. In IP Martins, A Castro-Caldas, HR Van Dongen, A Van Hout (1991) (eds) Acquired Aphasia in Children: Acquisition and Breakdown of Language in the Developing Brain. Dordrecht: Kluwer Academic Publications (in cooperation with NATO Scientific Affairs Division).

Aram DM, Rose DF, Rekate HL, Whitaker HA (1983) Acquired capsular/striatal aphasia in childhood. Archives of Neurology 40: 614-17.

Aram DM, Ekelman BL, Whitaker HA (1987) Lexical retrieval in left and right brain lesioned children. Brain and Language 27: 75-100.

Aram DM, Ekelman BL (1988a) Scholastic aptitude and achievement among children with unilateral brain lesions. Neuropsychologia 26: 903-16.

Aram DM, Ekelman BL (1988b) Auditory temporal perception of children with left or right brain lesions. Neuropsychologia 26: 931-5.

Aram DM, Ekelman BL, Gillespie LL (1989) Reading and lateralised brain lesions in children. In K Von Euler (ed) Developmental Dyslexia and Dysphasia. London: Macmillan.

Bax MCO (1964) Terminology and classification of cerebral palsy. Developmental Medicine and Child Neurology 6: 296-7.

Beaumanoir A (1985) The Landau-Kleffner Syndrome. In J Roger, C Dravet, M Bureua, FE Dreifuss, P Wolf (eds) Epileptic Syndromes in Infancy, Childhood and Adolescence. Paris: John Libbey, Eurotex.

Bishop DVM (1982) Comprehension of spoken, written and signed sentences in childhood language disorders. Journal of Child Psychology and Psychiatry 23(1): 1-20.

Bishop DVM (1983) The Test for Reception of Grammar. Published by the author at the University of Manchester, M13 9PL, UK.

Bishop DVM (1985) Age of onset and outcome in 'Acquired Aphasia with Convulsive Disorder' (Landau-Kleffner Syndrome). Developmental Medicine and Child Neurology 27: 705-12.

Bishop DVM (1988) Language development after focal brain damage. In D Bishop, K Mogford (eds) Language Development in Exceptional Circumstances. Edinburgh: Churchill Livingstone.

Bishop DVM (2003) Test for Reception of Grammar – version 2. Oxford: The Psychological Corporation.

Bishop DVM (2003b) Expression, Reception and Recall of Narrative Instrument. Oxford: The Psychological Corporation.

Bishop DVM (2003c) Children's Communication Checklist – 2nd edition. Oxford: The Psychological Corporation.

Bishop DVM, Edmundson A (1987) Specific language impairment as a maturational lag: evidence from languitudinal data on language and motor development. Developmental Medicine and Child Neurology 29: 442-59.

Bishop D, Rosenbloom L (1987) Classification of childhood language disorders. In W Yule, M Rutter (eds) Language Development and Disorders Oxford: Blackwell Scientific Publications/McKeith Press.

Bishop D, Mogford K (eds) (1988) Language Development in Exceptional Circumstanccs. Edinburgh: Churchill Livingstone.

Bloom L, Lahey M (1978) Language Development and Language Disorders. New York: John Wiley and Sons.

Bochner S, Jones J (2003) Child Language Development: Learning to Talk (2nd edition). London: Whurr Publishers.

Bray M (2001) Working with parents. In M Kersner and JA Wright (eds) Speech and Language Therapy: the decision making process when working with children. London: David Fulton Publishers.

Brimmer MA, Dunn LA (1973) English Picture Vocabulary Test. Gloucester: Education Evaluation Enterprises.

Brindley C, Cave D, Crane S, Lees J, Moffat V (1996) The Paediatric Oral Skills Package. London: Whurr Publishers.

Brookhouser PE, Auslander MC, Meskan ME (1988) The pattern and stability of post-meningitic hearing loss in children. The Laryngoscope 98: 940-47.

Brown JK, Hussain IHMI (1991) Status Epilepticus I: Pathogenesis. Developmental Medicine and Child Neurology 33: 3-17.

Budden S, Meek M, Henigan C (1990) Communication and oral-motor function in Rett Syndrome. Developmental Medicine and Child Neurology 32: 51-55.

Bzoch KR, League R (1970) The Receptive and Expressive Emergent Language Scale. Baltimore: University Park Press.

Caplan R, Guthrie D, Komo S, Siddarth P, Chayasirisobhon S, Kornblum H, Sankar R, Hansen R, Mitchell W, Shields WD (2002) Social Communication in Children with Epilepsy. Journal of Child Psychology and Psychiatry 43(2): 245-53.

Carter JA (2002) Epilepsy and developmental impairments following severe malaria in Kenyan children: a study of their prevalence, relationships, clues to pathogenesis and service requirements. Unpublished PhD thesis. University of London.

Carter JA, Neville BGR, Newton CRJC (2003a) Neuro-cognitive impairment following acquired central nervous system infections in childhood: a systematic review. Brain Research Reviews 43: 57-69.

Carter JA, Murira GM, Ross AJ, Mung'ala-Odera V, Newton CRJC (2003b) Speech and language sequelae of severe malaria in Kenyan children. Brain Injury 17(3): 217-24.

Carter RL, Hohengger MK, Satz P (1982) Aphasia and speech organisation in children. Science 218: 797-99.

Catsman-Berrevoets CE, Van Dongen HR, Zwetsloot CP (1992) Transient loss of speech followed by dysarthria after removal of posterior fossa tumour. Developmental Medicine and Child Neurology 34: 1102-17.

Chadwick O, Rutter M, Thompson J, Schaffer D (1981) Intellectual performance and reading skills after localised head injury in childhood. Journal of Child Psychology and Psychiatry 22: 117-39.

Chapman SB, Levin HS, Culhane KA (1995) Language impairment in closed head injury. In HS Kirshner (ed) Handbook of Neurological Speech and Language Disorders. New York: Marcel Dekker, Inc.

Chiat S, Law J, Marshall J (eds) (1997) Language Disorders in Children and Adults. London: Whurr Publishers.

Clarke M, Price K, Jolleff N (2001) Augmentative and Alternative Communication. In M Kersner and JA Wright (eds) Speech and Language Therapy: the decision making process when working with children. London: David Fulton Publishers.

Clinical Guidelines for Diagnosis, Management and Rehabilitation of Stroke in Childhood (2004). London: Royal College of Physicians, in press.

Collignon R, Hecaen H, Angelergues G (1968) A propos de 12 cas d'aphasie acquise de l'enfant. Acta Neurologica et Psychiatrica Belgica 68: 245-77.

Coombes K (1987) Speech Therapy. In W Yule, M Rutter (eds) Language Development and Disorders. Oxford: Blackwell Scientific Publications/ McKeith Press.

Cooper JA, Ferry PC (1978) Acquired auditory verbal agnosia and seizures in childhood. Journal of Speech and Hearing Disorders 43: 176-84.

Corbett J (1985) Epilepsy as part of a handicapping condition. In E Ross and E Reynolds (eds) Paediatric Perspectives on Epilepsy. Chichester: J Wiley and Sons.

Cross JA, Ozanne AE (1990) Acquired childhood aphasia: assessment and treatment. In BE Murdoch (1990) (ed) Acquired Neurological Speech/Language Disorders in Childhood. London: Taylor and Francis.

Crystal D, Fletcher P, Garman M (1981) The Grammatical Analysis of Language Disability. London: Edward Arnold.

Dennis M (1980) Strokes in childhood I: Communicative intent, expression and comprehension after left hemisphere arteriopathy in a right handed nine year old. In Language Development and Aphasia. New York: Academic Press.

Deonna T (1991) Acquired Epileptiform Aphasia in Children (Landau-Kleffner Syndrome). Journal of Clinical Neurophysiology 8(3): 288-98.

Deonna T, Beaumanoir A, Gaillard F, Assal G (1977) Acquired aphasia in childhood with seizure disorder: a heterogeneous syndrome. Neuropaediatrie 8: 263-73.

De Renzi E, Vignolo L (1962) The Token Test; a sensitive test to detect disturbances in aphasics. Brain 85: 665-78.

Dewart H, Summers S (1995) The Pragmatics Profile of Everyday Communication Skills in Children. Windsor: NFER-Nelson.

Dodd B, Crosbie S, Mcintosh B, Teitzel T, Ozanne A (2000) Preschool and Primary Inventory of Phonological Awareness. Oxford: The Psychological Corporation.

Dugas M, Grenet P, Masson M, Mialet JP, Jaquet G (1976) Aphasie de l'enfant avec epilepsie; evolution regressive sous traitement antiepileptique. Revue Neurologique (Paris) 132(7): 489-93.

Dugas M, Gerard CL, Franc S, Sagar D (1991) Natural History, Course and prognosis of the Landau and Kleffner Syndrome. In IP Martins, A Castro-Caldas, HR Van Dongen, A Van Hout (1991) (eds) Acquired Aphasia in Children: Acquisition and Breakdown of

Language in the Developing Brain. Dordrecht: Kluwer Academic Publications (in cooperation with NATO Scientific Affairs Division).

Dulac O, Billard C, Arthuis M (1983) Aspects electro-cliniques et evolutifs de l'epilepsie dans le syndrome aphasie-epilepsie. Archives Francaises de Pediatrie 40: 299–308.

Edwards S, Fletcher P, Garman M, Hughes A, Letts C, Sinka I (1997) Reynell Developmental Language Scales III. Windsor: NFER-Nelson.

Eisele JA (1991) Selective deficits in language comprehension following early left and right hemisphere damage. In IP Martins, A Castro-Caldas, HR Van Dongen, A Van Hout (1991) (eds) Acquired Aphasia in Children: Acquisition and Breakdown of Language in the Developing Brain. Dordrecht: Kluwer Academic Publications (in cooperation with NATO Scientific Affairs Division).

Enderby P (1983) The Frenchay Dysarthria Test. Windsor: NFER-Nelson.

Ewing-Cobbs L, Fletcher JM, Landry SH, Levin HS (1985) Language disorders after paediatric head injury. In Speech and Language Evaluation in Neurology: Childhood Disorders. New York: Grune and Stratton.

Fletcher P, Hall D (eds) Specific Speech and Language Disorders in Children. London: Whurr Publishers.

Freud S (1897) Die Infantile Cerebrallaehmung. (Infantile cerebral paralysis). Translated by LA Russin (1968) Coral Gables: University of Miami Press.

Gaddes WH, Crockett DJ (1975) The Spreen-Benton aphasia tests: normative data as a measure of language development. Brain and Language 3: 257–80.

Gathercole S, Baddeley A (1996) Children's Test of Nonword Repetition. Oxford: The Psychological Corporation.

Gerard CL, Dugas M, Sagar D (1991) Speech therapy in Landau-Kleffner Syndrome. In IP Martins, A Castro-Caldas, HR Van Dongen, A Van Hout (1991) (eds) Acquired Aphasia in Children: Acquisition and Breakdown of Language in the Developing Brain. Dordrecht: Kluwer Academic Publications (in cooperation with NATO Scientific Affairs Division).

German DJ (1986) National College of Education Test of Word Finding (TWF). Allen, TX: DLM Teaching Resources.

German DJ (2000) Test of Word Finding – 2nd edition (TWF-2). Allen, TX: DLM Teaching Resources.

Gillberg C (1986) Onset at age 14 of a typical autistic syndrome. A case reports of a girl with herpes simplex encephalitis. Journal of Autism and Developmental Disorders 16: 569–75.

Gillberg C (1988) The Neurobiology of Infantile Autism. Journal of Child Psychology and Psychiatry 29(3): 257–66.

Gillberg C, Ehlers S, Wahlstrom J (1990) The syndromes described by Kanner and Rett-Hagberg: Overlap in an extended family. Developmental Medicine and Child Neurology 32: 258-66.

Goodglass H, Kaplan E (1972) The Assessment of Aphasia and Related Disorders. Lea and Febiger, Philadelphia.

Gooding CA, Brasch RC, Lallemand DP, Wesbey GE, Brandt-Zawadzki MN (1984) Nuclear magnetic resonance imaging of the brain in children. The Journal of Pediatrics 104: 509-15.

Griffiths R (1954) The Abilities of Babies. Windsor: NFER-Nelson.

Griffiths R (1970) The Abilities of Young Children. Windsor: NFER-Nelson.

Grote C, Van Slyke P, Hoeppner J (1999) Language outcome following multiple subpial transection for Landau-Kleffner Syndrome. Brain 122: 561-66.

Guttman E (1942) Aphasia in children. Brain 65: 205-19.

Hand K (1996) Can we measure response to treatment in children with epileptic aphasias (Landau-Kleffner Syndrome)? MSc Thesis, Department of Human Communication Science: University of London.

Hattenstone S (1998) Out of it. London: Hodder and Stoughton (A Sceptre Book).

Haynes C (1992) A longitudinal study of language impaired children from a residential school. In Fletcher P and Hall D. (eds) Specific Speech and Language Disorders in Children. London: Whurr Publishers.

Hecaen H (1976) Acquired aphasia in children and the ontogenesis of hemispheric specialization. Brain and Language 3: 114-34.

Hertz-Pannier L, Chiron C, Jambaque I, Renaux-Kieffer V, Van De Moortele PF, Delalande O, Fohlen M, Brunelle F, Le Bihan D (2002) Late plasticity for language in a child's nondominant hemisphere: a pre- and post-surgery fMRI study. Brain 125: 361-72.

Hirsch E, Maquet P, Metz-Lutz M-N, Motte J, Finck S, Marescaux C (1995) The eponym 'Landau-Kleffner Syndrome' should not be restricted to childhood-acquired aphasia with epilepsy. In A Beaumanoir, M Bureau, T Deonna, L Mira, CA Tassinari (eds) Continuous Spikes and Waves during Slow Sleep. New York: John Libbey and Company.

Howard D, Patterson KE, Franklin S, Orchard-Lisle VM, Morton J (1985) Treatment of word retrieval deficits in aphasia; a comparison of two therapy methods. Brain 108: 817-29.

Howard S, Hartley J, Muller D (1996) The changing face of child language assessment. Child Language, Teaching and Therapy 11: 7-22.

Hudson LJ (1990) Speech and language disorders in childhood brain tumours. In BE Murdoch (1990) (ed) Acquired Neurological Speech/Language Disorders in Childhood. London: Taylor and Francis.

Hudson LJ, Murdoch BE, Ozanne AE (1989) Posterior fossa tumours in childhood: associated speech and language disorders post-surgery. Aphasiology 3: 1-18.

Huskisson JA (1973) Acquired receptive language difficulties in childhood. British Journal of Disorders of Communication 8(1): 54-63.

Irwin K, Birch V, Lees J, Polkey C, Alarcon G, Binnie C, Smedley M, Baird G, Robinson RO (2001) The effect of multiple subpial transection in the Landau-Kleffner Syndrome. Development Medicine and Child Neurology 43: 248-52.

Isaac K (2002) Speech Pathology in Cultural and Linguistic Diversity. London: Whurr Publishers.

Isler W (1971) Acute Hemiplegias and Hemisyndromes in Childhood. Spastics International Medical Publications. London: William Heinemann Medical Books.

Johnson D, Roethig-Johnson K (1987) Stopping the slide of head injured children. Special Children, November 1987: 18-20.

Jordan FM, Ozanne AE, Murdoch BE (1988) Long-term speech and language disorder subsequent to closed head injury in children. Brain Injury 2: 179-85.

Kanner L (1943) Autistic disturbance of affective contact. Nervous Child 2: 179-85.

Kelly JJ, Mellinger JF, Sundt TM (1978) Intracranial arteriovenous malformations in childhood. Annals of Neurology 3: 338-43.

Kirk SA, McCarthy JJ, Kirk, WD (1968) The Illinois Test of Psycholinguistic Abilities Illinois: University of Illinois.

Kirkham F, Edwards M, Lees J (1990) Recovery of cognitive and language skills after prolonged coma in childhood. Paper presented at the Fourth International Aphasia Rehabilitation Congress, 4-6 September 1990, Edinburgh.

Klein SK, Tuchman RF, Rapin I (2000) The influence of pre-morbid language skills and behaviour on language recovery in children with verbal auditory agnosia. Journal of Child Neurology 15: 36-43.

Knowles W, Masidlover M (1982) The Derbyshire Language Scheme. Available from: The Education Office, Grosvenor Road, Ripley, Derbyshire, United Kingdom.

Kurita H (1985) Infantile autism with speech loss before the age of thirty months. Journal of the American Academy of Child Psychiatry 24: 191-6.

Landau WM (1991) The conception and embarrassing birth of an eponym. In IP Martins, A Castro-Caldas, HR Van Dongen, A Van Hout (1991) (eds) Acquired Aphasia in Children: Acquisition and Breakdown of Language in the Developing Brain. Dordrecht: Kluwer Academic Publications (in cooperation with NATO Scientific Affairs Division).

Landau WM, Kleffner F (1957) Syndrome of acquired aphasia and convulsive disorder in children. Neurology 7: 523-30.

Lea J (1970) The Colour Pattern Scheme: a method of remedial language teaching. Available from Moor House School, Oxted, Surrey.

Lees JA (1988) What does acquired childhood aphasia say to late onset autism? Paper presented at the 16th International Study Group on Child Neurology and Cerebral Palsy, 26-30 September 1988, Cambridge.

Lees JA (1989) A Linguistic Investigation of Acquired Childhood Aphasia. Unpublished M Phil thesis: City University, London.

Lees JA, Neville BGR (1990) Acquired aphasia in childhood: case studies of five children. Aphasiology 4(5): 463-78.

Lees JA, Neville BGR (1996) Fit for Neurosurgery? Bulletin of the Royal College of Speech and Language Therapists 535: 9-10.

Lees J (1993a) Children with Acquired Aphasias. London:Whurr Publishers.

Lees J (1993b) Differentiating language disorder subtypes in acquired childhood aphasia. Aphasiology 7: 481-8.

Lees J (1993c) Assessment of receptive language. In JR Beech, LM Harding, D Hilton-Jones (eds) Assessment in Speech and Language Therapy. London: Routledge.

Lees JA (1993) Differentiating Language Disorder Subtypes in Acquired Childhood Aphasia. Aphasiology 7(5): 481-88.

Lees JA (2001) Children with acquired speech and language problems. In M Kersner, J Wright (eds) Speech and Language Therapy: The decision making process when working with children. London: David Fulton Publishers.

Lees JA (1993a) Children with Acquired Aphasias. London: Whurr Publishers.

Lees JA (1997) Longterm effects of acquired aphasias in childhood. Paediatric Rehabilitation 1(1): 45-9.

Lees J, Urwin S (1991) Children with Language Disorders. London: Whurr Publishers.

Lees J, Urwin S (1997) Children with Language Disorders (2nd edition). London: Whurr Publishers.

Lees J, Cass H, Waring M, Burch V, Neville BGR (1998) Monitoring response to pharmacological treatment in children with acquired epileptic aphasias (Landau-Kleffner syndrome). Paper presented at the 24th meeting of the BPNA, Manchester, January 1998. Developmental Medicine and Child Neurology 39 (supplement 77): 9.

Lees JA (1999) From 'which pig is not outside the field?' to 'which horse is not outside the field?': commentary of the Reynell Developmental Language Scales III (RDLS III). International Journal of Language and Communication Disorders 34(2): 174-80.

Leiter R (1969) Leiter International Performance Scale. Chicago: Stoelting.

Lesser R (1978) Linguistic Investigation of Aphasia. London: Edward Arnold.

Lesser RP, Luders H, Morris HH, Dinner DS, Klem G, Hahn J, Harrison M (1986) Electrical stimulation of Wernicke's area interferes with comprehension. Neurology 36: 658-62.

Levin HS, Maddison CF, Bailey CB, Meyers CA, Eisenberg HM, Guinto FC (1983) Mutism after closed head injury. Archives of Neurology 40: 601–6.

Loonen CB, Van Dongen HR (1990) Acquired childhood aphasia: Outcome one year after onset. Archives of Neurology 47: 1324–8.

Lowe M, Costello AJ (1976) The Symbolic Play Test. Windsor: NFER-Nelson.

Mandler JM, Johnson NS (1977) Remembrance of things parsed: story structure and recall. Cognitive Psychology 8: 111–51.

Mantovani JF, Landau WM (1980) Acquired aphasia with convulsive disorder: course and prognosis. Neurology 30: 524–9.

Marescaux C, Hirsch E, Fink S, Maquet P, Schlumberger E, Sellal F, Metz-Lutz MN, Alembik Y, Salmon E, Franck G, Kurtz D (1990) Landau-Kleffner Syndrome: A Pharmacologic Study of Five Cases. Epilepsia 31(6): 768–77.

Marshall JC (1986) The description and interpretation of aphasic language disorder. Neuropsychologia 24: 5–24.

Martins IP, Castro-Caldas A, Van Dongen HR, Van Hout A (1991) (eds) Acquired Aphasia in Children: Acquisition and Breakdown of Language in the Developing Brain. Dordrecht: Kluwer Academic Publications (in cooperation with NATO Scientific Affairs Division).

Martins IP, Ferro JM (1987) Acquired conduction aphasia in a child. Developmental Medicine and Child Neurology 29: 529–40.

Martins IP, Ferro JM, Trindade A (1987) Acquired crossed aphasia in a child. Developmental Medicine and Child Neurology 29: 96–100.

Martins I P, Ferro JM (1991) Recovery from aphasia and lesions size in the temporal lobe. In IP Martins, A Castro-Caldas, HR Van Dongen, A Van Hout (1991) (eds) Acquired Aphasia in Children: Acquisition and Breakdown of Language in the Developing Brain. Dordrecht: Kluwer Academic Publications (in cooperation with NATO Scientific Affairs Division).

McCabe RJR, Green D (1987) Rehabilitating severely head-injured adolescents: three case studies. Journal of Child Psychology and Psychiatry 28: 111–26.

McKeever M, Holmes GL, Russman BS (1983) Speech abnormalities in seizures: A comparison of absence and partial complex seizures. Brain and Language 19: 25–32.

McKenna P, Warrington E (1983) The Graded Naming Test. Windsor: NFER-Nelson.

McKinney W, McGreal DA (1974) An aphasic syndrome in children. Canadian Medical Association Journal 110: 637–9.

Metter EJ (1987) Neuroanatomy and physiology of aphasia: evidence from positron emission tomography. Aphasiology 1: 3–33.

Middleton J (1989) Annotation: Thinking about head injuries in children. Journal of Child Psychology and Psychiatry 30: 663–70.

Morrell F, Whisler WW, Bleck TP (1989) Multiple subpial transection: A new approach to the surgical treatment of focal epilepsy. Journal of Neurosurgery 70: 231–9.

Morrell F, Whisler WW, Smith MC, Hoeppner TJ, De Toledo-Morrell L, Pierre-Louis SJC, Kanner AM, Buelow JM, Ristanovic R, Bergen D, Chez M, Hasegawa H (1995) Landau-Kleffner syndrome: treatment with subpial intracortical transection. Brain 118: 1529–46.

Morris J (2002) A Lot to Say: a guide for social workers, personal advisors and others working with disabled children and young people with communication impairments. London: Scope.

Morton RE, Bonas R, Minford J, Kerr A, Ellis RE (1997) Feeding ability in Rett Syndrome. Developmental Medicine and Child Neurology 39: 331–5.

Murdoch BE (1990) (ed) Acquired Neurological Speech/Language Disorders in Childhood. London: Taylor and Francis.

Murdoch BE, Ozanne AE (1990) Linguistic status following acute cerebral anoxia in children. In BE Murdoch (1990) (ed) Acquired Neurological Speech/Language Disorders in Childhood. London: Taylor and Francis.

Murdoch BE (1998) Dysarthria: A Physiological Approach to the Assessment and Treatment. Cheltenham: Stanley Thornes.

Murdoch BE (1999) (ed) Communication Disorders in Childhood Cancer. London: Whurr Publishers.

Murdoch BE, Boon DL, Hudson LJ (1999) Major childhood cancers: leukaemia and brain tumours. In BE Murdoch (ed) Communication Disorders in Childhood Cancer. London: Whurr Publishers.

Murdoch BE, Hudson LJ (1999) Chapters 3, 4 and 5 in BE Murdoch (ed) Communication Disorders in Childhood Cancer. London: Whurr Publishers.

Mutter V, Hulme C, Snowling M (1997) Phonological Abilities Test (PAT). Oxford: The Psychological Corporation.

Nash P, Stengelhofen J, Brown J, Toombs L (2002) Improving Children's Communication: Managing Persistent Communication Difficulties. London: Whurr Publishers.

Neale MD (1958) Neale Analysis of Reading Ability. London: McMillan.

Neville BGR (1999) Reversible disability associated with epilepsy. Brain and Development 21: 82-5.

Neville BGR, Harkness WJF, Cross JH, Cass HD, Burch VC, Lees JA, Taylor DC (1997) Surgical treatment of severe autistic regression in childhood epilepsy. Paediatric Neurology 16(2): 137-40.

Neville BGR, Burch V, Cass H, Lees J (2000) Behavioural aspect of Landau-Kleffner Syndrome. In C Gillberg, G O'Brien (eds) Developmental Disability and Behaviour. Clinics in Developmental Medicine 149. Cambridge: MacKeith Press (distributed by Cambridge University Press).

Newton A, Thompson M (1976) The Aston Index. Wisbech: Learning Development Aids.

Nippold MA (1988) (ed) Later Language Development: Ages Nine through Nineteen. Boston: College Hill Press.

Nuffield Centre Dyspraxia Programme (2004) Windsor: The Miracle Factory.

O'Brien G, Cheeseburgh B (2000) Traumatic Brain Damage. In C Gillberg, G O'Brien (eds) Developmental Disability and Behaviour. Clinics in Developmental Medicine 149. Cambridge: MacKeith Press (distributed by Cambridge University Press).

Paget R, Gorman P, Paget G (1976) The Paget Gorman Sign System. London: Association for Experiment in Deaf Education.

Pahl J, Kara MB (1992) The Renfrew Word Finding Scale: application to the South African context. South African Journal of Communication Disorders 39: 69-73.

Paquier P, Saerens J, Parizel PM et al. (1989) Acquired reading disorder similar to pure alexia in a child with ruptured arteriovenous malformation. Aphasiology 3: 667-76.

Paquier P, Van Dongen HR (1991) Two contrasting cases of fluent aphasia in children. Aphasiology 5(3): 235-45.

Parmelee DX, O'Shanick GJ (1987) Neuropsychiatric intervention with head injured children and adolescents. Brain Injury 1: 41-7.

Passy J (1990) Cued Articulation. Australian Council for Educational Research. Available from ICAN, 10 Bowling Green Lane, London EC1R 0BD.

Payne KT, Taylor OL (2002) Multicultural influences on human communication. In GH Shames and NB Anderson (eds) Human Communication Disorders: An Introduction (6th edition). Boston: Allyn and Bacon.

Paediatric Stroke Working Group (2004) Stroke in Childhood: Clinical guidelines for diagnosis, management and rehabilitation. London: Royal College of Physicians.

Penfield W, Rasmussen T (1950) The Cerebral Cortex of Man. London: MacMillan

Pitchford N.J, Funnell E, Ellis AW, Green SH, Chapman S (1997) Recovery of spoken language processing in a 6-year-old child following a left hemisphere stroke: A longitudinal study. Aphasiology 11(1): 83–100.

Porch B (1972) The Porch Index of Communicative Ability in Children. Palo Alto: Consulting Psychologist Press.

Rapin I, Allen DA (1987) Developmental Dysphasia and Autism in Preschool Children; Characteristics and Subtypes. Proceedings of 1st Symposium on Speech and Language Disorders in Children, Reading UK. London: AFASIC.

Renfrew C (1977a, 1995a) The Word Finding Vocabulary Test. Oxford: Winslow Press.

Renfrew C (1977b, 1995b) The Bus Story Test. Oxford: Winslow Press.

Renfrew C (1988, 1997) The Action Picture Test. Oxford: Winslow Press.

Rett A (1966) Uber ein Zerebral-atrophisches Syndrom bei Hyperaemmonamie. Wien: Bruder Hollinek.

Rett A (1969) Hyperammonaemie und cerebrale atrophie im kindesalter. Folia Hereditaria et Pathologica 18: 115–24.

Reynell J (1977) The Reynell Developmental Language Scales. Windsor: NFER-Nelson.

Reynell J (1985) The Reynell Developmental Language Scales (revised) Winsdor: NFER-Nelson.

Rigaudeau-Mckenna B (1998) Metalinguistic awareness in a case of early-adolescent dysphasia. Clinical Linguistics and Phonetics 12: 281–304.

Riley O (2001) Managing children individually and in groups. In M Kersner, JA Wright (eds) Speech and Language Therapy: the decision making process when working with children. London: David Fulton Publishers.

Ripley K, Lea J (1984) Moor House School; a follow up study of receptive aphasic ex-pupils. Moor House School, Oxted Surrey.

Riva D, Pantaleoni C, Milani N, Devoti M (1991) Late sequelae of right versus left hemispheric lesions. In IP Martins, A Castro-Caldas, HR Van Dongen, A Van Hout (1991) (eds) Acquired Aphasia in Children: Acquisition and Breakdown of Language in the Developing Brain. Dordrecht: Kluwer Academic Publications (in cooperation with NATO Scientific Affairs Division).

Robinson RJ (1987) The causes of language disorder: introduction and overview. Proceedings of the First International Symposium of Specific Speech and Language Disorders in Children, Reading, England. London: AFASIC.

Robinson RJ (1991) Causes and association of severe and persistent specific speech and language disorders in children. Developmental Medicine and Child Neurology 33: 943–62.

Robinson RO (1988) Investigations in children with acquired autism. Paper presented at 'Syndromes of Acquired Autism'; meeting of the Royal Society of Medicine, 13th December 1988, London.

Robinson RO (1992) Brain imaging and language. In P Fletcher, D Hall (eds) Specific Speech and Language Disorders in Children. London: Whurr Publishers.

Robinson RO, Baird G, Robinson G, Simonoff E (2001) Landau-Kleffner Syndrome: a course and correlates with outcome. Developmental Medicine and Child Neurology 42: 243–7.

Ross EM, Peckham CS, West PR, Butler NR (1980) Epilepsy in childhood: findings from the National Child Development Study. British Medical Journal 1: 207–10.

Royal College of Speech and Language Therapists (1996) Communicating Quality 2. London: RCSLT.

Rutter M (1978a) Diagnosis and Definition. In M Rutter, E Schopler (eds) Autism: A Reappraisal of Concepts and Treatment. Plenum Press, New York.

Satz P. (1991) Symptom pattern and recovery outcome in childhood aphasia: a method-
ological and theoretical critique. In IP Martins, A Castro-Caldas, HR Van Dongen, A Van
Hout (1991) (eds) Acquired Aphasia in Children: Acquisition and Breakdown of
Language in the Developing Brain. Dordrecht: Kluwer Academic Publications (in
cooperation with NATO Scientific Affairs Division).

Scott RC, Neville BGR (1998) Developmental perspectives on epilepsy. Current Opinion
in Neurology 11: 115-18.

Semel E, Wiig E, Secord W (2000) Clinical Evaluation of Language Fundamentals – 3rd edition. Oxford: The Psychological Corporation.

Simoni F Di (1978) The Token Test for Children. Boston: Teaching Resources
Corporation.

Smith MC, Whisler WW, Morrell F (1989) Neurosurgery of Epilepsy. Seminars in
Neurology 9: 231-47.

Smyth V, Ozanne AE, Woodhouse LM (1990) Communicative Disorders in Childhood
Infectious Diseases. In BE Murdoch (1990) (ed) Acquired Neurological Speech/
Language Disorders in Childhood. London: Taylor and Francis.

Spreen O, Benton AL (1969) Neurosensory Centre Comprehensive Examination for
Aphasia. Australia: University of Victoria.

Stackhouse J, Wells B (1997) Children's Speech and Literacy Difficulties: a psycholinguistic framework. London: Whurr Publishers.

Staden U, Isaacs E, Boyd SG, Brandl U, Neville BGR (1998) Language dysfunction in children with Rolandic Epilepsy. Neuropediatrics 29: 242-8.

Super CM, Harkness S (1986)The developmental niche: a conceptualisation of the inter-
face of child and culture. International Journal of Behaviour Development 9: 545-69.

Swinburn K (1999) An informal example of successful therapy for a sentence processing
deficit. In S Byng, K Swinburn, C Pound (eds) The Aphasia Therapy File. Hove: The
Psychology Press.

Vance M (1991) Educational and therapeutic approaches used with a child with acquired
aphasia with convulsive disorder (Landau-Kleffner Syndrome). Child Language,
Teaching and Therapy 7: 41-60.

Vance M (1997) Christopher Lumpship: developing phonological representations in a
child with an auditory processing deficit. In S Chiat, J Law, J Marshall (eds) Language
Disorders in Children and Adults. London: Whurr Publishers (pp. 17-41).

Van Der Sandt-Koenderman WME, Smit IAC, Van Dongen HR, Van Hest JBC (1984) A case
of acquired aphasia with convulsive disorder; some linguistic aspects of recovery and
breakdown. Brain and Language 21: 174-83.

Van Dongen HR, Loonen MCB. (1977) Factors related to prognosis of acquired aphasia in
children. Cortex 13: 131-6.

Van Dongen HR, Loonen MCB, Van Dongen KJ (1985) Anatomical basis for acquired fluent
aphasia in children. Annals of Neurology 17: 306-9.

Van Dongen HR, Visch-Brink EG (1988) Naming in aphasic children: analysis of paraphasic
errors. Neuropsychologia 26: 629-32.

Van Dongen H, Meulstee J, Blauw-Van-Mourik M, Van Harskamp F (1989) Landau-Kleffner
Syndrome: A case study with a fourteen year follow-up. European Neurology 29:
109-14.

Van Dongen HR, Paquier P (1991) Fluent aphasias in children. In IP Martins, A Castro-
Caldas, HR Van Dongen, A Van Hout (1991) (eds) Acquired Aphasia in Children:
Acquisition and Breakdown of Language in the Developing Brain. Dordrecht: Kluwer
Academic Publications (in cooperation with NATO Scientific Affairs Division).

Van Dongen HR, Catsman-Berrevoets CE, Van Mourik M (1994) The syndrome of 'cerebellar' mutism and subsequent dysarthria. Neurology 44: 2040-46.

Van Harskamp F, Van Dongen HR, Loonen MCB (1978) Acquired aphasia with convulsive disorder in children; a case study with a seven year follow up. Brain and Language 6: 141-8.

Van Hout A (1991) Outcome of acquired aphasia in childhood: Prognostic factors. In IP Martins, A Castro-Caldas, HR Van Dongen, A Van Hout (1991) (eds) Acquired Aphasia in Children: Acquisition and Breakdown of Language in the Developing Brain. Dordrecht: Kluwer Academic Publications (in cooperation with NATO Scientific Affairs Division).

Van Hout A (1997) Acquired Aphasia in Children. Seminars in Pediatric Neurology 4(2): 102-8.

Van Hout A, Evrard P, Lyon G (1985) On the positive semiology of acquired aphasia in children. Developmental Medicine and Child Neurology 27: 231-41.

Van Slyke PA (2002) Classroom instruction for children with Landau-Kleffner Syndrome. Child Language Teaching and Therapy 18(1): 23-42.

Vargha-Khadem F, O'Gorman AM, Watters GV (1985) Aphasia and handedness in relation to hemispheric side, age at injury and severity of cerebral lesions during childhood. Brain 108: 677-96.

Vargha-Khadem F, Isaacs EB, Papaleloudi H, Polkey CE, Wilson J (1991) Development of language in six hemispherectomized patients. Brain 114: 473-95.

Vargha-Khadem F, Carr LJ, Isaacs E, Brett E, Adams C, Mishkin M. (1997) Onset of speech after left hemispherectomy in a nine-year-old boy. Brain 120: 159-82.

Vernon PE (1977) Graded Word Spelling Test. London: Hodder and Stoughton.

Volkmar FR, Cohen DJ (1989) Disintegrative Disorder or 'Late Onset Autism'. Journal of Child Psychology and Psychiatry 30(5): 717-24.

Walker M (1980) The Revised Makaton Vocabulary. Published by the author at St George's Hospital, London.

Ward JD, Alberico AM (1987) Paediatric head injuries. Brain Injury 1: 21-5.

Wechsler D (1974) Wechsler Intelligence Scale for Children (revised). New York: Psychological Corporation.

Whurr R (1974) An Aphasia Screening Test. London: Whurr Publishers.

Whurr R, Evans S (1995) The Children's Aphasia Screening Test. London: Whurr Publishers.

Whurr R, Lorch MP, Nye C (1992) A meta analysis of studies carried out between 1946 and 1988 concerned with the efficacy of speech and language therapy treatment for aphasic patients. European Journal of Disorders of Communication 27: 1-18.

Wiig E, Secord W, Semel E (2000) Clinical Evaluation of Language Fundamentals – Preschool UK edition. Oxford: The Psychological Corporation.

Wijngaert E De (1991) The Landau-Kleffner Syndrome: Rehabilitation. In IP Martins, A Castro-Caldas, HR Van Dongen, A Van Hout (1991) (eds) Acquired Aphasia in Children: Acquisition and Breakdown of Language in the Developing Brain. Dordrecht: Kluwer Academic Publications (in cooperation with NATO Scientific Affairs Division).

Woods BT, Teuber HL (1978) Changing patterns in childhood aphasia. Annals of Neurology 3(3): 273-80.

Worster-Drought C (1956) Congenital suprabulbar paresis. Journal of Laryngology and Otology 70: 453-63.

Worster-Drought C (1971) An unusual form of acquired aphasia in children. Developmental Medicine and Child Neurology 13: 563-71.

Yeates KO (2000) Closed Head Injury. In KO Yeates, MD Ris, HG Taylor (eds) Paediatric Neuropsychology: Research, Theory and Practice, London: The Guilford Press.

Ylvisaker M (1985) Head Injury Rehabilitation: Children and Adolescents. London: Taylor and Francis.

Index

ABA design 90
abscess 3
Acquire 104
acquired receptive aphasia with convulsive disorder 8, 105
Action Picture Test 24, 56-58, 124-125
acute 13, 39
acute disintegrative psychosis 152
adenoidectomy 122
ADHD 117
adult aphasia 15-16
adulthood 39
advocate 24
agnosia 16
aggression 141
aims 162-165
alphabet board 89, 90
alternative/augmentative communication 33, 34-35, 70-73, 88, 166
angiography 51, 59, 61, 80
angioma 60
anomalous 149
anomia 16, 18
anoxia 100-104
antibiotics 92, 93
anticoagulants 156
antiepileptic drugs 115, 139-140
Aphasia Screening Test 23
aphasic arrest 107, 129
aphasic syndromes 9
arterial cortical ischaemia 156
arterial disease 61
articulation 9
assertive 40
assessment 11-12, 19, 20-32, 68-69, 88, 94-95, 163-164, 168

Aston Index 74
astrocytoma 143
asylum-seeking 36, 94
asymmetrical 100, 139
ataxia 120
attention 11, 31, 69, 76, 108, 150
attention seeking 40
atypical 159
audiological 53
audiologist 114
auditory comprehension 9
auditory deprivation 111
auditory processing 72, 91, 110, 111, 112
autism 15, 116
autistic spectrum disorders 117

babbling 155
bacterial 92
baseline 11
behaviour 39-41, 53, 102, 108, 115, 117, 124, 142
benign 86, 130
Benign Rolandic Epilepsy 5, 75, 130-135
bilateral 100, 118, 139
bilingual 11, 36-37, 82, 153
body language 116
Boston Aphasia Test 24
Boston Diagnostic Aphasia Examination 50
brain lesion 1
brain stem 87, 94
Broca 6, 12
Broca's aphasia 16
Broca's area 6, 54, 55, 116
bullying 39-41
Bus Story Test 147
cardiac 45, 100

cerebellum 87, 100, 142
cerebral abscess 92–93, 138
cerebral atrophy 78, 135
cerebral cortex 6, 129, 155
cerebral malaria 3, 92, 93–94
cerebral palsy 46, 70
cerebral perfusion pressure 101, 102
cerebritis 98
cerebrospinal fluid 92
cerebrovascular lesion 3
Checklist of Everyday Communication
    Skills 29
Child Brain Injury Trust 76
child-centred 12
child-focused 162
Children's Aphasia Screening Test 23, 24,
    26, 69
Children's Communicative Checklist 29
Children's Test of Nonword Repetition 27
chemotherapy 87
circle time 40
classification 5, 158
classroom 35
cleft palate 40
Clinical Evaluation of Language
    Fundamentals 26, 87
clinical guidelines 14
cognitive processes 31
colour coding 38
coma 93, 100–104
communication aid 71
communication board 72
communicative intent 150
community worker/s 36
compliance 69
computed tomography scanning 12
concentration 31, 124
conduction aphasia 16
conductive hearing loss 61, 115, 122
confabulation 75
confrontational naming 49
congenital 105
contusion/s 65, 80, 81
conversation 171
convulsive 2
convulsive status 101, 128, 135–136, 140,
    161
coprolalia 78, 141
corpus callosum 86
counselling 138
critical period 158

crossed aphasia 86
CSWSS 128, 131
cue/s 50, 73, 170
cued Articulation 112–113
culture 13, 30–31, 36
curricula 88

daily routine 76
damage 3–5
deafness 92, 120
deficit-based 38
dementia 154
dentition 70
depressed 82
Derbyshire Language Scheme 24, 26, 73
deteriorating 149–159
deterioration 2–5,
developmental history 163
developmental invariance position 7
developmental language disorder 16–18,
    48
developmental language impairments 1
dietician 38
Different Strokes 64
discourse 73
disinhibited behaviour 77
disintegrative disorder 151
Dog Story 81, 82, 133–134, 142, 144, 147,
    171–172
doppler ultrasound 51
draw-a-man test 74
dysembroplastic neuroepithelial tumour
    9, 89
dysarthria 15, 69, 70, 87, 135
dysfluency 56
dysgraphia 8
dyslexia 8
dysphagia 15, 38
dysphonia 82
dyspraxia 16, 69, 123, 126
dystonic 82

echolalia 153
educational needs 53–54, 60, 76, 77, 78,
    82, 104, 124, 156
educational placement 101, 115
educational psychologist 41, 75, 102
educational strategies 113–114
Education Act 2, 66
EEG 4, 106, 109, 115, 139, 145
efficacy 38

electrical stimulation 130
electronic 34
embryological development 46
emotional 40
employment 109
encephalitis 3, 92, 93, 99, 101
Encephalitis Society 99
encephalopathy 93, 97
English Picture Vocabulary Test 24
environmental sounds 124
epidemiology 1, 109
epilepsy 58, 94, 102, 109
epileptic aphasia 3, 5, 128-148
errors 21
ESES 107
ethnicity 31
exclusion 39
experimental 46
expert model 36
Expression, Reception and Recall of
    Narrative Instrument 27
expressive aphasia 48
eye contact 141, 154

facial naevus 155
falciparum malaria 93
family 36, 71, 103, 114, 138, 154, 162
family history 75, 106, 123, 130, 146, 163
Farmer Story 96, 98, 121, 156-157,
    171-172
feeding difficulties 155
feeding programme 95, 104
fluctuating 108, 123, 137
formal 21, 26, 28, 29
Frenchay Dysarthria Test 24, 67, 69, 87,
    94, 103
friendship 40
Friends of Landau-Kleffner Syndrome 127,
    160
functional communication 26
functional hypothesis 105
functional MRI 46

gait 82, 89
gastroscopy 78
gastrostomy 38
genetic 78, 130
gestures 34, 72, 149
Glasgow Coma Score 66, 80
global aphasia 16
glucose metabolism 51

goal-orientated 81
Graded Naming Test 24, 30, 50, 81, 82,
    83, 143, 168-170
Graded Word Spelling Tes 74
grammar 22, 131
Great Ormond Street Hospital 29
grief 71
Griffiths Scale of Mental Ability 102
group 34, 35-36
group dynamics 35-36

haematoma/s 45, 51, 65
haemorrhage 38, 45, 51, 59, 137
hand control 34
headache 60, 83, 97
head injury 3, 65-85, 101, 106, 137, 161
head trauma 45, 109, 128
hearing impairment 28, 94, 115
hearing test 95
hemianopia 59, 87
hemiatrophy 156
hemiplegia 3, 45, 46, 54, 56, 59, 135, 144,
    156
hemispherectomy 9, 46-47, 158
Herpes Simplex encephalitis 15, 152
history 6-10
holistic 14
hydrocephalus 143

Illinois Test of Psycholinguistic Abilities 24
immunization 149
impairment/s 3-5, 21, 25, 38, 92, 131, 164
inclusion 41
independent living 77
individual 34, 35-36
Infantile Autism 151
infarction 45, 51, 144, 156
infection 3, 92-99, 161
informal 21, 26, 28, 29
input 28
intensive 37
intensive care 1, 66, 80, 104, 140
interaction 35
interpretor/s 31, 37
intervention 164-165
intonation 49
intracerebral 45
intracranial 66, 101
intraventricular 45
ischaemia 5, 46
jargon 7, 8, 56, 87, 118, 156

John Lea Colour Pattern Scheme 33, 38,
    73, 113, 124

ketogenic diet 120, 139
keyworker 14, 114

Landau-Kleffner syndrome 4, 5, 8, 12, 18,
    23, 29, 105–127, 150, 153, 161
language disorder subtypes 5
Language Remediation and Screening
    Procedure 24
Language Through Reading 33
language unit 55
late onset autism 4, 151–153
learning difficulties 78, 92, 100, 102, 155,
    156
left hemisphere 7
Leiter International Scale 122
lesional hypothesis 105
lesion-based 6
lexical-syntactic deficit 17, 18
life transitions 35
literacy 27
longitudinal 8, 19, 132, 148, 162
loss 2–5, 71
lymphoblastic leukaemia 86

magnetic resonance imaging 51, 65, 115
mainstream education 2
malaria 31
malignant 86, 129, 161
malformation 155
Makaton Vocabulary 54, 72, 111, 124
management 33–41
mastoid bone 93
mastoiditis 93
mathematics 113
measles 149
medical model 2, 36
memory 11, 53, 75, 101, 102, 116, 131
meningitis 3, 92, 97
meningoencephalitis 92
meta-analysis 166
metabolic rate 135
metalinguistic awareness 74
mid brain 98
migraine 109, 146
milestones 77, 149, 154, 155
minor epileptic status 137–138
mixed nonfluent aphasia 16
mobility 34

mood 53
morbidity 47, 92, 93
mortality 47, 92, 93
mother tongue 36
motivation 73
motor aphasia 7
motor cortex 53
motor development 54
motor neurone 70, 82
motor speech 28, 69
Moyamoya syndrome 47
multi-centre studies 11
multidimensional 21–22
multidisciplinary 14, 28, 32, 51–53, 85,
    114, 154, 162
multiple subpial transection 9, 10, 107,
    115, 124
mutism 3, 8, 49, 50, 71, 87, 138
myelination 51
myoclonic 142
myringotomies 122

naming 23
narrative 132, 133–134
nasogastric 38
National Child Development Study 135
National Head Injuries Association 76
natural history 15, 19, 31, 48, 66–68,
    107–110, 128–130
Neale Analysis of Reading Ability 74, 98,
    102, 120, 143
near-drowning 100
neologism 23, 49
neonatal 46, 48
neoplasm 51, 86–91
neurologist 114, 139
neuropsychiatry 77, 83
neuropsychology 77
Neurosensory Centre Comprehensive
    Examination for Aphasia 49–50
neurosurgeon 32
nonfluent 33
nonverbal 26, 34
normal language development 10
norms 168–170, 171
Nuffield Centre Dyspraxia Programme 28

occipital 142
occupational therapist 53, 76
oedema 51, 78
output 28

objects 34
opthalmological 53
oro-motor 131
outcome 90, 110
oxygen 51, 100, 135

Paediatric Oral Skills Package 24, 28, 70,
        94, 103
Paget Gorman Sign System 111, 123
paraphasia 8, 14, 23, 48–49
parasites 4
parental participation 36
partial seizures 89
peers 39
peer mediation 41
peri-natal 47
permanent 131
perseveration 97
persistent vegetative state 67
phonation 70
phonemic 112, 126
Phonological Abilities Test 27
phonological programming deficit 17
phonological-syntactic deficit 17
physiotherapy 54, 76
physiotherapist 38, 53
play 23, 26, 150
Porch Index of Communicative Ability in
        Children 22, 24
positron emission tomography 51
posterior fossa 87
post-ictal 136, 142, 161
post-natal 46
posture 104
pragmatics 23, 73–74, 94, 164
pre-natal 46
preschool 36
Preschool and Primary Inventory of
        Phonological Awareness 27
pressure monitoring 66
professional jargon 37
prognosis 3–5, 15, 152
prosody 110
protocol 63, 68, 163
psychiatry 82, 101, 117
psycholinguistic 28, 33, 112–113
psycholinguistic profiling 27
psychological 40, 138
psychologist 38, 74, 76
punctuation 83
pure tone audiometry 98, 118, 146

pure word deafness 16

qualitative 22
quality of life 131
questionnaire 132, 133

radiologist 38
radiotherapy 60, 87
randomized control trials 166
Rasmussen's encephalitis 46–47
reading 23, 33, 74, 113, 156
Receptive and Expressive Emergent
        Language Scale 24
receptive aphasia 14
recovery 13, 67
reflexes 70
refugee 36, 94
regression 5, 9, 89, 106, 109, 117,
        149–150, 152, 154
rehabilitation 41, 53–54, 64, 65, 67,
        75–77, 80, 81, 85, 95, 103, 160
re-referral 165
research 162
resection 9
residential 40, 126
residual 37
resources 20, 21
resource-poor countries 94
respiratory 100
Rett's syndrome 4, 154–155
Rett's Syndrome Association 155
reversible disability 91
Reynell Developmental Language Scales
        11, 21, 24, 54, 69, 122, 150
Rhesus incompatibility 142
right hemisphere 7
road traffic accident 78, 80
Rolandic areas 120
role play 51
Royal College of speech and Language
        Therapists 161, 165

saliva 70
scapegoating 39
school entry 40
scoring 21–23
school performance 132
selective mutism 37
self-confidence 40
self-cueing 169
self-esteem 40

self-monitoring 73
semantic 23, 38
semantic-pragmatic deficit 17, 18
sensory impairment 34
sensory aphasia 7
sentence repetition 9, 25
sequences 76
severity 26
sickle cell 45
sign/s 33, 34
single-case studies 166
single word 38
sinusitis 93
sleep 106, 117, 124, 137
social communication 29, 139
social development 151
social model 2
social services 103, 160, 165
socio-economic status 109
space-occupying lesion 86, 87
spasticity 80
specific language disorder 130
speech and language therapist 2, 33,
    49–51, 103–104, 138–139, 162–165
speech and language therapy 68–74, 89,
    111–113, 165
speech production 23
Spreen-Benton Aphasia Test 29
spelling 33, 74, 83
spike and wave 89, 91, 105, 146
standard deviation 168–169
state dependant epilepsy 91
story telling 25, 27, 38, 50, 60, 61, 63, 81,
    82, 118, 132, 171–172
stroke 45–64
Sturge-Weber Syndrome 155–158
subarachnoid 45
subdural abscess 95
suffocation 100
support group 160
suprabulbar paresis 105
surgery 115–117, 126
swallowing 164
Sylvian region 95
symbol/s 33, 34
Symbolic Play Test 24, 153
symbolic understanding 34
syntactic 23, 38
systemmatic literature review 167

teacher 74, 153
teamwork 39, 41
teenager/s 29, 38–39, 73, 168, 170

telegrammatic 58, 97, 146
temporal lobe 56, 92, 145
Test for Reception of Grammar 22, 23, 24,
    26, 29, 56, 102, 123
Test of Word Finding 23, 26
thrombus 45
'tip of the tongue' phenomenon 169
Todd's paralysis/paresis 106, 129,
    135–136, 161
Token Test 11, 24, 50, 87
tongue 154
total communication 33
tracheostomy 141
transcortical sensory aphasia 16, 87
traumatic 2
tremour 80, 82
tumour 3, 86, 137, 142

unconscious 78, 80, 82
urine test 140

vascular malformations 47
ventricles 51
ventriculo-peritoneal shunting 143
verbal auditory agnosia 8, 16, 17, 18, 110
verbal dyspraxia 17
Vernon Graded Word Spelling Test 102
video 73
videofluroscopic radiology 69, 155
viral 92, 97
virus 106
vision 143
visual evoked response 82
visual field 3, 56
vocabulary 168

Wernicke 6, 12
Wernicke's aphasia 16, 18
Wernicke's area 6, 116, 130, 145
Weschler Intelligence Scale for Children
    102
word-finding 14
Word Finding Vocabulary Test 24, 31, 81,
    83, 124–125, 141
Worster-Drought Syndrome 105
written language 74–75, 118, 121, 131, 147
writing 23, 83

youth training scheme 83

z-score 26